W9-BPL-608

EUREKA!

How to Fix California

Arthur B. Laffer, Ph.D.

with Wayne H. Winegarden, Ph.D.

PACIFIC
RESEARCH
INSTITUTE

Eureka! How to Fix California
Arthur B. Laffer with Wayne H. Winegarden

March 2012

ISBN 978-1-934276-18-1

Book Design by Dana Beigel

Pacific Research Institute
One Embarcadero Center, Suite 350
San Francisco, CA 94111
Tel: 415-989-0833/ 800-276-7600
Fax: 415-989-2411
Email: info@pacificresearch.org
www.pacificresearch.org

Nothing contained in this report is to be construed as necessarily reflecting the views of the Pacific Research Institute or as an attempt to thwart or aid the passage of any legislation.

©2012 Pacific Research Institute and Laffer Associates. All rights reserved. No part of this publication may be reproduced, stored in a retrieval system, or transmitted in any form or by any means, electronic, mechanical, photocopy, recording, or otherwise, without prior written consent of the publisher.

Dedication

I would like to dedicate the book to several mentors past and present:
Justin Dart, Bob Mundell, Ron McKinnon, Emile Despres, William G. Laffer,
George P. Shultz, Charles (Tex) Thornton, and Steve Moore

Contents

Exhibits

Chapter 4 When States Start an Income Tax

Chapter 5 Form 1040: Everything You Wanted to Know about Californian Taxpayers But Were Afraid to Ask

Chapter 7: California Real Estate Booms and Busts: A Chain Reaction

Chapter 8: The California Story: Karl Marx vs. Adam Smith

Chapter 9: A Man's Home Is His Castle: The Legacy of Proposition 13

Chapter 10: Proposition 13: Lost, Regained, and Lost Yet Again

Chapter 11: Bureaucrats Gone Wild, Politicians Gone Wilder

Chapter 12: Primum Primorum: A Low Rate Flat Tax for Californians

Chapter 13: Politics [pol-i-tiks]

Foreword

The California dream is the American dream. Back in 1941 fulfilling the California dream only required an idea, hard work, and in the case of CKE, owner of Carl's Jr. and Hardees Restaurants, $326 for a hot dog cart. Things are very different today.

Starting and running a business in California now requires an idea, hard work, and a lot more money. It also requires teams of lawyers, lobbyists, tax law experts, environmental law experts, zoning law experts, health regulation experts, labor law experts, etc.

Then, assuming you somehow overcome all of these regulatory costs and your business actually turns a profit, California imposes one of the highest state tax burdens in the country. These punitive tax rates lower the return on entrepreneurial risk-taking to a degree that is unique to California. As if that were not enough, if against these long odds a business is successful it becomes an inevitable target for plaintiff's class action lawyers who collectively bankroll state legislators all too willing to create new laws designed to trip up employers and give rise to the next great liability bonanza. In light of these impediments, is it any wonder that business and job creation are stagnating in California?

CKE currently has 720 restaurants in California. Each restaurant creates, on average, 25 jobs for a total of around 18,000 jobs that are directly attributable to our operations. CKE also spends about $1 billion a year on food and paper products, $175 million on advertising, $33 million on maintenance, and $60 million on capital projects, creating even more jobs in the communities where we operate.

Our company's history is tied directly to the days when California was the land of opportunity, "The Golden State." We love California and we would love to grow our California business. Nonetheless, due to the high cost of doing business in California, CKE is not expanding its operations in California and is choosing to place its bets on other states that have lower costs of doing business, such as Texas.

Our experience exemplifies California's current economic malaise. I have been a Californian since 1991. And since that time, I have seen California through the best of times—such as the dot.com boom that revolutionized the way businesses operate across the globe and through the worst of times—such as California's current economic crisis. California's bouts of prosperity and stagnation are not random events. As *Eureka!* clearly and succinctly demonstrates, prosperity in California follows good economic policies. The reverse is also true: economic decline and high unemployment in California follow bad economic and regulatory policies.

I first met Art Laffer in 1989 when I deposed him as an expert witness on the other side of a civil case I was trying. I was immediately impressed. His history as one of Ronald Reagan's economic advisors and one of our nation's leading economists is well known. His significant role in helping President Reagan right our nation's economic ship in the 1980s is also well known. On a personal note, Art wrote the foreword to my book back in 2010.

Carl Karcher was also a great friend of Art's beginning in the mid-1970s just after Art arrived in California to become the Charles B. Thornton Professor at USC. Carl even asked Art to join CKE's board of directors, but due to Art's active political and academic schedule it was infeasible—it's truly a small world, isn't it.

I am unable to think of anyone better suited to set the course for economic prosperity in California.

As Art and Wayne Winegarden persuasively show in *Eureka!*, righting California's economic course requires a careful examination of the tax and regulatory policies that have historically created economic prosperity in California as well as the other 49 states. In the first half of *Eureka!*, they convincingly demonstrate that economic prosperity is created when states do not implement high progressive income taxes, large overall tax burdens, high corporate income tax burdens, anti-growth regulations, and spending policies that discourage work and encourage unemployment. Unfortunately, California is currently committing all of these mistakes. Unless California reverses its anti-growth policies, its future will be what we see on the news each night out of European countries such as Greece or Italy that have pursued similar policies. It may be a slow decline, but it is a decline, nonetheless. If a pleasant climate was the determinant of economic success, Greece would lead the world in per capita GDP.

Importantly, *Eureka!* is designed to do more than merely complain about California's current economic policies. In the second half, the authors present a series of policy reforms that would correct the economic problems facing our state; and political reforms to ensure that California continues to implement sound economic policies thereby eliminating California's cycle of surging prosperity followed by deep economic despair. If followed, the reforms *Eureka!* suggests will put California on the path to economic prosperity; and keep her there.

Given the depth of California's current economic malaise, *Eureka!* is an important contribution that can help restore the California dream. Every elected official in our state should read it without delay.

Andrew F. Puzder
Chief Executive Officer of CKE Restaurants and
co-author of *Job Creation: How It Really Works and Why Government Doesn't Understand It*

Ya ever see the sun come up over the Rockies?
It hits all of a sudden, and below there's California.
And you swear you're lookin' at heaven.[1]
—Kurt Russell as Wyatt Earp, *Tombstone*

Introduction

"California Dreamin'" began long before the Mamas and the Papas sang about it in 1965 or even before the Joads pilgrimaged to California after the dustbowl of the 1930s. The first California dream actually began in the year 1500. It was around this time that Spanish writer Garci Rodríguez de Montalvo introduced the world to the fictional island of California ruled by the Amazonian Queen Calafia in *Las Sergas de Esplandián* (*The Adventures of Esplandián*).

After the publication of *The Adventures of Esplandián*, Spanish explorers learned of an actual "island" that lay just beyond Mexico. This island was said to have been ruled by Amazonian women. In honor of Montalvo's popular book, they named that island California. And thus, the dream of California began.

Since Montalvo's time, that dream has never waned. But the ability of Californians to fulfill their dreams has. When I first moved to California in 1963, I wondered why it was called the "Golden State." I had thought perhaps the rubric referred to the days of the California gold rush of the 1840s. But I was wrong—the answer turns out to refer to a different gold. Gold is the color of the dead grass that covers California from head to toe during the dry season. And unfortunately, despite its many natural advantages, California is no longer the country's economic growth leader.

Don't get me wrong—California is still the land of plenty. In every sense of the word California is a humongous state: the largest GDP (if it were a country it would have the eighth largest GDP in the world)[2]; the largest population (larger than Canada, Australia, and about the size of Poland)[3]; the largest number of beautiful people; and the largest Hispanic population. It probably has the largest-of-everything population. It's got the Beach Boys, the Rose Bowl, Hollywood, giant redwoods, lots of oranges, the Reagan Library, and all sorts of other treasures that are unique. California in many, many ways is special, and Californians like to think of themselves as special too.

But the truth is that California has a lot to learn from the rest of the world. What happens in Iowa may have some differences from what happens in California, but what happens with tax policy or other economic policies in Iowa will pertain just as well to California or any other state. This book examines the political and economic policies of successful states that time and again have generated growth and prosperity for its residents and the rest of the nation. But first, we must understand economics—supply side economics—the key to achieving that prosperity whether we're viewing the entire world, a country, a state, a city, or a family.

This isn't rocket surgery.
—Larry Gatlin

Chapter 1

Economics and Incentives: What Makes People Tick

People like doing things they find attractive and are repelled by things they find unattractive. Government policies change the attractiveness of activities. Taxes, for example, make activities less attractive and subsidies make activities more attractive. Don't be surprised when government raises taxes on work, output, and employment that the economy will produce less work, less output, and less employment. And when government increases subsidies to non-work, leisure, and unemployment, the economy will produce less work, less output, and less employment. It's the nature of people.

In their classic textbook *Economics,* my former Yale classmate Bill Nordhaus and his co-author Paul Samuelson produced a quote from an anonymous author as follows: "You cannot teach a parrot to be an economist simply by teaching it to say 'supply' and 'demand.'"[1] While Nordhaus and Samuelson are correct as far as they go, they should have added that without getting a person to understand supply and demand, they will never be an economist.

And what is supply and demand? A supply curve relates the quantity of a product supplied to the market price of that product. People supply more of a product when their incentive to supply that product (i.e. the price) is higher and they demand less of a product when the disincentive to buy that product (again the price) is higher. This is the essence of economics.

In any version of political economics, taxes have always played an important role in determining economic growth, the levels of output and employment, and other metrics of prosperity. In incentive economics, or what people may call supply-side economics, tax rates play as much of a separate role in the metrics of prosperity as do overall tax revenues. A tax rate changes the marginal rate of substitution between labor and leisure. It drives a wedge between wages received by the employee and wages paid by the employer.

Tax rates also drive a wedge between one set of goods and another set of goods, between one time period and another, and between one location and another location. Tax rates are prices pure and simple, and goodness knows what economics would be without prices. Economics would probably be no better than Professor Samuelson's parrot. The logic of how tax rates and government spending impact the economy is probably the premier logical step in the development of the field of growth economics. Taxes in the U.S. comprise some 19 percent of all gross domestic product (GDP) while government spending today is about 38 percent of GDP.[2] On a tax rate basis, if we look only at the highest marginal rates, we have the following sequence from work to goods. It's pretty impressive.

Exhibit 1

Total NIPA Government Taxes, Revenues, and Expenditures as a Percent of GDP
Quarterly, Q1 1960 to Q1 2011

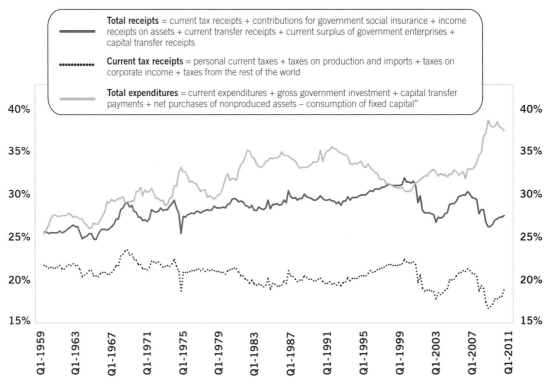

Total receipts = current tax receipts + contributions for government social insurance + income receipts on assets + current transfer receipts + current surplus of government enterprises + capital transfer receipts

Current tax receipts = personal current taxes + taxes on production and imports + taxes on corporate income + taxes from the rest of the world

Total expenditures = current expenditures + gross government investment + capital transfer payments + net purchases of nonproduced assets – consumption of fixed capital"

Source: Bureau of Economic Analysis, Federal Reserve Bank of St. Louis

Take a person, for example, who is working today in California. That worker has a federal payroll tax (employer and employee) of 15.3 percent[3], marginal federal income tax rate of 35 percent[4], a state payroll tax of 7.5 percent (highest unemployment insurance, employment training tax, and state disability insurance tax)[5], and a top state marginal income tax rate of 10.3 percent.[6] Soon that worker will have tax add-ons for ObamaCare.

In order to buy something, which is after all the point of working, the worker will have to pay sales taxes somewhere around 9 percent, as well as property taxes, excise taxes, state and local gas taxes, state and local liquor taxes, tariffs, and of course, corporate taxes of all sorts embedded in the price of the products and services that worker buys.

God forgive this worker if he or she wishes to save some of this income to give at a later date to grandchildren. In addition to corporate taxes (state and federal) there are dividend taxes (state and federal), capital gains taxes (state and federal), and federal estate taxes. And this doesn't even count how much the person will have to pay professionals to provide guidelines through the maze of rules and regulations.

On average, all these taxes probably add up to something in excess of 35 percent on income while for some people, on the margin, could be as high as 80 percent. In an address to the Economic Club of New York on December 14, 1962, John F. Kennedy presaged our view of the world when he said:

Whenever the government bails someone out of trouble, they put someone else into trouble. Every resource given to someone by the government represents that resource being taken away from someone else by the government.

> In short, it is a paradoxical truth that tax rates are too high today and tax revenues are too low. And the soundest way to raise the revenues in the long run is to cut the [tax] rates now. The experience of a number of European countries and Japan have borne this out. This country's own experience with tax reduction in 1954 has borne this out. And the reason is that only full employment can balance the budget, and tax reduction can pave the way to that employment. The purpose of cutting taxes now is not to incur a budget deficit, but to achieve the more prosperous, expanding economy which can bring a budget surplus.[7]

While tax rates and other tax variables are extremely important tools of government, they aren't the only government tools that are important. Government spending is also critical. In the most fundamental sense of the word, government spending is taxation. Father Christmas doesn't work at the Treasury department nor does the Tooth Fairy ever since the U.S. ran out of free land to give to its citizens. Governments don't create resources; they redistribute resources. Whenever the government bails someone out of trouble they put someone else into trouble. Every resource given to someone by the government represents that resource being taken away from someone else by the government.

To see clearly the logic that government spending is in fact taxation requires a simplification of the framework so that the essence of what is economics can easily be understood. It's hard for anyone to follow cause and effect in an economy with 310 million people: Chinese capital flows, credit default swaps, monetary base, multipliers, velocity, etc. All of the added complications that comprise a big modern economy are terribly confusing and only stand to obfuscate careful analysis. It is impossible for an individual to really keep track of all the T-accounts resulting from a change in economic policies. However, if the principles of economics are true, then those principles should be just as true in a two-person world as they are in a complicated 310-million-person world. The nice feature of a two-person world is that someone can actually understand just what the implications of those principles are.

Imagine, for example, that we have a world with only two farms and those two farms are the whole world. There's farmer A and farmer B and no one else in the world. If farmer B gets unemployment benefits, who do you think pays for those unemployment benefits? Obviously farmer A pays for farmer B's unemployment benefits. No less than 100 percent of government spending is taxation.

The Toll for the Troll

Milton Friedman used to argue that government spending is taxation nonstop.[8] But taxation may be substantially greater than all of government spending. Taxation is always equal to or greater than government spending…but never less. For example, there is always what we learned from children's fables—the famous "toll for the troll."

What one farmer pays in taxes may well be a lot more than the other farmer receives in government benefits. To file tax returns, to keep tax records, to accommodate audits, and to fund the IRS isn't cheap. Estimates are that taxpayers pay roughly 30-cents out-of-pocket for every dollar they pay in income taxes.[9] The government receives a lot less in taxes than taxpayers actually pay. While all government spending is tax, all tax isn't limited to government spending. There's always the toll for the troll.

Now tax rates, independent of the level of government spending, can also be important in determining an economy's tax burden. To see this point, imagine the same two farmers where there are 100 percent tax rates on everything each one of the farmers produces. Tax rates in this example would be so high that no matter how much each farmer works, that farmer will still receive nothing for his or her total production. Obviously, there would be no work, no output, and no government spending because there would be no tax revenue. Tax rates would be so high that no one would want to produce taxable income. Even though government spends nothing, the tax burden on the two farmers is enormous when tax rates are so high that they destroy all output.

In the pages that follow, we are going to look at the level and change in government spending. We will look at tax rates past, present, and future, as well as different forms of taxation. And, finally, we are going to look at regulations. We will then tease out of the data to understand how much each of these separately and collectively contributes to the path of an economy.

The current tax code is a daily mugging.
—Ronald Reagan

Chapter 2

Taxes: A Primer

The model we are going to examine in this chapter is a traditional economic model that includes various tax rates, total government spending, various forms of government spending, and a wide range of regulations. When examining a state or any other economic entity for that matter, it's not only the volume of taxes and spending that matters, but also how those taxes are collected and how the tax and borrowing proceeds are spent. As noted by 19th century American (also a Californian) economist Henry George,

> The mode of taxation is, in fact, quite as important as the amount. As a small burden badly placed may distress a horse that could carry with ease a much larger one properly adjusted, so a people may be impoverished and their power of producing wealth destroyed by taxation, which, if levied in any other way, could be borne with ease.[1]

Furthermore, regulations may be as important at the state level as they are at the federal level. Other factors that could also have considerable impact on a state's economic performance are whether or not a state is a right-to-work state, the level of its minimum wage, or the size of its welfare benefits.

That's the framework of the model that we are going to use in looking at California. It is also the framework that we are going to use to look at all the outside examples that might bear on the California economy. California can learn from other people's actions, successes, and failures to determine what will and will not work within California.

I am going to borrow a great deal from the research on cancer that has been done over the last forty or fifty years in the United States and elsewhere in the world.[2] The similarities between cancer research and macro-economic research are striking. It's impossible in any of these studies, whether one studies cancer or macro-economics, to conclusively demonstrate causation. To demonstrate causation requires controlled experiments and economists don't have this ability. Historically cancer research wasn't able to run controlled experiments either, although in recent years that has changed.

To prove causation requires three steps:
1. Show a strong correlation between the suspected cause A and the effect B;
2. Isolate the suspected cause A from all the other potential causes; and
3. The *pièce de résistance*: Be able to introduce the variable A into a system that doesn't already have variable A and have the system then produce the effect B.

You need correlation, isolation, and introduction to show causation. Obviously, we cannot do a double blind experiment on economies where some of them are given placebos and others get tax cuts or spending changes or some other economic variable.

Correlation

We are going to try to find out just how robust the correlations are between the policy variables we've selected and economic performance variables by looking at the relationship between taxes, tax rates, spending, regulation, and economic growth and other metrics of an economy's performance. We also are going to try to find correlation strength in many different areas. Repeated patterns across states and over different time periods only reinforce the logical connection between cause and effect. In effect, it's not only the strength of the correlation that matters but also the universality of that strength. Do other studies in other places find the same types of correlation, the same power of those correlations?

The more information we can assemble on the strength and the universality of these correlations raises our expectations that in fact A actually does cause B. Correlation doesn't prove causation, that's for sure, but pervasive universal strong correlation does raise what economists call their Bayesian prior (i.e. the likelihood of causation) that inferring causation is appropriate. If the correlation is only sporadic at best and unreliably strong, the force of the argument is reduced if not negated. The more universal the correlation and the stronger the correlation, the more likely it is that there is causation.

Intensity

In cancer studies, researchers were able to relate smoking to lung cancer in study after study. The correlations were strong and consistent. Populations of people who smoked for a period of time had a greater likelihood of developing lung cancer. By contrast, people who smoked for shorter periods of time were less likely to develop lung cancer. For those who once smoked and who now don't smoke, the probability of developing lung cancer depends on how long it has been since the ex-smoker last smoked. The number of cigarettes smoked affects the probability of contracting lung cancer.

Timing

Again, while the timing of events doesn't prove causation either, there is a presumption that causes precede effects and the longer the time elapsed between the two events the more likely the relationship is causal. While correlation doesn't prove causation nor does the time interval between the occurrence of one event and the other event with which the first event is correlated prove causation, they do increase the likelihood of causation.

There are all sorts of variables relating smoking to the likelihood of contracting lung cancer. The same type of factors may also be true in economics. How big are the tax cuts or tax increases? How long has the tax cut or tax increase been in place? What types of tax cuts or tax increases were made? It's not only the strength of the correlations; it's also the universality of the correlations and the intensity of the correlations that will make a difference.

Incentive Effects vs. Tax Cuts

At this point a quick digression is in order as to just how tax rates impact growth. In the models we use, tax rates don't directly affect economic performance, *per se*, instead tax rates affect taxpayer incentives and it is the change in the taxpayer incentives that affects economic performance. People don't work or save to pay taxes. Nor do firms invest or hire employees to pay taxes. People work and save to get what they can after tax. It's that very personal and private incentive that motivates people to quit one job and take another or to work in the first place.

Firms don't locate their plant facilities as a matter of social conscience. They locate their plant facilities to make an after-tax rate of return for their shareholders. Sometimes firms and individuals will actually choose activities that are higher taxed over other activities that are taxed less because their after tax returns are higher in the higher taxed activities. Not everyone has left California after all. But firms and individuals never choose activities where the after-tax returns are less. The distinction between tax rates and incentive rates will become important later. An example should help.

In the early 1960s President John Kennedy cut the highest tax rate on the highest income earners from 91 percent to 70 percent, which is a 23 percent cut in that rate (21 percent / 91 percent) and he cut the lowest income earners highest tax rate from 20 percent to 14 percent, a 30 percent cut (6 percent / 20 percent). Twenty-three percent and 30 percent are the tax rate effects. But look at this from the standpoint of the taxpayer.

In the highest income tax bracket prior to Kennedy's tax cut, the income earner was allowed to keep 9 cents on the last dollar earned. After Kennedy's tax cut the earner was allowed to keep 30 cents. That is a 233 percent increase in the incentive for the income earner after a 23 percent tax rate cut.

In the lowest income tax bracket prior to Kennedy's tax cut, the income earner was allowed to keep 80 cents on the last dollar earned and after Kennedy's tax cut the earner was allowed to keep 86 cents. That is a 7.5 percent increase in the incentive for that income earner to work after a 30 percent tax rate cut. In our analysis we look at how incentives are affected rather than how tax rates are affected. In the case above, the smaller percentage tax rate cut produced the larger incentive increase.

Likelihood

It's important to remember that not every long term heavy smoker of unfiltered cigarettes contracts cancer. Far from it. While in mathematics a counter example is sufficient to disprove a theorem, a counter example when it comes to probabilities and likelihood functions is to be expected. The relationship between smoking and cancer is one of likelihood, not one of certainty. The same type of likelihood relationship exists between tax rates and economic growth.

Not every tax cut increases economic growth, but cutting tax rates should raise the likelihood of higher economic growth. Showing an example where higher tax rates are associated with higher growth doesn't discredit the theory that tax rate increases reduce the likelihood of higher growth. But consistent repeated cases of an association between higher tax rates and higher growth would be sufficient to discredit the theory.

Specificity

In addition to strength, universality, and intensity, we are also going to look at the specificity of the correlations. For example, in lung cancer studies, researchers found results that make intuitive sense. The crude logic as to why lung cancer is caused by smoking is that tars from the smoke embed themselves in the smoker's lungs. Smoking tends to affect those areas where the smoke actually comes into contact with the body most. Thus one tends to find the incidence of lung cancer, throat cancer, mouth cancer, and lip cancer greater in smokers than in non-smokers. All the areas where the smoke touches the body are the same areas where the cancer is presumed to occur and also where it does occur.

The same principles are equally true with economics as they are in cancer research. Income taxes should have different effects than say estate taxes, or capital gains taxes, or payroll taxes, or sales taxes. Each of these taxes targets a different activity of an economy. We are going to try to ferret out and cull the data for specificity, intensity, universality, and strength of correlations. As an additional characteristic we will look at the durability of the tax/economic performance correlation, which is the power and uniformness of a correlation across different groups.

When it comes to taxation, individuals and businesses have a number of avenues they can choose to follow in order to reduce the impact of a tax. Of course the simplest way to reduce the taxes one has to pay is to change the volume of the taxed activity. In the extreme, a person can reduce taxes to zero by going out of business or becoming unemployed. No income, no taxes.

But businesses and people can also reduce their tax burden by changing the timing of their income through IRAs (Individual Retirement Accounts), Keogh plans, or 401(k) plans. By smoothing income over time, the incidence of tax can often be lowered. Some people and some businesses can also change the form of their income from high taxed forms such as ordinary income to lower taxed forms such as capital gains or dividends. And finally, people and businesses can change the location of their income by moving from high tax locations to low tax locations. My next observation is clearly not meant as a recommendation to the reader or anyone else, but people can also reduce the amount of taxes they pay by evading taxes, and I hear through the grapevine that evasion sometimes happens.

These are the types of data that we are going to try to present, and from these data we will try to infer the relationship between economic policies and state performance. Obviously we are going to look at many different metrics of what constitutes state performance. The most common metric is what used to be called gross state product, but which the Bureau of Economic Analysis (BEA) now calls state GDP (gross domestic product). We are going to look at the level of state GDP, the growth of state GDP, and the share of U.S. GDP comprised by a single state.

The share of U.S. GDP metric is especially important for those states that had no income tax at some time in the past but then introduced an income tax. What happens to the state share of U.S. GDP following the introduction of a tax is a key question. We will look at not only what happens to their share of total U.S. GDP, but also to state employment growth, population growth, and yes even tax revenues. We are going to focus heavily on taxes, tax revenues, and tax revenue stability. Finally, we are going to look at all of the state performance characteristics with respect to the economic variables that we have described above.

Roughly $30 of additional out-of-pocket expenses are incurred for every $100 of income taxes paid.

As I mentioned earlier, there are often expenses incurred by the taxpayer and the overall tax system that either add to the taxpayer's burden without providing any additional revenue or are a direct expense to the taxing authority and as a result, reduces the amount of funds available to the government for other purposes. Our study of these costs using IRS data showed that roughly $30 of additional out-of-pocket expenses are incurred for every $100 of income taxes paid.[3]

In addition, there are all sorts of inefficiencies in the tax codes that encourage people and businesses to choose inefficient instruments and production technologies purely for tax reasons. Likewise the beneficiaries of government services often have to go out-of-pocket to receive their benefits, thus reducing the net benefit of government spending. And finally, the beneficiaries of government programs often change their behavior as a response to government programs. Who doesn't believe that at least a few people choose to be unemployed in order to receive their unemployment benefits?

We are going to try to analyze these specific policy/performance correlation data in ways that provide comparisons of what a state is doing relative to the policies of the other states. To isolate the impact of a policy change in one state, we are going to try to standardize for what the other states are doing as well. For example, if every state raises income tax rates, you may get lower growth for all the states, but there is no reason why a single state that raises its income tax in conformity with every other state should have relatively worse or better performance. To isolate state effects, we are going to look at relative behavior with respect to relative performance on all of these metrics.

States: Good and Bad Neighbor Policies

When it comes to a specific state there are other sets of policy variables that rise to the fore. First, each state is part of the whole country and what the country does will impact the state. In general we would expect this country effect to dominate a state's performance simply because country policies are broader and more pervasive than are state and local policies. And some states may outperform or underperform as a consequence of country policies and the specific composition of output by industry in the state.

Exhibit 2

Percent Change in Real Annual Personal Income, U.S. and California, 1970 to 2010

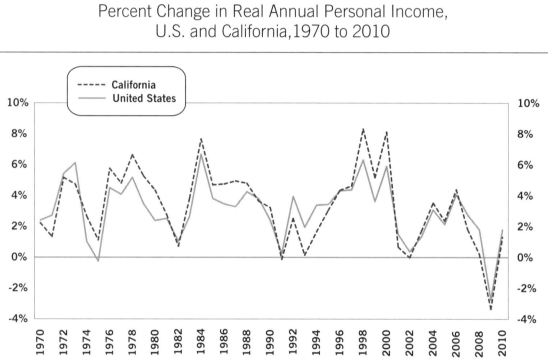

Source: Bureau of Economic Analysis

Back in 2005, California became a supernova sending out solar systems of economies in all directions.

Second, each state will be affected by its neighboring states and its competitor states. Where a business chooses to locate depends not only on one state's policies but also upon each of all the other states' policies. Choice means A versus B, not just whether A is good or not.

When state A employs sound policies and state B does not, the consequences are rarely beneficial for state B. For me, I left California in 2006 due to the poor policy decisions coming out of Sacramento.

I was not the only one. Back in 2005, California became a supernova sending out solar systems of economies in all directions. The predictable consequence was not only a mass exodus out of California, but the mass inflows of former Californians to the neighboring states. The 2005 data from United Van Lines creates a stunning picture that encapsulates the consequences from the policy implosion in California. Those states that had the largest inflows bordered on California, which had the largest outflow.

Exhibit 3

2005 Migration Trends Based on United Van Lines Data

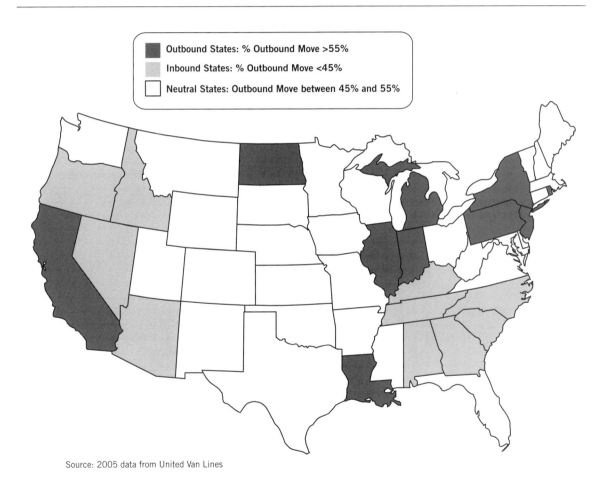

Source: 2005 data from United Van Lines

Lastly, states can, in part, affect their own destinies by the policies they choose. But the actual performance of any one state depends on lots of factors, not just on what that specific state does. A great example has to do with the recent increase in the price of hydrocarbons. There are a few states in the U.S. where deposits of coal, oil, and natural gas are significant components of a state's economy.

Higher oil prices tend to lead to higher output and usually greater taxes. These factors tend to be outside the reach of traditional policy actions.

At times we will look at property values, housing prices, and other variables, but the basic metrics that we will look at are state GDP, state GDP growth, share of U.S. GDP, employment, employment growth, population, population growth, tax revenues, and the stability of tax revenues over business cycles. We will carry out these studies in many different ways to extract information from variables that states control such as income tax rates, corporate tax rates, sales tax rates, and estate tax rates. For example, there are only 20 states currently that have a separate estate tax above and beyond the federal estate tax.[4] Estate taxes are important for certain groups of the population but not a huge deal for everyone else. We will have a couple of fun stories for you about the incentive effects of estate (death) taxes.

We are going to look at whether a state is a right-to-work state or a forced union state. One research study that I have performed recently focused on the state of Washington, which does not have an income tax but is not a right-to-work state.[5] I compared Washington State to the other states without income taxes and whether those states are right-to-work states or forced union states. As you will see, the results are amazing.

We will also look at welfare payments: how much does a state pay people for not working? We will look at the needs tests of government transfer payments, means tests, and income tests. Remember, it's not only how much a state taxes and spends, but it's also how states raise taxes and how they spend the money. The theory is that if you are going to tax people disproportionately for being successful and reward people disproportionately through government spending for not working, you are going to get worse results than if you don't disproportionately tax people who are successful and don't reward people disproportionately who are not working.

We are also going to look at policy variables like the minimum wage, which theory would argue really does remove people from the labor force. We are going to look at worker's compensation costs because they also matter. We are going to look at factors including spending and the types of spending, whether the state uses government funds to build bridges and libraries versus using that money for transfer payments and welfare. Lastly, we are going to look at different spending categories to the extent that we can uncover them. The following chapters will look at this information from all states that California can use to promote its own strong economic performance.

Away for the weekend
I've gotta play some one-night stands
Six for the tax man, and one for the band.
—"Success Story" The Who

Chapter 3

State Taxes: The Haves and Have Nots

It used to be that the sole purpose of the tax code was to raise the necessary funds to run government. But in today's world the tax mandate has many more facets including income redistribution, rewarding favored industries, and punishing unfavored behavior. And even with the greatly expanded tax mandate, finding an appropriate tax code would be relatively straightforward if only people would stop changing what they do when the tax code changes. It's like dodgeball; if only the other guy wouldn't duck when you threw the ball at him it would be easy to win. But, the other guy does duck and he almost always ducks just when you're throwing the ball at him. Damnit!

States provide a special environment to evaluate economic performance. Each state is subject to federal policies and each state exists in a virtually perfect free trade zone with all the other states. And yet each state also has a great deal of autonomy. States are free to enact all sorts of policies on their own and their political leaders are beholden only to their own electorate. As a result, states are often correctly described as crucibles for experiments in policies. Given the great variability of state policies over many years, there exists a huge reservoir of data reflecting past experiments. This reservoir allows us to explore the relative efficacy of a wide variety of state policies. Not only do we have a plethora of state data, we also have a fascinating interaction of state data with federal data. This repository of information and experiences should prove invaluable to the reform process in California.

Exhibit 4 lists several rows of data for all nine states that do not have a broad based personal earned income tax, the U.S. average for each of the metrics, and the same data for the nine states with the highest state marginal personal income tax rates, a group that includes California. In this instance, we chose nine states at the top and bottom of the policy ladder because there are only nine states with no earned income taxes.[1] We use a limited sample of the very top and bottom to accentuate the differences in policies in order to discern substantive differences in results.

To help California achieve the prosperity its citizens deserve, policies need to be developed based upon what actually will occur when those policies are put into place. Wishful thinking and political pandering has no place at the table. This chapter summarizes the experiences of all the states over the past half century with a whole host of economic experiments. These experiments have led to failures, successes, and inconclusive results that are described in the following pages. Untried and untested ideas and policies are exceptionally dangerous at this time due to California's extreme vulnerability. But worse than untried and untested ideas are ideas and policies that have been found wanting wherever they have been tried and yet continue to seduce politicians. The most immoral act a government can ever perpetrate on its citizenry is to enact policies that have the effect of destroying the production base from whence all beneficence ultimately flows.

Exhibit 4

The Nine States with the Lowest and the Highest Marginal Personal Income Tax (PIT) Rates, 10-Year Economic Performance

(performance between 2001 and 2010 unless otherwise noted)

State	Top PIT Rate*	Gross State Product Growth	Non-Farm Payroll Employment Growth	Population Growth	Net Domestic In-Migration as a % of Population	State & Local Tax Revenue Growth***
Alaska	0.00%	77.0%	12.2%	12.1%	-2.0%	452.6%
Florida	0.00%	47.7%	0.2%	15.0%	6.5%	82.3%
Nevada	0.00%	58.9%	6.1%	28.9%	14.1%	100.1%
New Hampshire	0.00%	35.2%	-0.7%	4.7%	2.5%	59.6%
South Dakota	0.00%	58.5%	6.4%	7.3%	0.8%	51.2%
Tennessee	0.00%	38.6%	-2.8%	10.3%	4.2%	61.7%
Texas	0.00%	57.7%	8.7%	17.9%	3.4%	75.5%
Washington	0.00%	47.8%	3.0%	12.3%	3.4%	57.8%
Wyoming	0.00%	105.6%	15.2%	14.3%	4.3%	172.2%
9 States with no PIT**	0.00%	58.54%	5.36%	13.65%	4.12%	123.66%
U.S. Average**	5.47%	46.61%	0.51%	8.63%	0.86%	70.23%
9 States with Highest Marginal PIT Rate**	9.92%	42.06%	-1.68%	5.49%	-1.91%	61.79%
Ohio	8.24%	24.8%	-9.3%	1.2%	-3.1%	44.5%
Maine	8.50%	35.4%	-2.5%	3.4%	2.3%	45.3%
Maryland	9.30%	50.9%	1.7%	7.4%	-1.5%	67.0%
Vermont	9.40%	36.1%	-1.6%	2.2%	-0.1%	64.5%
New York	10.50%	43.1%	-0.4%	1.5%	-8.3%	68.3%
California	10.55%	42.1%	-4.8%	8.0%	-3.9%	77.2%
New Jersey	10.75%	33.7%	-3.6%	3.6%	-4.8%	70.4%
Hawaii	11.00%	57.4%	5.7%	11.7%	-2.2%	72.1%
Oregon	11.00%	55.0%	-0.3%	10.4%	4.5%	46.8%

*Highest marginal state and local personal income tax rate imposed as of 1/1/2011 using the tax rate of each state's largest city as a proxy for the local tax . The deductability of federal taxes from state tax liability is included where applicable. New Hampshire and Tennessee tax dividend and interest income only.
**Equal-weighted averages
***1999-2008

For each of these states and the U.S. average of all states we have columns for the current:

- Top marginal personal earned income tax rate
- Gross state product growth
- Non-farm payroll employment growth
- Population growth
- Net domestic in-migration as a percent of population; and
- Growth of total state and local tax receipts

The economic, population, net domestic in-migration, and tax revenue data are all for the 10-year period 2001–2010.

The numbers are truly striking. For total gross state product (GSP) growth, the zero-personal-income-tax-rate states have, on average, outperformed those states with the highest personal income tax rates by 16.5 percent over the past decade and have outperformed the U.S. average by 12 percent.[2] The nine states without a personal income tax also outperformed California by 16.4 percent. In addition, there was not one single state in the nine highest tax rate states that performed as well as the average of the nine zero-income-tax states.

Now quite a bit of the extra growth in average gross state product between the highest and the lowest income tax rate states comes from higher population growth and higher employment growth. And here again California has been significantly trailing the rest of our sample.

For those states with no personal earned income taxes, average population growth over the past decade was about 13.7 percent, or 8.2 percentage points higher than the average of those nine states with the highest personal income tax rates, and over 5 percentage points higher than the U.S. average. And, for non-farm payroll employment growth, the average difference was a similar 7.0 percentage points higher (5.4 percent versus -1.7 percent) for the no-tax states versus the highest personal income tax rate states. No-tax state nonfarm payroll employment growth outperformed the U.S. average by 4.9 percentage points and outperformed California by a full 10.2 percentage points.

The nine states without a personal income tax outperformed California in terms of gross state product by 16.4 percent.

When it comes to population growth, people are voting with their feet. Not one of the high-tax-rate states had population growth as high as the average of the nine zero-income-tax-rate states. Guess who lost the election?

The growth premium of the no-personal-earned-income-tax states also benefits the government. Whereas the average growth of all states in tax revenues over the past 10 years was 70.2 percent, the no-income-tax states saw revenue growth 53.4 percentage points higher at 123.7 percent—double the 61.8 percent growth in revenue of the highest-personal-income-tax-rate states. Clearly, private sector growth matters a great deal for government revenues.

If the highest income tax rate states don't have those higher rates to collect more money, why then are those rates so high?

In the Long Term, the Analysis Still Lives

A possible criticism of the above analysis is that while it is true over the past 10 years, there may be something unique about this time period. To dispel this criticism, we evaluated the economic performance of the states with no income tax from as far back as 1971 through today.[3] However, the further back in time we go, there were more and more states that did not impose an income tax. In 1971, for example, 11 states did not levy an income tax—Alaska, which currently does not levy an income tax, did levy an income tax until 1980. Gradually over time, these 11 states plus Alaska dwindled down to the current nine (i.e. three states chose to impose an income tax while Alaska eliminated hers).

We compared the growth rate in personal income for those states that did not levy an income tax to the growth rates for those states with the highest marginal personal income tax rates.[4] The reader will note that our measure of economic activity switched from state GDP to personal income for our time series analysis. While state GDP is a more comprehensive measure of state economic activity, the switch from the Standard Industrial Classification (SIC) system to the North America Industry Classification System (NAICS) by the U.S. created a discontinuous break in the state GDP data as measured by the U.S. Bureau of Economic Analysis (BEA) in 1997. Due to this break, our analysis switches from state GDP to personal income for the longer time series analysis in order to preserve a consistent data series.

No-tax state nonfarm payroll employment growth outperformed the U.S. average by 4.9 percentage points and outperformed California by a full 10.2 percentage points.

The analysis also accounts for the changing composition of the states that did not levy an income tax, as well as the changing composition of the states that levied the highest income tax rates. For each year, each state is categorized into the zero-income-tax category, the highest-income-tax-rate category, or everyone else. It is the most recent year's data that determine in which category a state belongs. The average personal income growth rate over the previous 10 years for each category is calculated.

The changing composition of the state categories creates complications. For instance, Alaska levied an income tax until 1980. Therefore we classify Alaska as a no-income-tax state starting in 1981. Even though Alaska is considered a zero income tax state in 1981, it did have an income tax during the period in which its economic performance was measured. A similar dynamic applies to the states that became members of the highest income tax rate states during that period. Because economic performance changes in anticipation of a policy change, it is not clear what the "correct" timing should be, however. Because these effects are transitory, for simplicity we use the implementation date to guide the classification. We believe the conclusions we draw are not materially impacted by our date selections.

To smooth out yearly fluctuations, we compared the 10-year growth rates for the no-income-tax states to the 10-year growth rates for the states with the highest marginal personal income tax rates. As illustrated in Exhibit 5, the long-term growth rates of the states without an income tax are consistently higher than the long-term growth rates for the states with the highest marginal personal income tax rates.

The consistency and persistence of these results are overwhelming. Year in, year out, the average of the highest tax rate states are the losers and the zero-income-tax-rate states are the winners.

Personal income in the no-income-tax states has grown 55 percent more than has personal income growth in the nine states with the highest personal income tax rates between 1971 and 2010.

Moreover, persistently higher growth rates make a large aggregate difference over all states and over time. The magic of compound interest is nowhere more heart felt. Taking just the nine states that currently have no income tax compared to the nine states with the highest personal income tax rates over the entire period, personal income in the no-income-tax states has grown 55 percent more than has personal income growth in the nine states with the highest personal income tax rates between 1971 and 2010. By way of example, if both groups started off in 1971 with $100 of personal income, the highest personal income tax rate states would have $303.92 of personal income in 2010 and those nine states with no personal income tax would have $470.54 of personal income in 2010. Clearly, the lesson is that the right tax system matters and it matters a lot. Both poverty and prosperity are cumulative.

Exhibit 5

10-year Personal Income Growth Rate for No-Personal-Income-Tax-States
10-year Personal Income Growth Rate for States with the Highest Personal
Income Tax Rate and Premium for No Personal Income Tax States
1971-2010

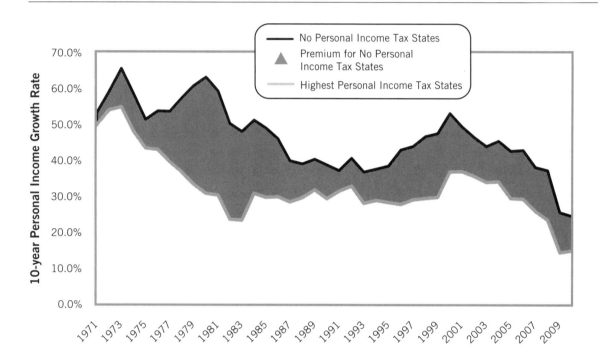

The Idiosyncracies of Oil Prices, Gas Prices, Mining Prices, and Severance Taxes

Another possible criticism of our analysis has to do with the mining sector of each state, commodity prices, and severance taxes. Severance taxes, or taxes on the removal of non-renewable resources such as oil and coal, are for most states an unimportant tax revenue source. Compared to total state and local tax revenues across all 50 states, total severance tax revenues accounted for approximately 1 percent of total state and local tax revenues between 1977 and 2008. For some states, however, severance taxes are a very important revenue source and mining is an important component of gross state product. It is important to remember that severance taxes really amount to a state tax on out-of-state taxpayers and thus have little direct effect on the specific state's growth. More on this later.

Exhibit 6 displays total severance tax revenues as a percentage of total state and local tax revenues from 1999 to 2008 for the 22 states with the highest severance tax revenues as a percentage of total tax revenues.

Exhibit 6

Severance Taxes as a Percentage of Total State and Local Tax Revenue
Average 1999 through 2008

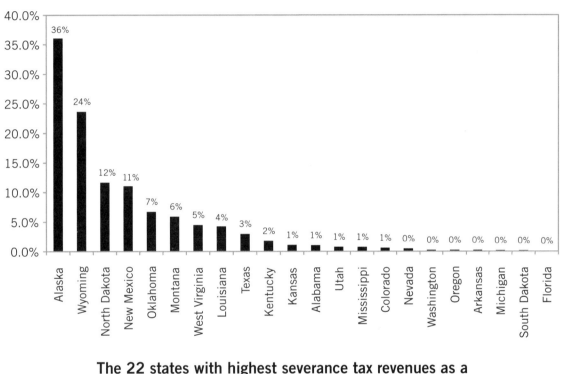

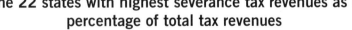

The 22 states with highest severance tax revenues as a percentage of total tax revenues

Exhibit 6 illustrates that although severance taxes are an unimportant revenue source nationally, for two states—Alaska and Wyoming—severance taxes account for one-quarter of total tax revenues. In seven other states—North Dakota, New Mexico, Oklahoma, Montana, West Virginia, Louisiana, and Texas—severance taxes account for between 3 percent and 12 percent of total tax revenues. Similar comments could also be made with respect to mining's contribution to each state's GDP.

With respect to our income tax comparisons, both Alaska and Wyoming are zero-income-tax states. Due to each state's relatively large mining component of GDP and heavy reliance on severance taxes during a period of rapidly rising oil, hydrocarbon, and raw materials prices, one criticism of our comparison is that Alaska and Wyoming are skewing the results. In fact, some argue being blessed with an abundance of oil, coal, or other natural resources is a necessary prerequisite for having no income tax. While the existence of oil, gas and other natural resources clearly make things easier for a state's government, they do not negate the impact of a state's income tax.

First, six of the no-income-tax states receive basically no revenues from severance taxes—Texas receives around 3 percent of its tax revenues from severance taxes. Second, and perhaps more important, having no income tax and relying heavily on severance taxes is not a necessary condition for economically outperforming the average state, or outperforming the states with the highest personal income tax rates. Admittedly, having lots of severance tax revenues does reduce the pressure on other tax revenue sources. But still, a zero income tax is a zero income tax.

Exhibit 7 reproduces the original personal income tax comparison for the zero-income-tax states that do not rely heavily on severance taxes (the nine previous states excluding Alaska and Wyoming) and the states with the highest marginal personal income tax rates. Exhibit 7 illustrates that Alaska and Wyoming are not the sole reason why we found the above results.

Exhibit 7

The Seven States with No Personal Income Taxes and Minimal Severance Tax
Revenues and the Highest Marginal Personal Income Tax (PIT) Rates
10-Year Economic Performance
(performance between 2001 and 2010 unless otherwise noted)

State	Top PIT Rate*	Gross State Product Growth	Non-Farm Payroll Employment Growth	Population Growth	Net Domestic In-Migration as a % of Population	State & Local Tax Revenue Growth***
Florida	0.00%	47.7%	0.2%	15.0%	6.5%	82.3%
Nevada	0.00%	58.9%	6.1%	28.9%	14.1%	100.1%
New Hampshire	0.00%	35.2%	-0.7%	4.7%	2.5%	59.6%
South Dakota	0.00%	58.5%	6.4%	7.3%	0.8%	51.2%
Tennessee	0.00%	38.6%	-2.8%	10.3%	4.2%	61.7%
Texas	0.00%	57.7%	8.7%	17.9%	3.4%	75.5%
Washington	0.00%	47.8%	3.0%	12.3%	3.4%	57.8%
7 States with no PIT**	0.00%	49.18%	2.98%	13.76%	4.98%	69.74%
U.S. Average**	5.47%	46.61%	0.51%	8.63%	0.86%	70.23%
9 States with Highest Marginal PIT Rate**	9.92%	42.06%	-1.68%	5.49%	-1.91%	61.79%
Ohio	8.24%	24.8%	-9.3%	1.2%	-3.1%	44.5%
Maine	8.50%	35.4%	-2.5%	3.4%	2.3%	45.3%
Maryland	9.30%	50.9%	1.7%	7.4%	-1.5%	67.0%
Vermont	9.40%	36.1%	-1.6%	2.2%	-0.1%	64.5%
New York	10.50%	43.1%	-0.4%	1.5%	-8.3%	68.3%
California	10.55%	42.1%	-4.8%	8.0%	-3.9%	77.2%
New Jersey	10.75%	33.7%	-3.6%	3.6%	-4.8%	70.4%
Hawaii	11.00%	57.4%	5.7%	11.7%	-2.2%	72.1%
Oregon	11.00%	55.0%	-0.3%	10.4%	4.5%	46.8%

*Highest marginal state and local personal income tax rate imposed as of 1/1/2011 using the tax rate of each state's largest city as a proxy effect of deductibility for the local tax. The effect of federal taxes on state tax liability is included where applicable. New Hampshire and and Tennessee tax dividend interest income only.
**Equal-weighted averages
***1999-2008

The seven states with no personal income tax that do not benefit from a heavy reliance on severance taxes still grow faster than the highest income tax rate states (49.2 percent versus 42.1 percent), still experience stronger employment growth (3 percent versus -1.7 percent), still experience faster population growth (13.8 percent versus 5.5 percent), and still have faster government revenue growth (69.7 percent versus 61.8 percent). One material change, however, is that the government revenue growth for the no-income-tax states is now the same as the U.S. average as opposed to being higher. What is encouraging is that these states generate the same tax revenue growth by growing the overall economy rather than imposing a higher marginal burden on income earners, the latter of which would cause the money the income earners earn to grow less rapidly. This is the Laffer Curve effect. A rising tide really does raise all boats!

Corporate Income Taxes

The states with the lowest corporate income tax rates are similarly associated with above average rates of economic growth while the states with the highest corporate income tax rates are associated with below average rates of economic growth. Exhibit 8 presents the latest comparison over the past 10 years for the nine states with the lowest corporate income tax rates compared to the nine states with the highest corporate income tax rates. It is important to note that only three states have no corporate income tax (Nevada, South Dakota, and Wyoming); therefore the competitive advantage between the lowest tax rate states and the highest tax rate states is not as great as was the difference for the zero tax states based on the personal income tax. And yet, the economic performance in those states with the lowest corporate income tax rates was still significantly better. It's noteworthy that a mining/severance tax adjustment makes almost no difference in the results for the corporate tax comparisons—pulling out Wyoming and Alaska does not change the results.

On average, the nine states with the lowest marginal corporate income tax rates saw state GDP growth rates that were 14.9 percentage points higher than the highest corporate tax rate states, employment growth that was nearly 7 percentage points higher and population growth that was also 7 percentage points higher. Tax revenue growth exceeded the national average by nearly 8 percentage points for the nine lowest corporate income tax rate states and except for Alaska, exceeded the average for the states with the highest marginal corporate income tax rates over time.

On average, the nine states with the lowest marginal corporate income tax rates saw employment growth that was nearly 7 percentage points higher.

With the exception of one or two anomalies in each category of metrics—South Carolina in the growth of gross state product, Mississippi in payroll employment growth, Delaware in population growth, and Delaware and Oregon in migration—the results are overpowering. Lower corporate tax rates are associated with higher state GDP growth, more rapid employment growth, increased population growth, and larger domestic in-migration without any (let alone catastrophic) revenue shortfall growth. Once again, common sense economics is confirmed overwhelmingly by the facts.

The lesson is clear: low corporate income tax rates encourage economic growth, and the tax revenues, if anything, are enhanced, while high marginal corporate income tax rates discourage economic growth.

Exhibit 8

The Nine States with the Lowest and the Highest Marginal Corporate Income Tax (CIT) Rates, 10-Year Economic Performance
(performance between 2001 and 2010 unless otherwise noted)

State	Top CIT Rate*	Gross State Product Growth	Non-Farm Payroll Employment Growth	Population Growth	Net Domestic In-Migration as a % of Population	State & Local Tax Revenue Growth***
Nevada	0.00%	58.9%	6.1%	28.9%	14.1%	100.1%
South Dakota	0.00%	58.5%	6.4%	7.3%	0.8%	51.2%
Wyoming	0.00%	105.6%	15.2%	14.3%	4.3%	172.2%
North Dakota	4.16%	81.5%	13.7%	5.7%	-3.4%	90.2%
Alabama	4.23%	43.7%	-2.1%	7.1%	1.9%	60.1%
Colorado	4.63%	42.4%	-0.3%	13.4%	3.7%	62.1%
Mississippi	5.00%	44.3%	-3.5%	4.0%	-1.1%	51.4%
South Carolina	5.00%	37.1%	-1.0%	13.8%	6.4%	45.2%
Utah	5.00%	58.2%	9.2%	20.6%	1.1%	71.4%
9 States with Lowest Marginal CIT Rate**	**3.11%**	**58.91%**	**4.86%**	**12.80%**	**3.08%**	**78.20%**
9 States with Lowest Marginal CIT Rate excluding WY**	**3.50%**	**53.07%**	**3.57%**	**12.61%**	**2.93%**	**66.45%**
U.S. Average**	**7.14%**	**46.61%**	**0.51%**	**8.63%**	**0.86%**	**70.23%**
9 States with Highest Marginal CIT Rate excluding AK**	**11.17%**	**39.88%**	**-3.36%**	**5.00%**	**-1.41%**	**48.94%**
9 States with Highest Marginal CIT Rate**	**10.97%**	**44.00%**	**-1.63%**	**5.79%**	**-1.48%**	**93.80%**
Michigan	9.01%	14.0%	-15.4%	-1.2%	-5.2%	25.9%
Alaska	9.40%	77.0%	12.2%	12.1%	-2.0%	452.6%
Illinois	9.50%	33.8%	-6.4%	2.6%	-4.8%	52.3%
Minnesota	9.80%	39.5%	-1.9%	6.4%	-0.9%	43.8%
Iowa	9.90%	51.7%	0.2%	4.0%	-1.4%	50.4%
Delaware	9.98%	41.9%	-1.6%	13.0%	5.2%	50.2%
Oregon	11.25%	55.0%	-0.3%	10.4%	4.5%	46.8%
Pennsylvania	13.97%	40.1%	-1.2%	3.3%	-0.3%	53.8%
New York	15.95%	43.1%	-0.4%	1.5%	-8.3%	68.3%

*Highest marginal state and local corporate income tax rate imposed as of 1/1/08 using the tax rate of each state's largest city as a proxy for the local tax. The effect of the deductibility of federal taxes from state tax liability is included where applicable.
  **Equal-weighted averages.
***1999-2008

Right-to-Work States

California cannot solely focus on its anti-growth personal income tax rate and corporate income tax rate. There is more to life than that. Every year, the Laffer-ALEC (American Legislative Exchange Council) State Competitiveness Index ranks the states on their economic competitiveness in a report called *Rich States, Poor States*. This ranking uses 15 fiscal, tax, and regulatory variables to determine which states have policies that are most conducive to prosperity. Several of these 15 policies have consistently stood out as the most important in predicting where jobs will be created and where incomes will rise. States with no income tax generally outperform high income tax rate states. This result holds equally true if not more so for the corporate income tax rate. We also find the overall tax burden an exceptionally important factor in determining whether a state is wining or losing the race for prosperity. In addition, right-to-work states grow faster than states with forced unionism.

Over the past decade the right-to-work states grew faster in nearly every respect than their union-shop counterparts.

As of today, there are 22 right-to-work states and 28 union-shop states (California is a union-shop state). Over the past decade (2001 to 2010) the right-to-work states grew faster in nearly every respect than their union-shop counterparts: 52.83 percent versus 41.72 percent in gross state product, 49.99 percent versus 38.78 percent in personal income, 2.80 percent versus -1.29 percent in payroll employment growth, and 11.85 percent versus 6.09 percent in population growth.

Exhibit 9

The 22 Right-To-Work States and the 28 Forced Union States
10-Year Economic Performance
(performance between 2001 and 2010 unless otherwise noted)

	Gross State Product Growth	Personal Income Growth	Nonfarm Payroll Employment Growth	Population Growth	Net Domestic In-Migration as a % of Population**
22 Right-To-Work States*	52.83%	49.99%	2.80%	11.85%	2.78%
U.S. Average*	46.61%	43.71%	0.51%	8.63%	0.86%
28 Forced Union States*	41.72%	38.78%	-1.29%	6.09%	-0.64%
*Equal-weighted averages ** 2000-2009					

In reality, the stampede of businesses from forced-union states has accelerated in recent years. The high profile court case *National Labor Relations Board (NLRB) v. Boeing* in which Boeing wanted to open a new production facility in the right-to-work state of South Carolina instead of the forced union state of Washington is just one example of many. The NLRB has enjoined Boeing from opening a facility in South Carolina claiming that Boeing has broken the law by moving to South Carolina as retribution against its Washington labor force for having called strikes in the past. To date, *NLRB v. Boeing* has not been fully resolved.[5]

A 2010 study in the *Cato Journal* by economist Richard Vedder of Ohio University found that between 2000 and 2008, 4.7 million Americans moved from forced-union states to right-to-work states.[6] That's one person every minute of every day. Right-to-work states are also getting richer over time. Professor Vedder found a 23 percent higher per capita income growth rate in right-to-work states than in forced-union states, which over the period between1977–2007 amounted to a $2,760 larger increase in per-person income in those states. That's a giant differential.

The unions are conceding that this migration is indeed happening, but they say that it is unhealthy and undesirable because workers in right-to-work states are paid less and get worse benefits than the workers in union states. Actually, when adjusting for the cost of living in each state and the fact that right-to-work states were poorer to begin with, a 2003 study in the *Journal of Labor Research* by University of Oklahoma economist Robert Reed found that wages rose faster in states that don't require union membership.[7]

Employers that move away from forced-union states mainly do so not to scale back wages and salaries—although sometimes that happens—but to avoid having to deal with intrusive union rules, the threat of costly work stoppages, lawsuits, worker paychecks going to union fat cats, aggressive anti-business union political activities, and so on. California, more than any state in the U.S., can appreciate the intrusive overpowering political actions carried out by unions. More on this later.

I am often accused of arguing that income tax rates are the only factors that influence where businesses and capital relocate. Taxes certainly matter. But taxes are not always the definitive factor in location decisions. Lucky are the six states—Texas, Tennessee, South Dakota, Nevada, Florida and Wyoming—that are both right-to-work states and have no income tax.

While there are only six right-to-work states that also have a zero-earned-income-tax rate and three zero-earned-income-tax rate states that have forced-union shops, their performance differences over the past decade (2001–10) are amazing. Of the nine zero-income-tax-rate states, those six that are also right-to-work have grown a lot faster than the three with forced-union shops: 61.15 percent versus 53.33 percent in gross state product, 54.99 percent versus 44.93 percent in personal income, 5.63 percent versus 4.84 percent in payroll, 15.61 percent versus 9.73 percent in population, and 5.54 percent versus 1.29 percent in net domestic in-migration. Enough written!

Exhibit 10

The Six No Income Tax/Right-To-Work States and the Three No Income Tax/Forced Union States
10-Year Economic Performance
(performance between 2001 and 2010 unless otherwise noted)

State	Gross State Product Growth	Personal Income Growth	Nonfarm Payroll Employment Growth	Population Growth	Net Domestic In-Migration as a % of Population**
Wyoming	105.6%	74.7%	15.2%	14.3%	4.3%
Nevada	58.9%	53.0%	6.1%	28.9%	14.1%
South Dakota	58.5%	49.8%	6.4%	7.3%	0.8%
Texas	57.7%	59.6%	8.7%	17.9%	3.4%
Florida	47.7%	51.5%	0.2%	15.0%	6.5%
Tennessee	38.6%	41.4%	-2.8%	10.3%	4.2%
6 No Income Tax Right-To-Work States*	**61.15%**	**54.99%**	**5.63%**	**15.61%**	**5.54%**
6 No Income Tax Right-To-Work States ex WY*	**52.27%**	**51.05%**	**3.72%**	**15.86%**	**5.79%**
U.S. Average*	**46.61%**	**43.71%**	**0.51%**	**8.63%**	**0.86%**
3 No Income Tax Forced Union States ex AK*	**41.48%**	**40.64%**	**1.16%**	**8.52%**	**2.95%**
3 No Income Tax Forced Union States*	**53.33%**	**44.93%**	**4.84%**	**9.73%**	**1.29%**
Alaska	77.0%	53.5%	12.2%	12.1%	-2.0%
Washington	47.8%	48.5%	3.0%	12.3%	3.4%
New Hampshire	35.2%	32.8%	-0.7%	4.7%	2.5%

*Equal-weighted averages
** 2000-2009

Union Membership

The flip side of right-to-work laws is union membership. Unions drive a huge wedge in the employment market. Consequently, unions' actual economic impact is depressed economic growth that ultimately leads to depressed income growth. It's just basic Econ 101. One only has to look at the devastation that the United Auto Workers brought to Detroit and the U.S. auto industry; or the crisis that state and local unions (in cahoots with compliant politicians) have created for state and local pension systems across the country to see the economic damage from unions.

Unions create a labor monopoly for those industries and firms unlucky enough to have to deal with them. Like all monopolies, the result is greater inefficiencies, higher costs, and economic rigidity, forcing the organizations that must work with the unions to create less output while using more labor. Economic growth, however, occurs when people, industries, and countries are able to create more output with fewer resources. The expected result of unions is reduced economic growth, reduced employment growth, and ultimately less income growth.

This is precisely what the evidence shows. The nine states with the lowest percentages of workers unionized—also all right-to-work states—significantly outperform the nine states with the highest percentages of workers unions—also all forced-union states.

Over the 1997–2006 period, the lowest unionized states saw state GDP growth that was 10.3 percentage points higher, personal income growth that was 14 percentage points higher, employment growth that was 4.0 percentage points higher, population growth that was 7.9 percentage points higher, net domestic migration growth that was 6.7 percentage points higher, and state and local tax revenue growth that was 13.8 percentage points higher. The lowest unionized states also outperformed the U.S. average across all of these categories, while the highest unionized states underperformed the U.S. average across all of these categories.

Exhibit 11

The Nine States with the Lowest and Highest Percent of Employed Who are Union Members

10-Year Economic Performance

(performance between 1997 and 2006 unless otherwise noted)

State	% of Employed who are Union Members***	Gross State Product Growth	Personal Income Growth	Right-To-Work? (1=Yes)**	Nonfarm Payroll Employment Growth	Population Growth	Net Domestic In-Migration as a % of Population	State & Local Tax Revenue Growth
North Carolina	3.3%	65.7%	65.2%	1	10.8%	15.8%	5.7%	69.2%
South Carolina	3.3%	53.7%	65.7%	1	11.0%	12.4%	5.3%	60.0%
Virginia	4.0%	77.6%	76.1%	1	15.3%	12.0%	1.8%	78.6%
Georgia	4.4%	60.9%	70.5%	1	13.1%	21.4%	6.2%	70.8%
Texas	4.9%	75.3%	76.8%	1	16.9%	18.4%	2.5%	73.8%
Arkansas	5.1%	56.3%	62.7%	1	8.5%	8.2%	2.4%	70.8%
Florida	5.2%	85.0%	85.5%	1	24.9%	19.1%	8.5%	87.2%
Utah	5.4%	77.8%	79.5%	1	21.2%	21.9%	-1.1%	77.1%
Mississippi	5.6%	48.5%	57.4%	1	3.1%	4.3%	-0.6%	52.6%
9 States with Lowest % of Employed who are Union Members*	**4.58%**	**66.74%**	**71.05%**	**1**	**13.85%**	**14.84%**	**3.41%**	**71.12%**
U.S. Average*	**11.15%**	**61.69%**	**63.92%**	**0.44**	**11.83%**	**9.04%**	**0.66%**	**63.39%**
9 States with Highest % of Employed who are Union Members*	**19.88%**	**56.44%**	**57.09%**	**0**	**9.84%**	**6.97%**	**-3.31%**	**57.35%**
California	15.7%	73.5%	73.8%	0	14.7%	10.8%	-3.5%	80.9%
Minnesota	16.0%	60.0%	60.3%	0	10.4%	8.1%	0.0%	43.0%
Illinois	16.4%	47.3%	49.3%	0	2.7%	4.4%	-5.2%	53.7%
Michigan	19.6%	29.5%	34.6%	0	-2.5%	2.8%	-2.8%	35.3%
Washington	19.8%	62.3%	67.9%	0	13.7%	12.3%	3.0%	53.8%
New Jersey	20.1%	51.5%	56.2%	0	9.3%	4.9%	-4.3%	72.6%
Alaska	22.2%	66.1%	60.4%	0	17.3%	10.5%	-3.0%	52.0%
New York	24.4%	56.2%	52.9%	0	6.8%	3.8%	-9.3%	63.9%
Hawaii	24.7%	61.6%	58.5%	0	16.1%	5.3%	-4.5%	61.1%

* Equal-Weighted Averages
** 2006   ***2006 Bureau of Labor Statistics

ALEC/Laffer Competitive Environment Ranking

Exhibit 12 accounts for many of the other key factors that also impact economic growth. It presents the economic performance of the top 10 and bottom 10 performers from the latest Laffer-ALEC State Competitive Environment ranking that accounts for the following 15 policy factors:

- Highest Marginal Personal Income Tax Rate
- Highest Marginal Corporate Income Tax Rate
- Personal Income Tax Progressivity
- Property Tax Burden
- Sales Tax Burden
- Tax Burden from All Remaining Taxes
- Estate Tax/Inheritance Tax (Yes or No)
- Recently Legislated Tax Policy Changes
- Debt Service as a Share of Tax Revenue
- Public Employees per 1,000 Residents
- Quality of State Legal System
- State Minimum Wage
- Workers' Compensation Costs
- Right-to-Work State (Yes or No)
- Tax or Expenditure Limits

Exhibit 12

Relationship between Policies and Performance:
Laffer State Competitive Environment Rank vs. 10-Year Economic Performance
Performance between 2000 and 2009

State	Rank	Gross State Product Growth	Personal Income Growth	Personal Income per Capita Growth	Net Domestic In-Migration as a % of Population	Nonfarm Payroll Employment Growth
Utah	1	62.2%	59.8%	35.2%	2.0%	11.8%
South Dakota	2	61.5%	56.1%	49.9%	0.8%	7.3%
Virginia	3	55.1%	54.5%	46.2%	2.2%	4.4%
Wyoming	4	119.8%	81.8%	70.7%	4.1%	19.4%
Idaho	5	48.2%	53.5%	33.4%	7.4%	10.7%
Colorado	6	45.9%	43.2%	30.8%	4.1%	2.6%
North Dakota	7	73.3%	60.6%	69.5%	-2.9%	12.5%
Tennessee	8	36.2%	41.8%	32.7%	4.3%	-4.3%
Missouri	9	30.8%	38.6%	34.2%	0.7%	-2.9%
Florida	10	51.6%	54.8%	40.1%	6.9%	3.9%
10 Highest Ranked States*		58.5%	54.5%	44.3%	3.0%	6.5%
U.S. Average*		48.8%	47.8%	41.4%	0.9%	1.5%
10 Lowest Ranked States*		41.6%	39.9%	41.2%	-2.4%	-0.9%
Pennsylvania	41	38.4%	36.9%	40.5%	-0.4%	-1.0%
Rhode Island	42	42.0%	40.7%	47.1%	-4.3%	-3.8%
Oregon	43	46.2%	40.5%	30.9%	4.6%	-0.6%
New Jersey	44	36.9%	33.5%	39.4%	-5.3%	-1.8%
California	45	43.0%	38.0%	34.7%	-4.0%	-2.3%
Hawaii	46	58.8%	55.0%	50.7%	-2.2%	8.6%
Maine	47	39.2%	41.3%	44.4%	2.0%	-0.7%
Illinois	48	30.9%	33.1%	34.8%	-5.1%	-7.0%
Vermont	49	39.3%	41.8%	46.8%	-0.5%	0.2%
New York	50	40.8%	38.2%	42.6%	-8.6%	-0.5%

*equal weighted averages
Sources: U.S. Census, Bureau of Economic Analysis, Bureau of Labor Statistics

The results at this point may be creating feelings of déjà vu for the reader. States that spend less—especially on income-transfer programs—and states that tax less—particularly on productive activities such as working or investing—and states that regulate less, experience higher economic growth rates, than states that tax, spend, and regulate more.

As we illustrate again later in the book, states that foster strong economic environments also benefit from a better housing market. As an example, the top nine states from the Laffer-ALEC ranking have not only experienced greater economic growth than the bottom nine states, they have also weathered the housing downturn better. The average house price in the top nine states have declined only 4.9 percent from the housing peak in the first quarter of 2006 compared to an 18.1 percent decline for the bottom nine. Exhibit 13 also includes a comparison of the top and bottom 10 states because the Laffer-ALEC survey ranked Florida—a state with a major housing decline— as number 10. Yet, even with Florida included the findings do not change—those states with the strongest economic policies did not experience as large of a decline in housing values as those states with the weakest economic policies.

Exhibit 13

Relationship between Policies and Housing Price Performance
Laffer State Competitive Environment Rank vs. Home Prices
Performance between 1Q 2006 and 2Q 2011

State	ALEC-Laffer Outlook Rank	Change in Home Price Index
Utah	1	-11.0%
South Dakota	2	5.1%
Virginia	3	-13.4%
Wyoming	4	5.7%
Idaho	5	-24.5%
Colorado	6	-5.5%
North Dakota	7	18.7%
Tennessee	7	-6.1%
Missouri	9	-12.7%
Florida	10	-44.9%
Top 9*		-4.9%
Top 10*		-8.9%
U.S. Average*		-11.9%
Bottom 10*		-16.6%
Bottom 9*		-18.1%
Pennsylvania	41	-3.1%
Rhode Island	42	-24.0%
Oregon	43	-21.8%
New Jersey	44	-17.7%
California	45	-46.3%
Hawaii	45	-20.1%
Maine	47	-9.5%
Illinois	48	-17.0%
Vermont	49	-0.5%
New York	50	-5.6%
*equal weighted averages		
Sources: Federal Housing Finance Agency and Laffer Associates calculations		

Sales Taxes

The same economic benefits we saw with income taxes, corporate taxes, and right-to-work states do not accrue to those states with low sales tax burdens (measured as sales tax revenues per $1,000 of personal income) compared to those states with the highest sales tax burdens. Because sales taxes are, by definition, flat taxes on consumption, these taxes should be less economically distorting than progressive income taxes, either personal or corporate. We find that sales taxes are economic performance neutral and therefore are far preferable as a means for a state to raise needed tax revenues. All taxes are bad in the sense that they impede a productive activity. But some taxes are a lot worse than others and the government does need revenues after all to carry out its appointed tasks. If tax they must, the sales tax is one of the least harmful taxes.

Exhibit 14 illustrates that the states with the lowest sales tax burdens have lower state GDP growth, lower employment growth, and less population growth than the states with the highest sales tax burdens. But in truth these measures are probably spurious when it comes to sales tax burden as a stand-alone tax. Oregon, which has no sales tax at all, has the single highest income tax rate in the nation. Mississippi, which has a high sales tax burden, has one of the lowest corporate tax rates in the nation, and Tennessee, Washington and Wyoming have no income tax at all and yet are high sales tax burden states.

Sales taxes affect where sales occur and income taxes—corporate and personal—affect where income occurs.

I remember doing a tax study for Governor Pete DuPont of Delaware back in the late 1970s when Delaware had no sales tax (and still has no sales tax) but had a 19.8 percent highest marginal personal income tax rate. If you can believe what I'm about to write, Delaware at that time had the highest sales to income ratio of any state in the nation. Today, Oregon has made itself the Delaware of the 1970s—one giant retail outlet mall. Go figure!

Exhibit 14

The Nine States with the Highest and Lowest Sales Tax Burden
10-Year Economic Performance
(performance between 2001 and 2010 unless otherwise noted)

State	Sales Tax Burden*	Gross State Product Growth	Non-Farm Payroll Employment Growth	Population Growth	Net Domestic In-Migration as a % of Population
Delaware	$0.00	41.9%	-1.6%	13.0%	5.2%
Montana	$0.00	56.0%	9.4%	9.2%	4.0%
New Hampshire	$0.00	35.2%	-0.7%	4.7%	2.5%
Oregon	$0.00	55.0%	-0.3%	10.4%	4.5%
Alaska	$7.31	77.0%	12.2%	12.1%	-2.0%
Massachusetts	$12.41	34.2%	-4.6%	2.1%	-4.7%
Virginia	$13.79	51.4%	3.2%	11.3%	1.7%
Maryland	$13.89	50.9%	1.7%	7.4%	-1.5%
Vermont	$14.31	36.1%	-1.6%	2.2%	-0.1%
9 States with Lowest Sales Tax Burden**	**$6.86**	**48.62%**	**1.97%**	**8.06%**	**1.06%**
U.S. Average**	**$24.58**	**46.61%**	**0.51%**	**8.63%**	**0.86%**
9 States with Highest Sales Tax Burden**	**$43.03**	**55.47%**	**3.07%**	**10.63%**	**1.90%**
Mississippi	$35.16	44.3%	-3.5%	4.0%	-1.1%
Arkansas	$40.09	44.6%	0.8%	8.4%	2.5%
Tennessee	$40.59	38.6%	-2.8%	10.3%	4.2%
Arizona	$40.89	49.0%	5.0%	20.5%	10.7%
New Mexico	$42.35	53.1%	5.9%	12.6%	1.5%
Louisiana	$43.37	58.7%	-1.6%	1.6%	-6.1%
Wyoming	$47.50	105.6%	15.2%	14.3%	4.3%
Hawaii	$48.56	57.4%	5.7%	11.7%	-2.2%
Washington	$48.73	47.8%	3.0%	12.3%	3.4%

*State and local Sales tax imposed as of 1/1/11 using the tax rate of each state's largest city as a proxy for the local tax. Sales tax burden of $1,000 of personal income.
**Equal-weighted averages.

Sales taxes affect where sales occur and income taxes—corporate and personal—affect where income occurs.

Total Tax Burden

As we've seen with our analysis of corporate and personal income taxes, sales taxes, and severance taxes, the manner in which a tax is imposed matters. The size of the burden on the state residents also matters. Referring back to the Henry George quote cited, it is both the placement and the size of the load that matters to a horse and to an economy.[8] Even if optimally developed (such as a flat rate income tax), a state cannot impose a tax burden equivalent to 100 percent of state GDP. Such a tax burden, no matter how well placed, will simply destroy the tax base from which all tax revenues are generated. The overall tax burden is, consequently, relevant as well as the form of the tax.

The average employment growth for all nine low-tax burden states is 4.72 percent. For California, employment growth is -4.8 percent. California needs a wake-up call, now!

As alluded to above, care must be taken in measuring a state's actual tax burden. For instance, dividing Alaska's total state tax revenues by total state personal income equals a burden of nearly 15 percent on average. However, because most of the revenues come from severances taxes, which are not paid by Alaskans, the actual tax burden paid by Alaska's resident producers and earners is much lower. Similarly, states with a large number of visitors and tourists—such as Florida, Nevada, Louisiana, or California—export a portion of the state's sales tax burden to these visitors and tourists. The correct tax burden measure for residents in each state, consequently, should adjust the state and local tax revenues for tax "exports" and tax "imports". The Tax Foundation creates yearly estimates of each state's state and local tax burden that adjusts for tax exports and tax imports.[9] Returning to our comparisons of the top nine versus the bottom nine, the same pattern also holds— those states that imposed the smallest tax burden in 2008 experienced higher rates of economic growth than both the average state and those nine states that imposed the largest tax burden. And again, while the strong Alaskan and Wyoming economies' increased the performance of the low tax states, the stronger economic performance of the low tax burden states holds even when the results from Alaska and Wyoming are excluded. Tax revenues are changed a lot by Alaska and Wyoming, but the other variables are not.

Exhibit 15

The Nine States with the Highest and Lowest Tax Burden as a Percent of Personal Income, 10-Year Economic Performance

(performance between 2001 and 2010 unless otherwise noted)

State	State & Local Gov't Tax Burden as a % of Personal Income*	Gross State Product Growth	Non-Farm Payroll Employment Growth	Population Growth	Net Domestic In-Migration as a % of Population	State & Local Tax Revenue Growth***
Alaska	6.3%	77.0%	12.2%	12.1%	-2.0%	452.6%
Nevada	7.5%	58.9%	6.1%	28.9%	14.1%	100.1%
South Dakota	7.6%	58.5%	6.4%	7.3%	0.8%	51.2%
Tennessee	7.6%	38.6%	-2.8%	10.3%	4.2%	61.7%
Wyoming	7.8%	105.6%	15.2%	14.3%	4.3%	172.2%
Texas	7.9%	57.7%	8.7%	17.9%	3.4%	75.5%
New Hampshire	8.0%	35.2%	-0.7%	4.7%	2.5%	59.6%
South Carolina	8.1%	37.1%	-1.0%	13.8%	6.4%	45.2%
Louisiana	8.2%	58.7%	-1.6%	1.6%	-6.1%	70.4%
9 States with Lowest Tax Burden as a % of Personal Income**	**7.67%**	**58.57%**	**4.72%**	**12.34%**	**3.05%**	**120.94%**
9 States with Lowest Tax Burden as a % of Personal Income Excluding AK & WY**	**7.84%**	**49.22%**	**2.17%**	**12.08%**	**3.60%**	**66.24%**
U.S. Average**	9.38%	46.61%	0.51%	8.63%	0.86%	70.23%
9 States with Highest Tax Burden as a % of Personal Income**	**11.02%**	**38.24%**	**-2.89%**	**3.78%**	**-2.48%**	**57.46%**
Maine	10.1%	35.4%	-2.5%	3.4%	2.3%	45.3%
Vermont	10.2%	36.1%	-1.6%	2.2%	-0.1%	64.5%
Minnesota	10.3%	39.5%	-1.9%	6.4%	-0.9%	43.8%
California	10.6%	42.1%	-4.8%	8.0%	-3.9%	77.2%
Rhode Island	10.7%	38.1%	-4.1%	-0.5%	-3.8%	52.4%
Wisconsin	11.0%	35.3%	-2.8%	5.1%	-0.1%	39.9%
Connecticut	12.0%	40.9%	-4.3%	4.2%	-2.6%	55.3%
New York	12.1%	43.1%	-0.4%	1.5%	-8.3%	68.3%
New Jersey	12.2%	33.7%	-3.6%	3.6%	-4.8%	70.4%

*State & Local Government Tax Burden as of 2008 from Tax Foundation
**Equal-weighted averages.

The reader will quickly notice that patterns are evolving across the various measures of policy variables. Seven of the nine lowest tax burden states are also zero-income-tax states. It's really hard to over-tax when one of the major tax sources is denied. Likewise, there is a significant clustering of bad behavior on the high end of the tax burden. Some states just can't get out of their own way. Take a state like Michigan, which has had such bad policies for so long that all the targets of the high taxers have left the state and left it in a shambles. Michigan may not now be in the highest tax burden states category, but believe me when I write it is the poster child of bad state economies.

California, New York, and New Jersey are chasing after the Michigan model as fast as they can. Unfortunately for California, New York, and New Jersey as of late appear to have gotten a little religion so to speak. Governors Andrew Cuomo and Chris Christie are polar opposites of their predecessors Governors David Paterson and Jon Corzine. Governor Jerry Brown has yet to make his move but his predecessor Governor Arnold Schwarzenegger couldn't have been worse if he had actually played the role of America's worst governor. Deception, deceit, and dissembling have no meaning until you've studied Arnold Schwarzenegger.

Not one of the high tax burden states has grown as fast as the average of the low tax burden states—with or without the inclusion of Wyoming and Alaska—not one. In fact, there is not one high tax burden state that has grown as fast as the average state in the nation—again *not one*.

Every single high tax burden state has lost jobs over the past decade. How's that for egg in your beer. The average employment growth for all nine low tax burden states is 4.72 percent and excluding Alaska and Wyoming it is 2.17 percent. The average for all 50 states is 0.51 percent whereas the nine highest tax burden states it is -2.89 percent. For California, employment growth is -4.8 percent. California needs a wake-up call, *now!*

When it comes to population growth, California's right at about the national average of 8 percent. But these are largely immigrants from Latin America and Asia while domestic in-migration is -3.9 percent compared to the average of the high-tax burden states of -2.48 percent, the national average of 0.9 percent and the lowest tax burden states to 3.6 percent. California is in deep trouble. California's tax receipts are up because the state keeps raising tax rates but that won't last forever. A lot of people are following my lead and getting out of California.

Estate Tax and Inheritance Tax

Only 20 states levy an estate tax or inheritance tax in addition to the federal estate tax—California is not one of them, a very good thing. The estate tax and inheritance tax are some of the most anti-family, unjust taxes ever levied. California's estate tax was eliminated in a statewide ballot proposition in the early 1980s while Jerry Brown was governor.

One reason is that Americans believe that estate taxes are inherently unjust—that it rewards vice and punishes virtue. Take the example of two hypothetical successful people—Jerry and Mary—each of whom has worked and paid taxes on his or her income and has now accumulated $10 million of wealth during their years of starting and growing a family business. Now, Jerry sells the company and spends all his money capriciously eating, drinking, gambling, carousing, and otherwise living high on the hog as if the world were Las Vegas at night. He dies broke and leaves his children not a penny after enjoying his final 15 years of life on his self-indulgent spending binge.

Meanwhile, Mary lives thriftily. She continues to work to expand the business with the help of her two children and her firm's value grows to $20 million. She wants to leave this business, her life's legacy, to her children and grandchildren who are her most cherished assets. Mary has clearly engaged in what most people would view as a more virtuous lifestyle than has Jerry, but Mary is clobbered with a hefty estate tax at death while Jerry is taxed not a penny more. Very few Americans would regard this situation as just or fair.

Americans also understand that this is a double or even triple tax. In our example, note that Mary has already been taxed on the money that is subject to the death tax. Hence, Mary paid up to 50 percent in federal, state, and local income taxes on her money when she earned it, yet she'll pay more when she goes to her grave on the 50 percent that was not taxed away already. Hence, for every after-tax dollar that she is able to pass to her children, the government keeps more. Again, this notion of taxing the same income twice is at the heart of the unfairness of this tax.

The economic case that there should be no state level estate tax, state level inheritance tax, federal estate tax, or federal inheritance tax is straightforward: These punitive taxes raise very little revenues yet do significant harm to the economy, impose very high compliance costs, and fail to achieve its objective of curtailing the transmission of wealth from one generation to the next. They are arguably the most counterproductive taxes.

The core economic problem with the estate tax and inheritance tax is that they penalize saving and investment and unjustly force the break-up of thousands of closely held family-owned businesses, farms, ranches, and other properties. The estate tax and inheritance tax also cause the misallocation of tens of billions of dollars a year away from the highest wealth producing investments into entirely unproductive tax shelters (and into the hands of estate planners, tax accountants, and life insurance salesmen). The compliance costs relative to the dollars raised are enormous.

One study published in the *Seton Hall Law Review* indicated that in 1992, the compliance costs were more than half the total amount raised by the estate tax.[10] According to the Newspaper Association of America (NAA), for every dollar the government eventually collects, the government and individuals collectively spend 65 cents on enforcement, compliance, and legal bills.[11] It is important to realize that less than half of the estates that must go through the burden of complying with the paperwork and reporting requirements of the tax actually pay even a nickel of the tax. These small-sized estates sometimes are forced to spend tens of thousands of dollars to comply with a tax that they don't even owe. No wonder the estate lawyers and tax accountants love this tax.

The U.S. Joint Economic Committee estimated that the estate tax has reduced U.S. wealth creation by $500 billion because the tax raises the cost of capital and thus dramatically reduces the savings rate of seniors and reduces reinvestment in family businesses.[12] Douglas Holtz-Eakin, former Congressional Budget Office director, calculates that the current death tax raises the cost of saving by

8 percent for the richest 10 percent of entrepreneurs and business owners and by 14 percent for the richest 1 percent. That is a highly significant deterrent to saving.[13]

There is a clear Laffer Curve angle to this tax: the government would lose a trivial amount of revenues if the tax were abolished. Because of the high economic and compliance costs of the death tax, a 2006 study by the Joint Economic Committee found that there was "...no compelling reason to keep the tax and a number of reasons to reduce or abolish it."[14] In a 1995 study on the estate tax, economist Dick Wagner of George Mason University calculated that the estate tax may actually cost the federal government more money than it raises.[15]

But even if there were no Laffer Curve effect from the estate tax and inheritance tax, and abolition of the estate tax and inheritance tax led to a 100 percent loss of the revenue collected, the fact is that the revenues are fiscally irrelevant. On average, over the 1999–2008 period, estate and gift taxes accounted for only 0.6 percent of tax revenues. In Pennsylvania, the state with the highest estate and gift tax revenues over the past 10 years, the estate and gift taxes accounted for only 1.8 percent of tax revenues.

At the state level, the estate tax and inheritance tax also reallocate people. Because 30 states do not levy an additional estate tax or inheritance tax on top of the federal estate tax, wealthy individuals can save millions of dollars from relocating their estates—along with their incomes, spending, and possibly businesses—to states that do not levy an estate tax or inheritance tax. The late Senator Howard Metzenbaum exemplifies this incentive. According to Americans for Prosperity:

> Though a lifelong Ohioan, the Senator moved to Florida in 2002, according to a declaration of domicile filed with the Broward County Clerk's office in 2003. In doing so, he avoided paying his home state's income tax (top rate: 6.55 percent).
>
> More important as he neared the end of his life, the former Senator also saved his family from paying Ohio's death tax, which features one of the highest state rates (7 percent) and lowest asset thresholds—$338,333—in the country. Florida famously has no income or estate tax, which is one reason other than the climate that it is home to so many northern-born retirees.
>
> Howard Metzenbaum thus denied the state in which he lived most of his life a parting financial gift. But he has at least provided the rest of us with a teaching moment in tax policy. If a liberal lion like Metzenbaum is willing to relocate late in life to avoid his state's death tax, maybe living politicians in Ohio will better understand how their confiscatory tax laws are driving its citizens to warmer climes.[16]

The epilogue to this story is that Ohio repealed its estate tax in 2011 and is slated to become effective in 2012. Go Buckeyes!

All of the above argues that those states that levy an estate tax should experience weaker economic growth than those states that do not levy an estate tax. This is the case. The following table continue our comparisons by breaking the states into the non-estate/non-inheritance tax states, and the estate tax/inheritance-tax states. In each one of the categories, the states that did not levy an estate tax or inheritance tax experienced stronger economic growth than the states that levied an estate tax or inheritance tax—gross state product growth (8.27 percent), personal income growth (7.53 percent), employment growth (3.77 percent), population growth (3.94 percent), and net domestic in-migration (1.99 percent).

The results hold in other periods as well. Additionally, because the majority of states do not levy an estate tax or inheritance tax, it is remarkable that these states exceed the national average as they represent 60 percent of the states.

Exhibit 16

The 30 States Without Estate Tax or Inheritance Tax and the 20 States With Estate Tax and/or Inheritance Tax
10-Year Economic Performance
(performance between 2001 and 2010 unless otherwise noted)

	Gross State Product Growth	Personal Income Growth	Nonfarm Payroll Employment Growth	Population Growth	Net Domestic In-Migration as a % of Population**
30 States without Estate Tax or Inheritance Tax*	49.92%	46.73%	2.02%	10.20%	1.66%
U.S. Average*	46.61%	43.71%	0.51%	8.63%	0.86%
20 States with Estate Tax and/or Inheritance Tax*	41.65%	39.20%	-1.75%	6.26%	-0.33%
*Equal-weighted averages ** 2000-2009					

Welfare Spending and Poverty

The Tooth Fairy does not work at any state revenue department across the country; neither does Father Christmas or the Easter Bunny. Therefore, if a state government is going to provide welfare benefits to one person, it must take these resources away from another person. Sometimes our complicated world obscures this very basic point. It is helpful, therefore, to return to our hypothetical two-person economy. Remember, if something doesn't work in a two-person economy, it's not good economics.

Take two farmers who comprise the whole world. If one of those farmers gets welfare benefits, guess who pays for those welfare benefits? The answer is the other farmer, of course. My colleague Milton Friedman was correct when he said, "There ain't no such thing as a free lunch."

This simple story illustrates that there are two anti-growth effects created by welfare spending. Taking the resources away from productive workers, savers, and investors reduces the incentive to work, save, and invest (anti-growth effect number one) and paying people not to work increases the incentive to not work (anti-growth effect number two). The combination of these two effects implies that those states that spend a larger amount on welfare programs should experience slower economic growth. And, this is precisely what the data confirm.

Compared to those states that spent a larger amount on welfare per poor person, the states that spent less experienced faster growth in state GDP (8.42 percent), faster employment growth (4.15 percent), faster population growth (4.83 percent), and a slower increase in the poverty rate (-0.30 percent).

These results do not mean that state governments should not provide a safety net to those who truly need assistance or a helping hand. However, there is a cost to providing these services. As stated above, welfare always reduces total output. But often that cost is well worth the benefits to those who are aided. Providing overly-generous benefits, however, increases these costs and quite perversely can ultimately begin to hurt those individuals the policies were actually designed to help through the creation of fewer economic opportunities and the encouragement of greater poverty. Ideally, government policies designed to address the real problem of poverty incorporate the impact that government policies have on incentives by implementing programs such as enterprise zones, which we will touch upon in our policy reforms section.

Exhibit 17

The Nine States with the Lowest and Highest Welfare Spending per Person in Poverty
Five-Year Economic Performance
(performance between 2004 and 2008 unless otherwise noted)

State	Welfare Spending per Person in Poverty ($1000s)*	Gross State Product Growth	Nonfarm Payroll Employment Growth	Population Growth	Net Domestic In-Migration as a % of Population	Change in Poverty Rate
Texas	$6.05	33.3%	11.7%	8.4%	2.4%	-0.6%
Alabama	$6.33	19.9%	4.8%	3.7%	1.8%	-0.5%
Nevada	$6.34	32.0%	9.6%	12.3%	8.9%	-0.3%
Georgia	$6.73	19.7%	5.2%	8.8%	3.7%	0.7%
Montana	$6.80	30.5%	8.4%	4.6%	3.2%	0.2%
Mississippi	$7.19	26.4%	2.0%	1.9%	-0.3%	1.1%
Louisiana	$7.63	30.6%	1.0%	-0.8%	-4.9%	-2.0%
Arizona	$7.73	34.6%	10.0%	12.8%	7.5%	-0.4%
Colorado	$7.76	28.8%	7.8%	7.3%	2.0%	0.8%
9 States with Lowest Welfare Spending per Person in Poverty**	**$6.95**	**28.44%**	**6.73%**	**6.55%**	**2.71%**	**-0.12%**
U.S. Average**	**$11.41**	**24.22%**	**4.88%**	**3.92%**	**0.60%**	**0.26%**
9 States with Highest Welfare Spending per Person in Poverty exAK**	**$18.12**	**17.51%**	**2.17%**	**1.44%**	**-2.05%**	**0.30%**
9 States with Highest Welfare Spending per Person in Poverty**	**$18.64**	**20.02%**	**2.58%**	**1.72%**	**-2.01%**	**0.18%**
Delaware	$16.40	12.2%	3.1%	6.0%	3.2%	0.4%
Connecticut	$16.81	24.1%	3.0%	0.8%	-2.2%	-0.2%
New York	$16.93	23.7%	3.9%	0.9%	-5.1%	-0.9%
New Jersey	$17.05	17.9%	1.3%	0.6%	-3.5%	0.2%
Rhode Island	$17.63	12.6%	-1.3%	-1.7%	-4.1%	0.2%
Massachusetts	$19.59	19.2%	3.0%	1.4%	-3.4%	0.0%
Vermont	$20.07	12.8%	1.4%	0.5%	-0.7%	1.4%
Minnesota	$20.45	17.6%	3.1%	3.0%	-0.7%	1.3%
Alaska	$22.87	40.1%	5.9%	4.0%	-1.7%	-0.8%

*2008
**Equal-weighted averages

Looking at welfare spending per person in poverty brings in a somewhat new aspect to our economic analysis much as the issue of the right-to-work. Texas and Nevada, to be sure, are in the top nine just as they were when we viewed the nine states with no income tax. Alabama, Nevada, Mississippi, and Colorado were also in the nine lowest corporate income tax rate states as well. But this variable catches a metric that does not precisely match the other tax rate variables and yet has a great deal of explanatory power.

Only Alaska of the highest welfare states has state GDP growth as high as the average of the nine states with the lowest welfare spending. Employment metrics match the GDP metrics as do population growth and poverty growth. Shockingly there is a decrease in poverty the less a state pays people who are in poverty and an increase in poverty in the nine states with the highest payments for poverty. If this doesn't show economics at its strongest, we don't know what does. The idea that paying people more for doing something elicits more people doing that activity is just common sense—basic Econ 101. But to see this principle at work when it comes to welfare benefits is unpleasantly shocking to most people. Somehow, people want to believe that the world doesn't work this way when it comes to poverty. Well it does and we've got to live with it and adjust our policies accordingly. Higher welfare payments increase the number of people on welfare.

Shockingly, there is a decrease in poverty the less a state pays people who are in poverty and an increase in poverty in the nine states with the highest payments for poverty.

Summary of Tax Effects on Gross State Product Growth

We have reviewed a great deal of data, and summarizing all of this information is a daunting task. While there are many policies that matter, a number of measures have shown themselves to be the most significant in a 50-state review: the top corporate income tax rate, the top personal income tax rate, the overall tax burden, percentage of employees represented by a union, and whether or not a state is a right-to-work state.

The following graph summarizes much of our previous discussion of the impacts on policy on economic growth by combining four of the variables into one chart. We did not include the percentage of employees represented by a union. For illustrative purposes, Exhibit 18 summarizes the impacts we have found through this review. While we all know state economies are affected by all sorts of variables, we are also well aware of the simplistic nature of the variables we've used in this chapter. Yet when all is said and done it is astounding to me at how much of state performance is explained by these simple variables. State economic performance is significantly impacted by the types of economic policies states implement.

Exhibit 18

50 States PIT + CIT + Tax Burden as Percent of PI + RTW (RTW=0, no-RTW=+10%)

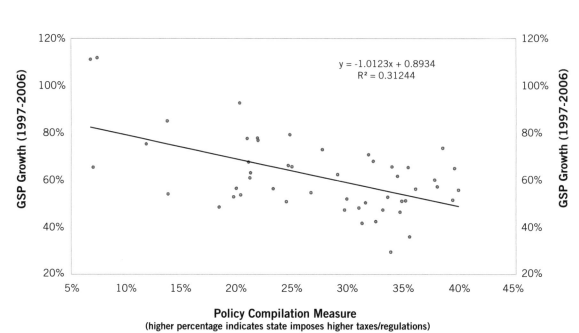

$y = -1.0123x + 0.8934$
$R^2 = 0.31244$

Policy Compilation Measure
(higher percentage indicates state imposes higher taxes/regulations)

Source: Bureau of Economic Analysis, Tax Foundation, author calculations

California would proceed at its own risk if they chose to ignore what's obvious. Just because it's simple doesn't make it wrong.

The Stability of Tax Receipts

Another major issue that state and local governments face is the stability of tax receipts. When tax receipts are volatile that usually means an abnormally great shortfall of revenues when times are tough when spending needs are the greatest, and excess revenues when times are good and some government spending is superfluous. State and local governments spend too much during good times on marginal projects solely because they can. And when bad times come, they are forced to raise taxes and cut back on desperately needed projects. In the case of California, in good times, automatic spending increases were put into law, and when the bad times came, the state went into spiraling deficits. Volatility of revenues and spending needs is anathema to good governance. Therefore, the best tax system is one where revenues are least volatile.

Exhibit 19 illustrates the percent change in the rolling 12 month sum of state and local tax revenues at the end of each quarter for every state's personal income tax revenues, corporate income tax revenues, sales tax revenues, and property tax revenues from 1998 through 2010.

Exhibit 19

Percent Change in 12-Month State and Local Tax Revenues
Individual Income, Corporate Income, Property and Sales Taxes

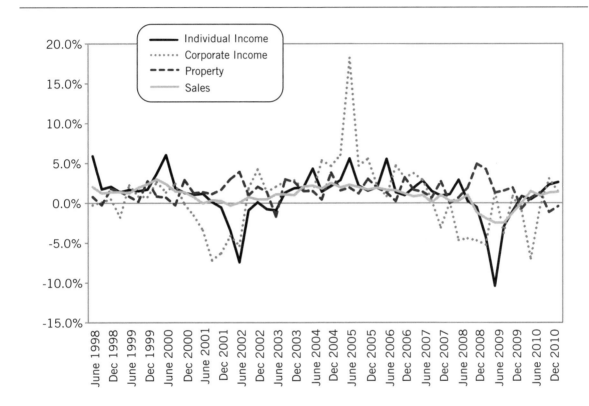

Source: U.S. Census, Quarterly Summary of State and Local Tax Revenues[8]

Exhibit 19 illustrates that personal income taxes and corporate income taxes show larger than average government revenue fluctuations. During bad economic times, individual and corporate income tax revenues fall further, and during good economic times individual and corporate income tax revenues surge higher. Simply put, revenues from sales and property taxes are more stable and reliable tax sources than are income taxes.

Combining this with our earlier results, progressive corporate and personal income taxes do far more harm and damage than do other taxes such as sales taxes, property taxes, and severance taxes

If you start me up,
If you start me up, I'll never stop.
—Rolling Stones

Chapter 4

When States Start an Income Tax

In the previous chapters we defined how much the economic performance of the nine states with no personal income tax exceeded the economic performance of the nine highest personal income tax rate states. Similarly the economic performance of the nine states with the lowest corporate income tax rates exceeded the economic performance of the nine highest corporate income tax rate states. While the results were as robust and conclusive as we could have imagined, there are a number of lingering concerns.

Each state in the U.S., for example, has its own unique characteristics and even when characteristics are shared with a few other states, it is difficult to disentangle exactly what has caused what. One could question the reliability of our previous section's comparison of the nine no-income-tax states with the highest income tax rate states because of differences in the two samples of states. In cliché form, are we really comparing apples with apples? In this chapter we narrow the focus in another way by comparing the performance of states that have actually implemented a state income tax before and after. In this case, the before and the after pictures are 180 degrees reverse of those of weight loss advertisements. The states that introduced an income tax look a helluva lot worse after they put in the income tax than they did before they put in an income tax—each of them.

Over the past 50 years 11 states have, at differing times, instituted a progressive state income tax. This chapter focuses on what the consequences have been for those states that have actually put in an income tax. In this way we can control for variations across states, which was not possible in the previous sections.

The 11 states where income taxes were initiated beginning with the most recent are: Connecticut (1991), New Jersey (1976), Ohio (1972), Rhode Island (1971), Pennsylvania (1971), Maine (1969), Illinois (1969), Nebraska (1968), Michigan (1967), Indiana (1963), and West Virginia (1961).

Exhibit 20 examines the economic consequences for each one of the 11 states that instituted a progressive state income tax within the past 50 years. Each state is measured by three key metrics:

- The state's share of total U.S. GDP;
- The state's share of U.S. population, and
- The state's share of total state tax revenue collected across all 50 states.

Exhibit 20

Economic Consequences from the Introduction of State Income Tax

State		Economic Performance			Top PIT	
		% of U.S. GDP	% of U.S. Population	State Tax Revenues % of U.S.	Introduced	Current
Connecticut	5 Years Prior	1.74%	1.33%	1.70%		
	2010	1.63%	1.16%	1.81%	1.50%	6.50%
	Change	**-0.11%**	**-0.17%**	0.11%		5.00%
New Jersey	5 Years Prior	3.66%	3.47%	2.77%		
	2010	3.35%	2.85%	3.79%	2.50%	8.97%
	Change	**-0.31%**	**-0.62%**	1.02%		6.47%
Ohio	5 Years Prior	5.42%	5.25%	3.61%		
	2010	3.28%	3.74%	3.35%	3.50%	5.93%
	Change	**-2.14%**	**-1.51%**	**-0.26%**		2.43%
Rhode island	5 Years Prior	0.44%	0.46%	0.47%		
	2010	0.34%	0.34%	0.36%	5.25%	5.99%
	Change	**-0.10%**	**-0.12%**	**-0.11%**		0.74%
Pennsylvania	5 Years Prior	5.72%	5.88%	5.59%		
	2010	3.91%	4.11%	4.21%	2.30%	3.07%
	Change	**-1.81%**	**-1.77%**	**-1.38%**		0.77%
Maine	5 Years Prior	0.39%	0.51%	0.43%		
	2010	0.35%	0.43%	0.49%	6.00%	8.50%
	Change	**-0.04%**	**-0.08%**	0.06%		2.50%
Illinois	5 Years Prior	6.52%	5.53%	4.64%		
	2010	4.48%	4.16%	4.09%	2.50%	5.00%
	Change	**-2.04%**	**-1.37%**	**-0.55%**		2.50%
Nebraska	5 Years Prior	0.67%	0.75%	0.45%		
	2010	0.62%	0.59%	0.54%	2.60%	6.84%
	Change	**-0.05%**	**-0.16%**	0.09%		4.24%
Michigan	5 Years Prior	5.08%	4.34%	5.03%		
	2010	2.64%	3.20%	3.18%	2.00%	4.35%
	Change	**-2.44%**	**-1.14%**	**-1.85%**		2.35%

Indiana	5 Years Prior	2.61%	2.55%	2.09%		
	2010	1.89%	2.10%	2.08%	2.00%	3.40%
	Change	**-0.72%**	**-0.45%**	**-0.01%**		1.40%
West Virginia*	5 Years Prior	0.79%	0.97%	1.01%		
	2010	0.48%	0.60%	0.67%	5.40%**	6.50%
	Change	**-0.31%**	**-0.37%**	**-0.34%**		1.10%

* Due to State GDP data limitations, West Virginia's economic activity is measured as a share of national personal income
** Statutory rate was 6.0% of U.S. tax liability applied to top rate of 91%

What we find absolutely astonishing is how the size of the economy in each one of these states has declined as a share of the total U.S. economy compared to a time just prior to when each state introduced its income tax. Some of the declines are quite large. Connecticut, for example, went from 1.74 percent of U.S. GDP in the 1986–1990 period to 1.63 percent in 2010. New Jersey fell from 3.66 percent of U.S. GDP from the 1971–1975 period to 3.35 percent in 2010. From 1967 to 1971 Ohio was 5.42 percent of total U.S. GDP yet in 2010 it fell to 3.28 percent. Rhode Island and Pennsylvania respectively went from 0.44 percent and 5.72 percent of the U.S. in the 1966–70 period to 0.34 percent and 3.91 percent in 2010. Maine's and Illinois' pre-tax period was 1964–68 and they dropped respectively from 0.39 percent and 6.52 percent of the total U.S. GSP to 0.35 percent and 4.48 percent in 2010. Our beloved Michigan, which seems never to get a break, went from 5.08 percent in the 1962–1966 period to 2.64 percent in 2010. Leaping Lizards! And lastly, Indiana in 1963 and West Virginia in 1961 went from 2.61 percent and 0.79 percent to 1.89 percent and 0.48 percent, respectively. And, who could have thought that West Virginia could actually decline further from its state of abject poverty in the early 1960s? But it did.

A similar pattern also holds for these states' share of the national population. What is perhaps even more surprising to some is that the introduction of an income tax did not universally increase the share of tax revenues going to these states. In fact, more times than not, the share of tax revenues fell despite that top marginal personal income tax rate rising in each one of these states. And do these states ever lower income tax rates once they got their nose in under the tent? *Never!*

It's more than depressing—it's an absolute tragedy when you realize just how much opportunity the citizens of these eleven states have lost following their adoption of a progressive income tax. On a human level it's appalling. Of course, there are many other factors impacting the economies of these states. Certainly the woe of the auto industry helps explain Michigan's decline. But surely the rise of unions, the absence of being a right-to-work state, and other state government policies cannot be held blameless for the demise of the auto industry. In the same manner, growth in agriculture helps explain Nebraska's steady share of U.S. GDP. Overall, it is the preponderance of the effect that is of interest. And, from this perspective, the introduction of a personal income tax is associated with declining relative economic growth.

The income experiments for each and every state that has instituted a personal income tax has been a total failure. In each case the state's economy has become a smaller portion of the overall U.S. economy and the state's citizens have seen their prosperity dramatically reduced. And the population of each of these states has given their state government a big raspberry by voting with their feet and leaving. California are you listening?

Bilateral Comparisons: Tennessee v. Kentucky, Texas v. California

Some states also provide a natural experiment due to their similarities. For instance, California and Texas are geographically and economically diverse states with huge populations (number one and two) and the largest state economies in the country. Kentucky and Tennessee are also geographically similar states with smaller less diverse economies.

While many of the attributes of these states are similar, the economic policies of the states vary widely. Tennessee and Texas have each pursued pro-growth economic policies consistent with the top growers—low tax rates, low tax burdens, and right-to-work states. Kentucky and California have pursued the opposite strategy. At this point, the reader will not be surprised by the results—both Tennessee and Texas outperform Kentucky and California as shown in Exhibits 21 and 22.

Exhibit 21

Tennessee v. Kentucky
Policy Instruments and Economic Consequences

	Tennessee	Kentucky
	Policy Instruments	
Top Marginal Personal Income Tax Rate	0.00%	8.20%
Top Marginal Corporate Income Tax Rate	6.50%	8.20%
Total State & Local Tax Revenue as % of State GDP (2008)	7.67%	9.10%
Right-to-Work?	Yes	No
	Economic Outcomes	
Change in Personal Income (1981-2010)	430.90%	338.50%
Unemployment Rate (2010)	9.70%	10.40%

Exhibit 22

Texas v. California
Policy Instruments and Economic Consequences

	Texas	California
	Policy Instruments	
Top Marginal Personal Income Tax Rate	0.00%	10.30%
Top Marginal Corporate Income Tax Rate	5.56%	8.84%
Total State & Local Tax Revenue as % of State GDP (2008)	7.19%	9.73%
Right-to-Work?	Yes	No
	Economic Outcomes	
Change in Personal Income (1981-2010)	494.90%	**403.10%**
Unemployment Rate (2010)	8.20%	**12.40%**

There it is in black and white. California, cutting taxes won't make you wear boots and cowboy hats but it will create jobs and prosperity for your citizens, y'all.

A Look at Stock Performance and State Competitive Environments

As the evidence above indicates, states that increase taxes above the national average experience weaker economic performance. These states find it difficult to retain existing facilities and to attract new businesses. Mobile capital and labor emigrate away from high tax states to seek higher after-tax returns in other states. Immobile factors of production are left behind to bear the burden of the state and local taxes. As a result, states that increase their relative tax burdens exhibit a slower pace of economic expansion, while those that lower their relative burdens experience accelerated economic growth.

A combination of the level as well as changes in relative tax burden truly characterizes the cost of doing business in a state. Overtaxed states *per se* restrain growth, while states that raise taxes—even if they currently aren't overtaxed—clearly inhibit growth.

The connection between state and local tax policy and economic performance assures us that the values of assets located in states will change in predictable directions. With respect to stock prices, a company's stock price should reflect all known information that could impact a company's performance—including the current economic policy environment(s) where the company operates. When the policy environment of a state improves, the profitability of the companies operating in that state improves and should be reflected in each company's stock price. The reverse should also hold: when the policy environment of a state worsens, the profitability of the companies operating in that state worsens and should be reflected in each company's stock price. Because the changes to the company's outlook are dependent upon changes in the policy environment, the analysis below focuses on changes in state tax policies.

If the stock prices of companies located in states that are cutting tax rates tend to rise (reflecting the stronger underlying economic fundamentals), while the stock prices of companies located in states that are increasing tax rates will tend to fall, then this will provide additional support to our story that pro-growth economic policies improve a state's economic outlook.

As simple as this test is, it is relatively difficult to apply in practice because most major corporations operate in many states and in a number of countries as well. An investment strategy based on changes in the state competitive environment is especially clear, however, if that strategy is applied to small companies where operations are concentrated in one state. With knowledge of the economics and knowledge of the policies, *voilà* we have a forecast of changes in state competitiveness. From there it's a small step to test whether a portfolio of companies located in more pro-growth states outperforms a portfolio of companies located in less pro-growth states.

The test period for our analysis was based on data from 1984 through Q1 1999. The universe of stocks considered to demonstrate the state portfolio effect was all U.S.-based companies in the lowest market-value decile of the New York, American, and NASDAQ stock exchanges. The lowest

A combination of the level as well as changes in relative tax burden truly characterizes the cost of doing business in a state. Overtaxed states per se restrain growth, while states that raise taxes— even if they currently aren't overtaxed— clearly inhibit growth.

market-value decile was examined because we wanted small-cap stocks that would represent accurately the economy of the state in which they were headquartered. For practical purposes, any stock priced for less than $1 per share at the beginning of the year— identical to the minimum price requirement the NASDAQ stock exchange uses—was removed from the stock universe.

In addition, stocks without a closing price at both the beginning and end of the year were dropped from the universe. This definitely adds a survivor bias to the performance results because who could know *ex ante* that a year later there would be no closing price? No one! However, because the strategy predicts that more companies will go bankrupt in states with rising tax burdens than with falling tax burdens, this survivor bias would be expected to hurt, not help, the strategy performance.[3] Finally, any stocks headquartered in Alaska or Wyoming were dropped from consideration, due to these states' unique reliance on oil and gas severance taxes, which makes interstate comparisons problematic.

This process resulted in a unique universe each year, which over the period examined the performance of 364 stocks per year. These were truly super small-cap companies: for the 1999 universe, their average market cap was $7.0 million at the beginning of the year. For comparison purposes, the average market cap of the Russell 2000 was $592 million, and $516 million for the S&P SmallCap 600.

For each of these super small-cap companies the state in which the company is located was identified, or, if located in more than one state, the state which possessed the greatest percentage of the company's production facilities, employees, etc. Small-cap companies located in the states with declining relative tax burdens were assigned to the "buy" portfolio, and companies based in states with rising relative tax burdens were assigned to the "sell" portfolio. For the purposes of our results, each stock in the portfolio carried the same weight.

The results for the 1984-99 time period are very promising (Exhibits 23 and 24). In eleven out of sixteen years, those companies located in states with falling relative tax burdens (i.e., the "buy" portfolio) experienced a higher average price appreciation than those companies located in states with rising relative tax burdens (i.e., the "sell" portfolio). Overall, the "buy" portfolio has appreciated at a compound annual rate of 24.65 percent versus 20.46 percent for the "sell" portfolio, and 22.78 percent for the universe as a whole.

Because the changes to the company's outlook are dependent upon changes in the policy environment, the analysis below focuses on changes in state tax policies.

Exhibit 23

Small Cap Stock Portfolio Performance, 1984–1Q 1999

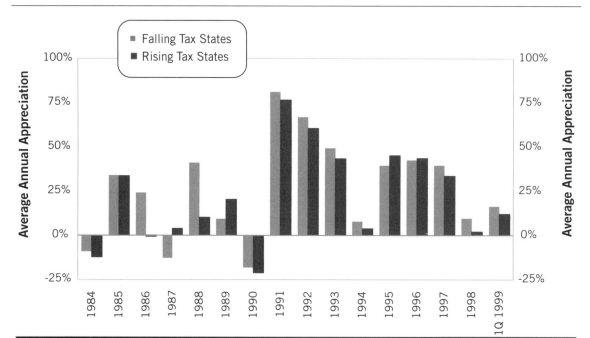

Year	Falling Tax State "Buy" Portfolio	# of stocks	Rising Tax State "Sell" Portfolio	# of stocks	Stock Universe	# of stocks
1984	-9.12%	179	-12.19%	107	-10.27%	286
1985	34.06%	168	33.65%	68	33.94%	236
1986	24.22%	145	0.06%	109	13.86%	254
1987	-12.76%	195	3.86%	85	-7.72%	280
1988	41.10%	126	10.12%	92	28.02%	218
1989	9.39%	132	20.38%	116	14.53%	248
1990	-18.15%	178	-21.14%	92	-19.17%	270
1991	81.20%	124	76.54%	78	79.40%	202
1992	67.00%	192	60.54%	108	64.68%	300
1993	49.34%	189	43.34%	211	46.18%	400
1994	7.87%	189	3.77%	288	5.39%	477
1995	39.57%	352	45.12%	136	41.12%	488
1996	42.55%	265	43.53%	259	43.04%	524
1997	39.61%	292	33.59%	274	36.69%	566
1998	9.57%	296	2.00%	273	5.94%	569
1Q 1999	16.38%	322	12.04%	184	14.80%	506
Compound Annual Rate	24.65%		20.46%		22.78%	
Source: Compustat						

Exhibit 24

Cumulative Performance of the Falling Tax State "Buy" Portfolio vs. the Rising Tax State "Sell" Portfolio, 1984–1Q 1999

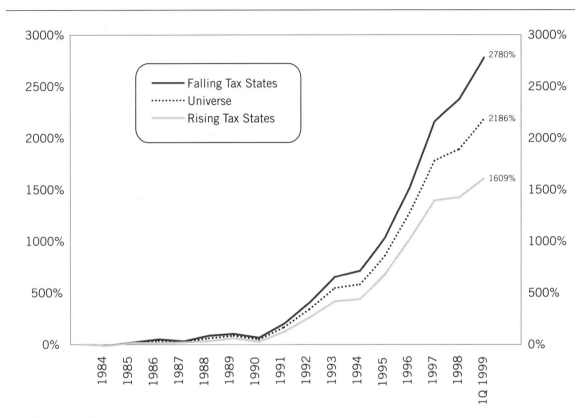

Source: Laffer Associates, Compustat

But those people keep a movin'. . .
and that's what tortures me.
—"Folsom Prison Blues", Johnny Cash

Chapter 5

Form 1040: Everything You Wanted to Know about California Taxpayers But Were Afraid to Ask

When filing federal tax returns, the filer reports a great deal of information including all of their financial information, such as adjusted gross income (AGI), number of dependents, and all sorts of deductions and categories of income. The filer also reports his or her state and county of residence. The U.S. Internal Revenue Service (IRS) provides these tax data tracking people over time and their states (as well as counties) of location, with all personal or identifying data removed of course. While these data are federal data, they provide incredible insight into the impact of state policies. These data are the unbiased adjudicators of state actions. They tell the story of how people "vote with their feet," so to speak, and their economic circumstances at the time. Talk is cheap but when you walk, there's a real cost. I personally can attest to that.

This chapter examines the U.S. IRS data by state from the Statistics of Income (SOI) databases. While available at a county level, we have kept our focus on California's relationship with the other 49 states and the District of Columbia. The IRS data cover a period from 1992 through 2008 and include the number of tax returns filed in California by people who filed in California the previous year, the number of tax returns filed in California by people who filed in a different state the previous year, and the number of tax returns that were filed in a different state this year by people who filed in California last year by the state of this year's filing.

We not only have the number of returns, but we also have the aggregate adjusted gross income and the average adjusted gross income per household for each of these groups. These data allow us to compile the net movements of filers between any state and California and the net flows of aggregate adjusted gross income between any state and California for each of the years from 1992 through 2008. By way of example, these data allow us to know by groups the number who filed tax returns in say Alabama last year who are filing tax returns this year in California and the average adjusted gross income of this group of migrants. On the reverse, we know the number of people who are filing tax returns this year in Alabama, who filed tax returns last year in California, and their average adjusted gross income.

There is a lot of information contained in these IRS files and it borders on overwhelming. While this section is not very long, don't let its length fool you as to its significance. No summary report card grade should be more meaningful to evaluate state government than the following pages.

Exhibit 25 shows the period between 1992 through 2008 where we list in separate columns for each of the 49 non-California states and the District of Columbia:

- the state
- the net flow of tax filers out of California in parentheses, and into California without parentheses
- the total number of filers moving into California from the state
- the total number of filers moving out of California into the state
- the net flow of adjusted gross income: out of California in parentheses and into California without parentheses
- the net adjusted gross income for the aggregate of all filers from the state in question who move into California
- the net adjusted gross income of the aggregate of all filers leaving California to the state in question
- the per filer average adjusted gross income of those who move into California
- the per filer average adjusted gross income of those who move out of California
- the per filer premium of filers who leave versus those who enter California

Also listed is each state's top corporate income tax rate, top personal income tax rate, whether it is a right-to-work state, the percentage of employees represented by unions, and lastly, the total state and local tax burden.

A negative number or a number in parentheses in the exhibit indicates that either the households or income left California over this period and went to another state. A positive number in the table indicates movement into California. What is striking is that over this period, more tax filers and income chose to leave California for another state than tax filers and income choosing to leave another state for California. Because more income over time has left California, the numbers in Exhibit 25 understate the actual loss of income to California. For instance, a tax filer that left California in say 1992 will likely have earned income in 1993 and beyond. Had the tax filer not left California in 1992, that tax filer would have continued to earn income in California for as long as he or she worked. Thus, all future income for this person will have been lost by California. As a result, by leaving California, the tax filer deprives the state of his or her income in the year he or she left as well as each subsequent year that he or she works but does not reside in California. These numbers are enormous and are a great loss to California.

Looking at the destination states of California taxpayers and comparing those states to the origin states where California filers came from reveals important trends as well. Overall, the top destination states had lower combined top personal income tax rates and corporate income tax rates, tended to be right-to-work states, and tended to have far lower overall tax burdens. In other words, Californians are choosing to relocate to the states that more closely adhere to the pro-growth tax lessons described above.

But not only are the absolute number of taxpayers responding to the incentives described above, the average income of a California out-migrant far exceeds the average income of a California in-migrant. Moreover, a lot more people are leaving California than are entering California. It's a double hex on California's bad policies.

AAGI/HHD Sum 1992-2008 ix. Outflows	x. Outflow Premium	xi. Top CIT Rate 2008	xii. Top PIT Rate 2008	xiii. R-T-W State?	xiv.) % of Emp. Covered by Unions (2008)	xv.) State & Local Tax Burden as a % of Pers. Income 2008
43173.69	22.5%	0.00%	0.00%	Yes	18.2%	7.5%
42286.26	14.2%	6.97%	4.54%	Yes	9.8%	9.2%
42326.38	23.9%	6.60%	9.00%	No	17.4%	9.5%
45781.72	0.8%	5.00%	0.00%	Yes	5.6%	7.6%
47076.62	10.6%	0.00%	0.00%	No	21.5%	9.4%
49291.19	15.4%	4.63%	4.63%	No	9.2%	8.7%
48910.79	17.9%	5.50%	0.00%	Yes	7.9%	9.1%
42392.05	28.0%	7.60%	7.80%	Yes	8.0%	9.8%
41021.71	14.7%	5.00%	5.00%	Yes	7.1%	10.0%
45058.50	16.3%	6.90%	7.75%	Yes	5.0%	10.1%
44369.66	-3.2%	6.00%	6.00%	Yes	4.6%	9.3%
43531.63	18.1%	6.50%	0.00%	Yes	6.6%	7.7%
39309.56	14.5%	7.60%	4.90%	No	11.6%	9.1%
41673.60	45.4%	6.75%	6.90%	No	15.7%	8.7%
41068.58	20.2%	6.40%	8.25%	No	25.5%	9.9%
51416.62	1.7%	6.00%	5.75%	Yes	5.0%	9.6%
30805.22	12.3%	6.50%	7.00%	Yes	7.3%	9.8%
30884.75	5.3%	6.00%	5.50%	Yes	8.3%	8.7%
39727.23	0.0%	6.25%	6.00%	No	12.8%	9.3%
42608.94	18.9%	5.00%	7.00%	Yes	5.8%	8.3%
47465.97	51.1%	0.00%	0.00%	Yes	8.9%	7.2%
37788.79	10.5%	6.50%	5.00%	Yes	10.7%	8.8%
38455.45	2.2%	6.00%	6.00%	No	9.6%	9.8%
40544.63	5.8%	8.50%	3.40%	No	13.7%	9.4%
36205.98	-2.8%	7.35%	6.45%	Yes	8.7%	9.6%
33948.19	6.8%	12.00%	8.98%	Yes	13.0%	9.2%
32515.65	-4.3%	7.81%	6.84%	Yes	10.7%	9.7%
44528.15	40.2%	8.93%	8.50%	No	14.7%	10.6%
32406.15	1.4%	8.00%	6.00%	Yes	5.6%	8.7%
37839.65	7.8%	0.00%	0.00%	Yes	6.4%	7.2%
32083.64	4.6%	5.00%	5.00%	Yes	7.3%	8.8%
42932.71	36.5%	8.50%	6.50%	No	15.3%	9.5%
31349.04	-3.0%	9.40%	0.00%	No	24.7%	6.1%
43275.27	33.9%	8.50%	9.50%	No	12.8%	10.5%
30363.44	0.7%	6.50%	5.54%	Yes	8.2%	8.7%
52083.43	11.6%	8.70%	5.95%	No	14.7%	9.8%
53890.49	0.0%	8.84%	10.30%	No	19.5%	11.0%
40854.02	4.5%	7.90%	6.75%	No	16.0%	10.7%
56508.31	12.7%	9.25%	0.00%	No	12.4%	7.7%
44508.96	-0.2%	9.00%	9.90%	No	17.4%	10.6%
47101.13	-3.1%	9.80%	7.85%	No	17.0%	10.3%
45802.86	-19.2%	9.98%	8.50%	No	14.3%	10.7%
50539.45	-2.9%	8.30%	6.25%	No	14.5%	10.8%
73335.98	6.2%	7.50%	5.00%	No	17.9%	11.9%
51408.49	5.5%	9.99%	3.07%	No	16.3%	10.5%
44390.91	-3.5%	8.50%	6.24%	No	15.5%	10.2%
41947.55	-5.8%	8.01%	4.35%	No	19.6%	9.6%
56758.17	2.8%	9.50%	5.85%	No	16.9%	10.2%
62962.51	-5.1%	9.00%	8.97%	No	19.0%	12.3%
47813.24	-10.2%	7.30%	3.00%	No	17.5%	9.7%
52847.20	-7.6%	8.31%	6.85%	No	26.6%	11.9%
2,237,170	**Average: 9.3%**	**6.94%**	**5.34%**		**12.9%**	**9.5%**

	Households Sum 1992 - 2008			AAGI (000's $) Sum 1992 - 2008			
	ii. Net	iii. Inflows	iv. Outflows	v. Net	vi. Inflows	vii. Outflows	viii. Inflows
Nevada	(183,311)	183,791	367,102	(9,371,283)	6,477,866	15,849,149	35245.83
Arizona	(157,429)	225,631	383,060	(7,846,092)	8,352,084	16,198,176	37016.56
Oregon	(111,445)	142,514	253,959	(5,878,682)	4,870,482	10,749,164	34175.46
Texas	(121,074)	282,907	403,981	(5,650,368)	12,844,577	18,494,945	45402.12
Washington	(89,098)	219,750	308,848	(5,185,093)	9,354,426	14,539,519	42568.49
Colorado	(63,626)	135,916	199,542	(4,031,568)	5,804,094	9,835,662	42703.54
Florida	(23,941)	175,996	199,937	(2,476,052)	7,303,025	9,779,077	41495.40
Idaho	(39,502)	35,253	74,755	(2,001,471)	1,167,547	3,169,018	33119.08
Utah	(32,648)	68,142	100,790	(1,697,408)	2,437,170	4,134,578	35766.05
North Carolina	(26,740)	74,570	101,310	(1,676,169)	2,888,708	4,564,877	38738.21
Georgia	(31,479)	77,987	109,466	(1,283,511)	3,573,458	4,856,969	45821.20
Tennessee	(19,790)	40,524	60,314	(1,132,089)	1,493,478	2,625,567	36854.16
New Mexico	(20,251)	45,771	66,022	(1,023,634)	1,571,662	2,595,296	34337.51
Montana	(11,621)	20,885	32,506	(755,967)	598,675	1,354,642	28665.31
Hawaii	(2,643)	88,439	91,082	(717,856)	3,022,752	3,740,608	34178.95
Virginia	(11,860)	112,553	124,413	(707,746)	5,689,150	6,396,896	50546.41
Arkansas	(19,858)	22,878	42,736	(688,941)	627,551	1,316,492	27430.33
Oklahoma	(19,740)	39,556	59,296	(671,529)	1,159,813	1,831,342	29320.79
Missouri	(14,828)	56,583	71,411	(588,930)	2,248,031	2,836,961	39729.80
South Carolina	(6,977)	26,317	33,294	(475,502)	943,120	1,418,622	35836.91
Wyoming	(4,453)	10,902	15,355	(386,366)	342,474	728,840	31413.87
Alabama	(6,679)	22,979	29,658	(334,954)	785,786	1,120,740	34195.83
Kentucky	(5,667)	22,097	27,764	(235,919)	831,758	1,067,677	37641.22
Indiana	(2,994)	47,541	50,535	(226,830)	1,822,093	2,048,923	38326.77
Kansas	(6,400)	34,100	40,500	(196,074)	1,270,268	1,466,342	37251.26
Iowa	(3,817)	27,627	31,444	(189,234)	878,233	1,067,467	31788.94
Nebraska	(5,714)	22,210	27,924	(153,263)	754,704	907,967	33980.37
Maine	437	12,108	11,671	(135,068)	384,620	519,688	31765.77
Louisiana	(3,267)	38,166	41,433	(122,511)	1,220,173	1,342,684	31970.16
South Dakota	(2,364)	8,818	11,182	(113,532)	309,591	423,123	35108.98
Mississippi	(2,602)	18,202	20,804	(109,161)	558,307	667,468	30672.84
West Virginia	(726)	6,080	6,806	(100,934)	191,266	292,200	31458.22
Alaska	(2,705)	23,828	26,533	(61,882)	769,902	831,784	32310.81
Vermont	805	7,809	7,004	(50,810)	252,290	303,100	32307.59
North Dakota	(591)	7,424	8,015	(19,596)	223,767	243,363	30141.03
Delaware	631	6,756	6,125	(3,585)	315,426	319,011	46688.28
California	-			-			53890.49
Wisconsin	2,270	44,831	42,561	14,608	1,753,396	1,738,788	39111.24
New Hampshire	2,328	15,684	13,356	31,764	786,489	754,725	50145.94
Rhode Island	887	12,326	11,439	40,657	549,795	509,138	44604.49
Minnesota	2,098	56,848	54,750	184,144	2,762,931	2,578,787	48602.08
D.C.	(56)	20,062	20,118	215,925	1,137,387	921,462	56693.60
Maryland	2,744	64,069	61,325	234,372	3,333,704	3,099,332	52033.03
Connecticut	9,922	42,293	32,371	547,608	2,921,567	2,373,959	69079.21
Pennsylvania	17,137	91,132	73,995	636,119	4,440,090	3,803,971	48721.52
Ohio	13,058	87,123	74,065	719,213	4,007,026	3,287,813	45992.75
Michigan	17,777	86,908	69,131	971,712	3,871,588	2,899,876	44548.12
Massachusetts	26,203	109,449	83,246	1,315,501	6,040,392	4,724,891	55189.10
New Jersey	24,563	88,260	63,697	1,843,904	5,854,427	4,010,523	66331.60
Illinois	27,828	162,909	135,081	2,218,197	8,676,857	6,458,660	53261.99
New York	38,544	218,391	179,847	2,984,024	12,488,435	9,504,411	57183.84
Sum:	(868,664)	3,492,895	4,361,559	(44,341,862)	151,962,411	196,304,273	2,081,363

Does not include Foreign

Exhibit 25

State Summary
Part A

Exhibit 25

State Summary
Part B

m 1992-2008	x.) Outflow Premium	xi.) Top CIT Rate 2008	xii.) Top PIT Rate 2008	xiii.) R-T-W State? Yes=1	xiv.) % of Emp. Covered by Unions (2008)	xv.) State & Local Tax Burden as a % of Pers. Income 2008
596	16.4%	4.59%	3.44%	0.67	11.6%	9.0%
556	-2.3%	8.49%	5.51%	0.00	18.2%	10.8%
636	14.9%	5.56%	4.80%	0.65	10.7%	9.1%
634	2.7%	8.64%	6.02%	0.05	16.8%	10.1%

i.) State	Households Sum 1992 - 2008			AAGI (000's $) Sum 1992 - 2008			AAGI/HHD - S	
	ii.) Net	iii.) Inflows	iv.) Outflows	v.) Net	vi.) Inflows	vii.) Outflows	viii.) Inflows	ix.) Ou
Top 9 Average	(91,342)	163,322	254,664	(4,904,224)	6,512,363	11,416,588	38,610	44,
Bottom 9 Average	19,753	105,615	85,862	1,274,517	5,737,121	4,462,604	54,705	53,
Top 20 Average	(50,393)	103,798	154,191	(2,692,995)	4,121,383	6,814,378	37,448	42,
Bottom 20 Average	9,136	60,641	51,024	586,047	3,177,723	2,560,831	47,915	48,

Over this 16-year period, California has on balance lost some 869,000 tax filers. About 3.5 million tax filers have moved into California while some 4.4 million tax filers have fled the state *(moi aussi)*. The numbers of people these tax returns represent is far greater than the number of tax returns because many returns have more than one dependent.

The key states to which Californians most frequently move represents both geography and economics. The top three destination states are the neighboring states of Nevada, Arizona, and Oregon, and four other states in the top nine are close as well—Washington, Colorado, Idaho, and Utah. The other two top destination spots of the top nine come as no surprise—Texas and Florida—both zero-income-tax, pro-growth states.

Of these nine top destination states, the average adjusted gross income (remember this is over 16 years) of out-migrants was $44,700 while for in-migrants the average adjusted gross income was $38,600, yielding an income premium to the out-migrants of 16 percent.

For the nine destination states, the average top personal income tax rate of 3.44 percent versus California's 10.3 percent, top corporate tax rate was 4.59 percent versus California's rate of 8.84 percent. Six of the nine destination states are right-to-work states and have an average 11.6 percent of their workforce represented by unions versus California's 19.5 percent. And finally, the nine top destination states have an average state and local tax burden of 9 percent versus California's 11 percent. This says it all.

Of the nine top destination states, the average adjusted gross income of out-migrants was $44,700 while for in-migrants the average adjusted gross income was $38,600, yielding an income premium to the out-migrants of 16 percent.

And for those top nine states that lost tax filers to California over this 18 year period? They include New York, Illinois, New Jersey, Massachusetts, Michigan, Ohio, Pennsylvania, Connecticut, and Maryland. Need I write more? California is quickly devolving into the league of losers.

One important point to note when using these data is that while tax filers are cumulative, lost adjusted gross income only applies to one year. Once lost to California most tax filers keep on earning income in their new state. Therefore the total adjusted gross income losses to California per year are far greater than the number reported which stands for only one year's adjusted gross income. My guess is that the $44 billion number really should average about $500 billion for each of the 16 years California is hemorrhaging.

The patterns of net out-migration vary considerably over time in ways that also make sense. During good times the lure of better economic policies in other states pushes lots of people out of California while during bad times it's the welfare that keeps them home.

Exhibit 26

Net Household and Average Adjusted Gross Income Migration
Annual, 1992-2009

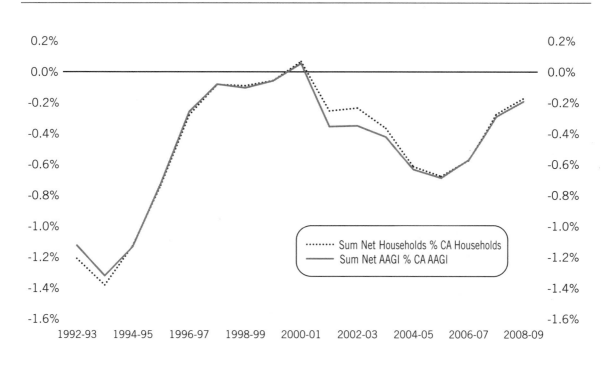

Source: IRS

In summary, using the IRS SOI data, the same picture emerges for California as it did using the cross-section time series data for all states, for those states that adopted a progressive income tax, as well as for the historical pairings of similar states. California really isn't very different from the rest-of-the-nation when it comes to economics.

The disaster that is California's economy is a direct consequence of excessive taxation, over-regulation, inappropriate state and local spending, pandering to job killing unions, and over-compensating people who don't work. The record is clear.

Implications for California

California is in economic disrepair. Change is needed. If California could make herself one of the no-income-tax states it would be in much better economic shape. Had California just caught up with the average of the no-tax-states over the past decade, the average California resident's income would be more than $1,807 higher. Taxes really do matter. And, it is not just taxes. Our review shows that regulations and spending matter a great deal too. As we will see in the next chapter, California's own economic history confirms our findings from our examination of all 50 states.

Had California just caught up with the average of the no-tax-states over the past decade, the average California resident's income would be more than $1,807 higher.

Sheriff of Nottingham: Wait a minute. Robin Hood steals money from my pocket, forcing me to hurt the public, and they love him for it?

—From "Robin Hood, Prince of Thieves"

Chapter 6

The Tale of Robin Hood (A Supply-Side Adaptation)

The last chapters illustrated the overwhelming correlations between sound fiscal and regulatory policies and economic performance. On average, the states that implement pro-growth economic policies prosper more than the states that do not. Paramount among these policies are the top corporate income tax rate, the overall tax burden imposed on the state's citizens, whether the state is a right-to-work state, the percentage of employees who are represented by unions, the top personal income tax rate, and welfare spending per person in poverty. Local regulations—especially zoning regulations—while not discussed in the last chapter—are also important.

However, the reader may still wonder—is California different? After all, California's climate is arguably the best in the U.S. California has beaches, great ports, fertile farmland, and abundant natural resources (including oil). Perhaps all of these natural advantages exempt California from the economic constraints that other states face. California's own history of implementing policies that vacillate between Karl Marx and Adam Smith, and then back again, dispels this notion. The laws of supply-side economics are of particular importance in California.

The Golden State's economic prosperity, consequently, depends upon learning the correct lessons from supply-side or incentive economics. Due to the pivotal role that incentive economics plays in creating prosperity in California, it is worth reviewing both the theory of incentives and the application of the theory of incentives to state economic outcomes before reviewing the connection between California's economic policies and California's economic outcomes.

The Theory of Incentives

Incentives can be either positive or negative. They are alternatively described as carrots and sticks or pleasure and pain. Whatever their form, people seek positive and avoid negative incentives. If a dog is scolded, for example, the animal's whereabouts will not be known, but the dog is certain not to be where the scolding took place. If, however, a dog is fed, we know exactly where the dog will be. The principle is simple enough: If an activity should be shunned, a negative incentive is appropriate. Positive incentives come into play in order to make activities attractive. When the dog is fed you can be fairly certain that the dog will be where the food is at feeding time. Positive incentives tell you what to do while negative incentives tell you what not to do.

> **In America today, if a company makes a great product everyone wants, produces that product at a really low cost, and eschews the use of tax dodges, our government will tax the bejabbers out of that company.**

In the realm of political economics, taxes are negative incentives and government subsidies are positive incentives, subject to all the subtleties and intricacies of the general theory of incentives. People attempt to avoid taxed activities—the higher the tax, the greater their attempt to avoid. As with all negative incentives, no one can be sure how the avoidance will be carried out. It's like a hot stove. You don't know where people's hands will be, but they won't be on the hot stove.

The government taxes cigarettes to stop people from smoking, not to get them to smoke. It fines speeding drivers so they won't speed, not to encourage them to drive faster. And, ridiculously enough, the government pays farmers not to grow food to raise food prices, not lower them. And yet contrary to common sense, it seems perfectly natural that government would tax people who work or companies that are successful only to give that money, and a whole lot more borrowed from the future, to people who don't work and to bail out losing companies. The thought never crosses their minds that these policies are the very reason why our economy is in such bad shape. It's absurd.

In America today, if a company makes a great product everyone wants, produces that product at a really low cost, and eschews the use of tax dodges, our government will tax the bejabbers out of that company. And, if another company makes a lousy product no one wants, does it at squanderously high cost, and uses multitudes of lawyers to milk our system dry, our government will subsidize that company whether it be the big banks, General Motors, or AIG with bailouts such as TARP. What do people honestly believe these policies will do to the quality of American companies? If companies can be more profitable hiring lobbyists, lawyers, and tax accountants to avoid taxes and receive bailouts and subsidies than they can be by developing and marketing better products, they will do it. And we suffer as a nation.

I'm beginning to think that Irving Kristol was correct when he wrote, "It takes a PhD. in Economics not to be able to understand the obvious." It shouldn't surprise anyone why the economy isn't getting better.

In the case of taxable income, people try to shift income from higher-taxed categories to lower-taxed categories. They purchase tax shelters, move to a lower tax region, and in the extreme, they may even earn less income or literally evade the tax at considerable personal risk. Because taxation is necessary to sustain government spending, one canon of taxation has always been to have the largest possible tax base coupled with the lowest possible tax rate. By so doing, people are provided the least opportunity to avoid paying taxes and the lowest incentive to do so.

Changes in marginal tax rates are important because they change incentives to supply and demand, work, effort, and capital. For example, firms base their decisions to employ workers, in part, on their total cost to the firm. Holding all else equal, the greater the cost to the firm of employing each additional worker, the fewer workers the firm will employ. Conversely, the lower the marginal cost per worker, the more workers the firm hires. For the firm, the decision to employ is based upon gross wages paid, a concept that encompasses all costs borne by the firm.

Workers, on the other hand, care little about the cost to the firm of employing them. Of concern from a worker's standpoint is how much the worker receives for providing work effort, net of all deductions and taxes. Workers concentrate on net wages received. The greater net wages received, the more willing a worker is to work. Conversely, if net wages fall, workers will find work effort less attractive and they will do less of it.

The difference between what it costs a firm to employ a worker and what that individual receives net, is the tax wedge. From the standpoint of a single worker, a tax cut has two types of effects. Because a decrease in marginal tax rates lowers the cost to the employer in the form of lower wages paid, clearly, firms will employ more workers. On the supply side, a reduction in marginal tax rates raises net wages received. Again, more work effort will be supplied. In sum, tax rate cuts increase the demand for and the supply of productive factors. In dynamic formulations, as tax rates fall, output growth increases, and vice versa. Regulations, restrictions, and requirements, along with explicit taxes, are all parts of the wedge that is driven between wages paid and wages received.

And, if another company makes a lousy product no one wants, does it at squanderously high cost, and uses multitudes of lawyers to milk our system dry, our government will subsidize that company.

And don't for a moment think that our highly progressive tax structure here in California helps the poor, the minorities, or the disenfranchised—it doesn't. Intuitively, it should be self-evident that if a government taxes people who work and pays people who don't work, there will be more people who don't work and fewer people who do work. The more workers are taxed and the more non-workers are paid, the more people there will be who don't work. It's as straightforward as one, two, three. The best form of welfare has always been and always will be a good high paying job.

The important question to address, and one critical to California and the U.S., is what is the best way to help the poor? All of us understand the importance of helping those who really do have difficulty helping themselves. The question is not whether you want to help the poor. The question is, how can you, literally, make the poor better off?

If the rich are taxed and the money is given to the poor, do not be surprised if there are a lot more poor people and fewer rich people. All people respond to incentives. Whether incentive economics fits with your view of what the world should be or not, it is the way the world actually works. If governments make an activity less attractive, people will do less of it. If governments make an activity more attractive, people will do more of it. Taxes make an activity less attractive and subsidies make an activity more attractive. It's as simple as that.

The Supply-Side Version of Robin Hood

Everyone knows the story of Robin Hood—the hero of Sherwood Forest—who stole from the rich and gave that contraband to the poor. I like to retell this story of Robin Hood, only my version is the supply-side version of the story. If you'll remember, it begins with Robin Hood and his band of merry men in the English town of Nottingham. They would wake up in the morning and don their light green leisure suits and go zipping off into Sherwood Forest, where they would wait for hapless travellers by the trans-forest throughway hiding amongst the trees.

If a rich merchant came by—and by rich I mean a super-richie (this guy didn't have a silver spoon in his mouth, he had a golden goblet down his throat)—Robin Hood would stop him, chat with him for a few minutes, and then take everything the guy had. The guy had to run naked back into the forest. But before you feel sorry for him, remember he is so rich that by the time he gets back to his castle, there will be lots of other golden goblets, lots of other jewels, and the medieval version of a security force to protect him. He'll be just fine, none the worse for the wear.

Robin Hood had a progressive stealing formula when dealing with the merchants who came through the forest. You recognize the model, don't you? Doesn't it sound like the California government?

If a prosperous merchant came through the forest, one who was just rich but not super-rich, Robin Hood would take almost everything the guy had, but not quite everything. If a normal, everyday average businessman came through the forest, Robin Hood would take just a moderate chunk of what the man had. And if a poor merchant came through the forest, one who could barely make it, Robin Hood would just take a little token from that guy.

In the vernacular of our modern day society, Robin Hood had a progressive stealing formula when dealing with the merchants who came through the forest. You recognize the model, don't you? Doesn't it sound like the California government to you?

At the end of the day, Robin Hood and his men would take their contraband and go back into Nottingham where they'd wander the streets. If they found someone who was down-and-out and had absolutely nothing, Robin Hood would stop him and say, "Hi, my name's Robin Hood. I'm your local redistributionist agent and I'd just like to tell you how much I love you." And then Robin Hood would give the destitute man a whole pile of goodies.

When Robin Hood and his men found another person whom we'd call "working poor," with an income around $14,500 a year (2,000 hours at about minimum wage), they would give him a smaller bundle of goodies than they gave to the guy who had nothing. And if Robin Hood found some normal, everyday average citizen walking around the streets of Nottingham, Robin Hood would give the man a small token equivalent to our modern day tax rebate. Robin Hood would add, "You and your wife go out to dinner and the wine's on me." If Robin Hood happened to bump into a rich person, he might just rip him off.

Once again using today's words, the more a person makes, the less Robin Hood gives him, and the less a person makes the more he gives him. You follow the model: he stole from the rich and gave to the poor. The richer you were the more he'd steal from you, the poorer you were the more he'd give you.

This is the story of Robin Hood.

Now, put on your supply-side economics hat and imagine for a moment that you are a merchant back in the ancient days of Nottingham: *How long would it take you to learn not to go through the forest?*

Those merchants who couldn't afford armed guards would have to go around the forest in order to trade with the neighboring villages. The route around the forest is a lot longer and full of rocks, bumps, logs, holes, and so forth—it was far more costly doing commerce when you're travelling around the forest rather than going through the forest.

Those merchants who could afford armed guards (and by the way, today we call these armed guards lawyers, accountants, and lobbyists) would go through the forest and Robin Hood couldn't rip them off. And believe me when I tell you that those armed guards were as expensive then as they are today. So at the end of the second day, Robin Hood had no contraband whatsoever to give to the poor. All he had succeeded in doing was driving up the cost of doing business, which meant the poor had to pay higher prices and were literally worse off. By stealing from the rich and by giving to the poor, Robin Hood made the poor literally worse off.

And so it is in California. The poor, who have relied on the state for so long for their sustenance, are now having their benefits cut to the bone. Because of our state's business-unfriendly policies, our unemployment rate is higher than the national average. Because of our bad governance, we have one of the worst K-12 education systems in the nation. I could go on and on, but the point is simple enough. Our progressive tax structure is not benefiting the truly needy.

Let me put the theorem to you precisely (and I could prove it to you mathematically if need be): By trying to redistribute income, government never, ever succeeds in redistributing income. What government does accomplish is the destruction of the volume of income. Government cannot change the distribution of income with taxes but it always lowers the volume of income with taxes. As we look at the progressive tax structure of California and of other international economies, it's amazing how the distribution of income, if anything, is made worse. And that's where we are today.

Let me write it again: To me the best form of welfare is still a good, high paying job. There is no alternative to economic growth.

I have a mansion
Forget the price
Ain't never been there
They tell me its nice.
"Life's Been Good"
—Joe Walsh

Chapter 7

California Real Estate Booms and Busts:
A Chain Reaction

Our story, if you'll allow me a little poetic license, begins with the end—the price of the ultimate immovable asset—California's housing market. The changing fortunes of California's housing market are linked to changing population flows, which directly follow from changing incomes and employment opportunities. And these factors result from changes in California's economic policies. Ultimately, a state's economic performance goes through a number of stages concluding with changes in real estate values. Simply described, the process is as follows:

- California's taxes and regulations affect California's business climate
- California's business climate affects California's income growth, economic output, employment growth, and population growth (economic activity)
- California's growth in economic activity affects California's home prices.

In this chapter, we attempt to create an economic "cause and effect" picture of California—with all of the appropriate caveats regarding *cause* and *correlation* discussed earlier. With tax increases, higher regulatory costs, and the state's fiscal weakness, it is easy to visualize a continuation of California's economic difficulties. More Californians are choosing to leave the state according to the Census Bureau's measure of net-internal migration, which has been negative in California for many years. Without having to shout or draw pictures, the prognosis for California virtually jumps off the pages. Because population growth and income are stagnant, the consequence will be continued weakness in California's real estate values.

Because population growth and income are stagnant, the consequence will be continued weakness in California's real estate values.

California's relative housing values and housing affordability are key economic welfare measures for California due to the housing market's reflection of a region's underlying economic value.

Exhibit 27

Linkage among California's Economic Conditions, California's Population Growth, Home Prices, and Affordability

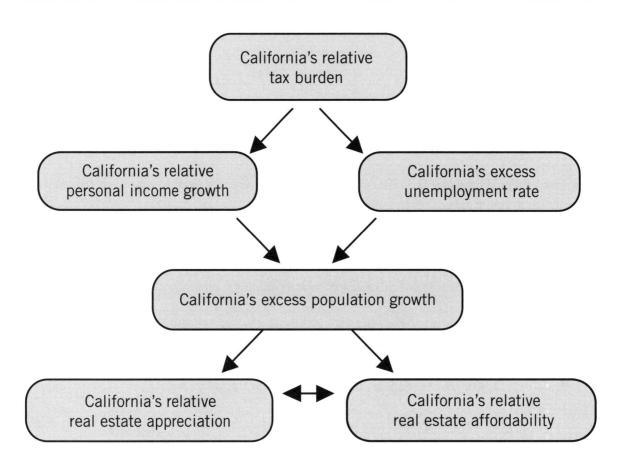

In the grand scheme of things, housing in the near and intermediate term is a relatively fixed factor. Only at great expense can houses or other forms of real estate be transported. In the very long run, however, new construction combined with depreciation can relocate enormous quantities of real estate at a relatively low cost. This long-run mobility of factors all but vanishes in the nearer term.

In the case of the real estate market, the importance of long-run forces is altogether too easy to overlook. While during any day, week, month or year, long-run forces appear to be irrelevant, they do ultimately prevail over all else. In the long run, equivalent houses should cost roughly the same everywhere. Betting against these long-run forces is literally betting against "the house": You do win from time to time, but the odds are not in your favor.

Whether in the long or short run, adjustments to market shocks occur through changes in price and/or changes in quantity. Increases in demand result in higher price and greater quantity. If the supply curve is elastic, then the increase in price will be small and the increase in quantity great. If on the other hand, the supply curve is inelastic, almost all of the adjustment will be with price. For developed real estate, the supply curve is inelastic over periods of several years but highly elastic over decades.

In the near term, changes in housing demand invariably come up against relatively inelastic supplies. Therefore, real estate prices provide a great deal of the buffer for near-term adjustments to changes in market conditions, while the quantity of homes accounts for less. The long-run tendency, however, is still worth keeping in mind. Over long periods of time, housing prices should equilibrate across different locations. All long-run changes in locational demand should be accommodated by changes in supply—not relative prices.

Exhibit 28 plots the median current dollar price of an existing single family California house for the period between the first quarter of 1970 through the first quarter of 2011. The same data series is also plotted for the U.S. When trying to figure out relationships between the California data and the U.S. data, it is important to remember that the California data are part of the U.S. data.

Exhibit 28

Median Home Prices of Existing Single Family Homes
California vs. United States
1970 QI through 2011 QI Semi-log

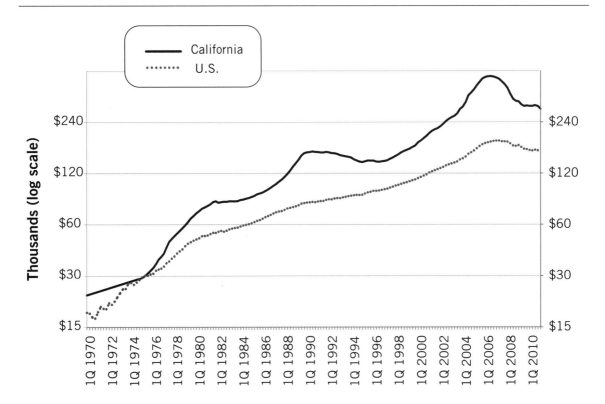

Source: California Association of Realtors, National Association of Realtors, U.S. Census and OFHEO.

What jumps out at the viewer is just how close to the rest of the country California housing prices were back in the early 1970s; how far they diverged by 1989, how they drew closer to U.S. housing prices in the 1990s; diverged again through the late part of the 1990s and mid-2000s; and finally how the recent, and rapid declines, in California housing prices have once again drawn them closer to the U.S. average. California's houses, however, still sell at a significant premium compared to the national average.

The difference in price trends between California's houses and those of the rest of the nation varies dramatically and begs for an explanation. In 1968, California's median-priced house was about 16 percent more expensive than that same house was for the U.S. as a whole. In 1989 California's median-priced house was nearly twice that of the median-priced house for the U.S. as a whole. But by 1997, California's median-priced house had fallen to less than 50 percent more expensive than the U.S. median-priced house. From this bottom, California's housing prices surged, even relative to the U.S. rise, peaking at nearly 150 percent higher than the U.S. average. From this height, California's prices have crashed and are currently at a significantly lower 80 percent premium over the average U.S. price. By the way, we are assuming here that the house could actually be sold (i.e. these are all transaction prices).

But this story isn't over yet. There's a lot more to come and none of it is pretty. In order to get our arms around the trunk of the tree, we need to first understand the dynamic of the California economy.

First let me describe what used to be called the Keynesian accelerator—not to be confused with the Keynesian multiplier. The accelerator principle shows how changes in population and income growth have an exaggerated (or accelerated) impact on output growth which then, in turn, feeds back on population growth. This dynamic feedback loop can have an enormously expansive beneficial effect when it works in the right direction but can also have a devastating impact when it reverses. First the principle.

Imagine a population of 100 families with each family living in one home. In our scenario, homes depreciate by 1 percent per year on average. If population is static, then the housing industry will produce one house per year to offset the 1 percent depreciation on the 100 homes. And that's that. Now, if you would, imagine that there had been no population growth for years and years and that economy was fully stable.

Now if population all of a sudden were to start growing at 1 percent per year instead of zero percent, the housing industry would have to produce two homes per year—one to replace the depreciation and one new home to add to the housing stock. Thus, a 1 percent increase in population growth leads to a 100 percent increase in housing construction. That's the accelerator, but the story doesn't end there.[1]

With a doubling of housing construction more jobs are created, wages rise, housing prices rise and prosperity comes. If you think of a California home costing several hundreds of thousands of dollars and the new resident's annual income being substantially less than that, then each new home creates enough income to employ several new families. And the economy is off to the races. People move to where the action is. Population growth increases even more, and a very powerful dynamic ensues, pushed even further and faster by the accelerator effect. But forever and infinity aren't real numbers. Sooner or later it all comes to an end, usually precipitated by ignorant public policy that panders to you-know-who. Sound familiar?

With building codes, regulations and requirements, inspection schedules, environmental impact statements and the like, the time between recognizing the need for a new home and completing construction of a new home can take as long as seven or more years.

What's exceptionally interesting about housing and the accelerator effect is that it takes a lot longer and costs a lot more to build a house today than it did previously. In some regions of California, just the permit fees alone are higher than the price of an equivalent home in other regions of the country. Effectively, the construction process for homes has been lengthened considerably as well as having been made generally more expensive. Taking far longer to construct homes means that the accelerator process is exaggerated even beyond its natural exaggeration.

When the market signals the construction industry that more new homes are warranted, the construction industry starts the process of accommodating that need. However, by the time those homes actually are available for purchase, a considerable amount of time has elapsed. And, by the way, not only has a lot of time elapsed, but new demands are piled on top of older demands. What these delays cause are exaggerated swings in unfulfilled demands for housing—especially in California.

As you can see, the exaggeration on the upside will cause larger than normal increases in housing prices to allocate the shortage of housing to the existing population. Speculators will get into the fray causing the upswing to be even greater yet. But once the existing population has been sated with houses, demand must taper, especially if population growth begins to slow, as it is today. The housing pipeline cannot be turned off quickly, so new homes will continue to stream onto the market well past the need. So housing prices not only go much higher than warranted in good times but in bad times they go much lower. And in California the housing cycle lasts a long, long time.

Exhibit 28 illustrates just how volatile California's housing prices are relative to the rest of the nation. The swings in relative housing prices are striking and are a direct consequence of the accelerator and the prolonged construction process in California. The swings and misses of California's economic history couldn't be more clearly expressed than they are in relative housing prices. And it's worse today than it ever was before.

One reason for the state government's budget deterioration is falling home prices. The housing bubble sent the median home price to $594,530 in May of 2007 in California.[2] At the height of this real-estate euphoria, fewer than one in 20 residents could afford to buy the average home in San Diego and Los Angeles Counties. Now the state is enduring the inevitable correction, with prices tumbling by double digits in some markets. Homeowners are demanding a revision of their property tax assessments, which is only adding to the revenue drought.

Now the accelerator is working in reverse. Just as the accelerator increases the rate of growth during the rising market, it accelerates the rate of decline during a falling market. Due to the accelerator effect alone, California's housing still faces a rough road ahead.

Housing Affordability: California and the United States

Up to now, we have only looked at housing prices, but prices are only part of the story. High prices coupled with even higher incomes could lead to even greater affordability. But, even this is an incomplete list. Other things matter too. For instance, housing values in California today are likely even lower than they appear due to changes in the number of people per household, the continued rise in housing foreclosures, and the size of the shadow inventory of unsold houses. While many considerations should go into the concept of affordability, income and home prices appear to be the essential ingredients across time.

Many measures of affordability exist, each with its own special features and nuances. Lacking universal "truth," we have chosen to relate the median house price to per capita personal income for both California and the U.S. (Exhibit 29).[3]

Exhibit 29

Median Home Prices Relative to Per Capita Personal Income: California vs. United States

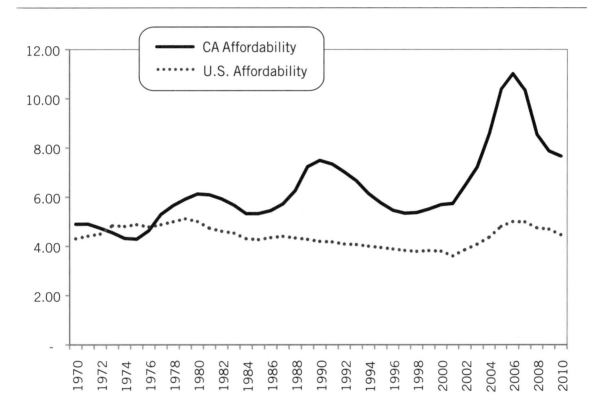

Source: Bureau of Economic Analysis, California Association of Realtors, National Association of Realtors, U.S. Census and OFHEO.

The differences in median home prices between California and the rest of the nation are not explained away by personal income differences. When income is taken into account, California median home prices look cheap in the 1970–75 period. For most of that period California home prices appear a smidgeon low in relation to income as compared to the rest of the nation.

But, from 1975 onward, California's median housing price relative to California's per capita personal income takes off vis-à-vis the rest of the country. In 1990, California's median house price relative to California's per capita personal income was nearly 80 percent higher than the U.S. By 1997 the California premium of median housing prices relative to per capita personal income had fallen in half—only about 40 percent higher than the U.S.

Virtually all of the increase in this measure of "un-affordability" of California homes relative to the U.S. from 1975 to 1990 comes from the increase in the price of a house in California relative to the rest of the nation. Relative per capita personal income in California stayed roughly the same over the period 1975–1990. In 1975, for example, California's per capita personal income was 15.6 percent greater than the per capita income for the nation as a whole. In 1990 California's per capita personal income was 10.5 percent above the nation's per capita personal income.

The increase in the "affordability" of California's housing prices in the early– and mid–1990s can be attributed to decreases in the price of houses in California, and not to any change in California's relative per capita income. In fact, the changes in California's relative per capita personal income worked to make California homes relatively less "affordable." By 1997, California's per capita personal income was only 5.5 percent higher than the nation's.

The final surge in California's housing prices was not matched by similar per capita personal income growth. Thus, rising house prices during the housing bubble of the early to mid–2000s, and its decline during the "housing bust" starting in 2006 explains the final surge and drop in Exhibit 30 that made homes first relatively less "affordable" by 2006; and then relatively more affordable through 2010.

California's Housing Prices and Population Growth

Part of the change in California's home prices is due to California's population growth relative to the rest of the nation. Because the supply of houses is relatively inelastic in the near term, in-migration and immigration can reasonably be expected to have a major impact on housing prices. Not only should in-migration and immigration affect housing prices in absolute terms, but also housing prices relative to income. Relative prices are determined by relative scarcity.

From 1975 to 1990, as California's population grew, so did California's median home price. When California's population growth slowed, as it did during the period 1990 to 1995, California's median home price also dropped. This is why we titled our 1990 paper on California's housing market "Either California's Housing Prices are Going to Fall or California's in for One Helluva Rise in Personal Income." When excess population growth once again was on the rise in California during the late 1990s and early 2000s, California's median home price rose right along with it. Along with the current housing bust since 2006, California's population growth once again slowed.

Over the past forty years, there has been a close relationship between California's excess population growth and our measure of affordability: California home prices divided by per capita personal income. In Exhibit 30 the two series are plotted using annual data for the period 1970 through 2010. Our measure of California's excess population growth is the annual percent change in California's population less the percent change in the population of the United States.

Exhibit 30

California Median Home Price Relative to Per Capita Personal Income vs. California Excess Population Growth

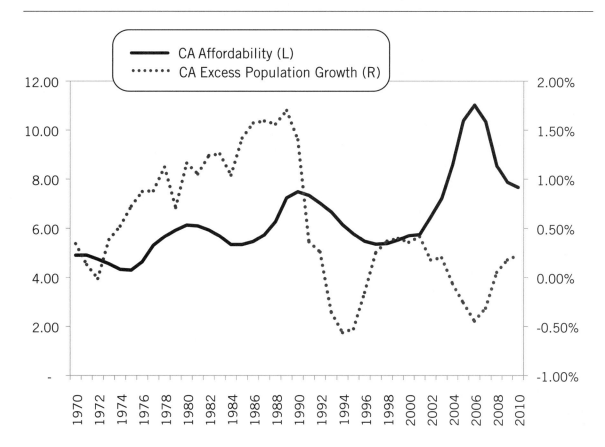

Source: Bureau of Economic Analysis, California Association of Realtors, National Association of Realtors

Given the crude nature of the data, the statistical fit is really quite exceptional. The graph looks like a spider doing push-ups on a mirror. Excess population growth goes a long way in "explaining" California's periods of real estate appreciation and depreciation.

Closer scrutiny of this relationship highlights a number of additional interesting features of these data. For example, California's population growth had always been higher than U.S. population growth until 1993. Back in the early 1970s and 1990s, the differences in the growth rates between California and the U.S. as a whole were far smaller than they had been in the 1980s. The leveling-off period for differences in relative population growth from, say 1978 to 1985, was also a period of a flat housing price "affordability" index. The surge in California's relative population growth in the late 1980s was accompanied by an equivalent or even bigger surge in California's home prices. In 1989, homes in California were less "affordable" than at any time in recent history, save over the current housing bubble. Ironically, for the rest of the nation homes were relatively "affordable". The fall in excess population growth between 1990 and 1995 was accompanied by a fall in California's relative home prices, making them more "affordable."

The analysis so far shows that California's real estate values are directly related to California's population growth. The question becomes, what drives California's population growth. In fact, it is changes in population growth that link changes in economic activity, and ultimately changes in economic policies, to the housing sector.

Economic Determinants of California's Population Growth

Taking our story the next step adds a new economic dimension. The question to answer now becomes why are people now moving away from California? Clearly the weather, mountains, beautiful coastline and other natural endowments should have had the same siren's lure year in year out. And yet California's excess population growth has shown a great deal of variation over the years. It's the economy.

There is no lemma in supply-side economics more powerful than the lemma that economic incentives motivate people to relocate. State economic policies don't reallocate income, they reallocate people. Imagine two locations: A and B. Then ask yourself what would happen to migration patterns if B's per capita income rose relative to A's per capita income? In the absence of other extenuating circumstances, B's population growth should increase relative to A's population growth. People like to get paid, and they'll even move to get paid more. The more they get paid the better they like it and the faster they'll move.

In Exhibit 31, California's population growth and California's relative per capita income are plotted for the years 1970–2010.

Exhibit 31

California Median Home Price Relative to Per Capita Personal Income vs. California Excess Population Growth

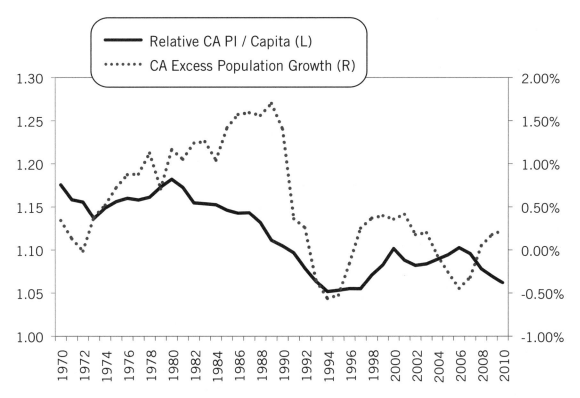

Source: Bureau of Economic Analysis, U.S. Census Bureau.

Exhibit 31 provides strong corroboration of the basic supply-side lemma that people move for economic reasons. The lemma simply makes sense and it's always nice when the data confirm common sense. Higher per capita incomes in California relative to the U.S. are closely associated with more rapid population growth in California.

Exhibit 32 displays yet another version of the same basic supply-side lemma that people move for economic advantage. The only two differences between Exhibit 31 and Exhibit 32 are that the economic advantage variable is California's relative per capita income in Exhibit 31 and California's excess unemployment rate in Exhibit 32.

Exhibit 32

California Excess Unemployment Rate vs. California Excess Population Growth

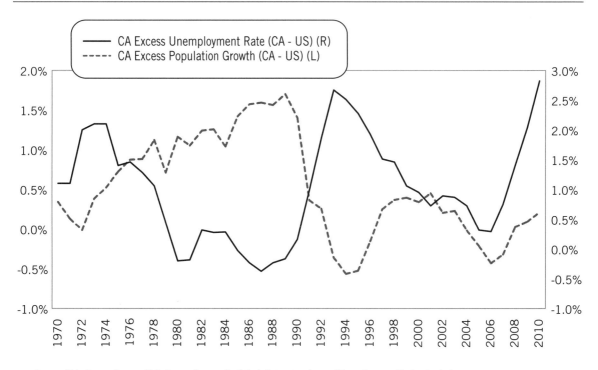

Source: U.S. Census Bureau, U.S. Census Bureau *Statistical Abstract*, various editions; Bureau of Labor Statistics

The more jobs California has, the lower California's unemployment rate; and the higher is the pay for those jobs relative to the U.S. which in turn increases California's population.

Unemployment being a disadvantage for people seeking high paying jobs, there should be an inverse relationship between California's excess population growth and California's excess unemployment. The numbers once again confirm supply-side economic logic. Simple common sense vanquishes complex error.

Whether one uses relative per capita income or California's excess unemployment, economics does have a role to play. No one need ever deny that non-economic factors also play roles in determining California's population growth. We're sure they do. But what we have established is the simple proposition that California's relative population growth, in part, depends upon California's economic climate relative to the rest of the nation. The more jobs California has, the lower California's unemployment rate; and the higher is the pay for those jobs relative to the U.S. which in turn increases California's population.

Taxes and Economic Growth: California and the United States

We have everything now in place save for the original cause. Economic conditions do cause migration, and migration and economic conditions together do cause changes in housing prices. But what causes changes in economic conditions?

Again it is clear that a lot of factors come into play when it comes down to the economy—whether on a national, state, or local level. And even though a policy may be a national policy, it still may have different regional effects. And California arguably could be near one extreme when it comes to defense spending, gas taxes, etc. But still it's a good bet that state and local policy differences will affect the relative performance of the different states.

For example, take two similar companies, one in California and one elsewhere. If these two companies compete in the U.S. market, then a tax decrease in California that would not be shared by the company outside of the state, will improve the California company's ability to compete. Whether the California company passes the tax decrease forward to its customers or backwards to its workers and suppliers, or just increases the return on its capital, the California company will benefit.

Lower taxes will make the California company more competitive. California-based companies will gain business. With a gain in business there soon will be higher wages, higher profits and lower unemployment. The incentives for people and capital to migrate into California will be increased. As a consequence, migration into California and investment in California will increase.

As we illustrate in the next chapter, each one of these changes in direction in California's housing prices, employment growth, and income growth coincides with changes in California's pro-growth environment. When the policy improved, these economic variables improved. And, unfortunately, when economic policies worsened, these economic variables worsened too.

The logical sequence is now complete. Measures of income growth, employment growth, population growth and housing values are all linked through a chain of events to the economic policies California implements. The next chapter reviews California's history, illustrating that this logical sequence explains the changes in California's relative economic fortunes. Once completed, the economic reforms necessary to reverse California's current economic funk become clear. These reforms are discussed in the final chapters.

I bet you're wondering how I knew
About your plans to make me blue
With some other guy you knew before.
"Heard it through the Grapevine"
—Marvin Gaye

Chapter 8

The California Story: Karl Marx vs. Adam Smith

California has many policy success stories. From rolling back and capping property taxes via Proposition 13, to the Gann spending limit, indexing the personal income tax for inflation, and repealing the state estate tax, California has often been the pro-growth policy leader of the U.S. But, then there are periods like today. First, a little history.

California was one of the many states that adopted both a sales and an income tax during the Great Depression. And this perverted thinking of raising taxes during bad times has persisted to this very day. California's implementation of sales and income taxes was the primary enabler that fostered the explosive growth of California's government. Progressive personal and corporate income taxes are the necessary policy precursors to empower big government. The California state sales tax took effect in 1933 at a rate of 2.5 percent and its state income tax began in 1935.

> California's income tax had a difficult birth. Although voters decisively rejected in 1932 Proposition 9 that would have required the Legislature to adopt an income tax to fund schools, among other things, the Legislature approved a proposal (AB 2429) for an income tax in 1933. However, the bill was vetoed by Governor James "Sunny Jim" Rolph.

> Due to the transfer of a considerable amount of state taxes to counties in 1935, the Joint Committee on Revenue and Taxation urged the Legislature to adopt an income tax. The proposal, introduced by Assemblyman Ford Chatters from the San Joaquin Valley as AB 1182, was subjected to numerous amendments drawn by University of California Professor Roger J. Traynor (who later became chief justice of the California Supreme Court).

As passed and signed into law (Statutes of 1935, Chapter 329) by Governor Frank Merriam, the bill was modeled after the federal income tax (as embodied in the Federal Revenue Act of 1934) and had rates of 1 percent of the first $5,000 of net income up to 15 percent on net income in excess of $250,000 (approximately one-fourth of federal rates). Definitions of taxable income differed somewhat with federal law, however. Net income generally included wages, profits, and gains.[1]

Exhibit 33

California Historical Tax Rates, Selected Taxes
(where applicable, rates are top marginal rates)

Year	Personal Income	Corporate Income	State Sales & Use	Combined State & Local Sales & Use	Insurance	Estate	Vehicle License Fee (VLF)	Gasoline	Cigarette	Beer	Distilled Spirits
1970	10.00%	7.00%	4.00%	5.00%	2.35%	24.00%	2.00%	$0.07	$0.10	$0.04	$2.00
1971	10.00%	7.00%	4.00%	5.00%	2.35%	24.00%	2.00%	$0.07	$0.10	$0.04	$2.00
1972	10.00%	7.60%	3.75%	5.00%	2.35%	24.00%	2.00%	$0.07	$0.10	$0.04	$2.00
1973	11.00%	7.60%	4.75%	6.00%	2.35%	24.00%	2.00%	$0.07	$0.10	$0.04	$2.00
1974	11.00%	9.00%	4.75%	6.00%	2.35%	24.00%	2.00%	$0.07	$0.10	$0.04	$2.00
1975	11.00%	9.00%	4.75%	6.00%	2.35%	24.00%	2.00%	$0.07	$0.10	$0.04	$2.00
1976	11.00%	9.00%	4.75%	6.00%	2.35%	24.00%	2.00%	$0.07	$0.10	$0.04	$2.00
1977	11.00%	9.00%	4.75%	6.00%	2.35%	24.00%	2.00%	$0.07	$0.10	$0.04	$2.00
1978	11.00%	9.00%	4.75%	6.00%	2.35%	24.00%	2.00%	$0.07	$0.10	$0.04	$2.00
1979	11.00%	9.00%	4.75%	6.00%	2.35%	24.00%	2.00%	$0.07	$0.10	$0.04	$2.00
1980	11.00%	9.60%	4.75%	6.00%	2.35%	24.00%	2.00%	$0.07	$0.10	$0.04	$2.00
1981	11.00%	9.60%	4.75%	6.00%	2.35%	24.00%	2.00%	$0.07	$0.10	$0.04	$2.00
1982	11.00%	9.60%	4.75%	6.00%	2.35%	24.00%	2.00%	$0.07	$0.10	$0.04	$2.00
1983	11.00%	9.60%	4.75%	6.00%	2.33%	16.00%	2.00%	$0.09	$0.10	$0.04	$2.00
1984	11.00%	9.60%	4.75%	6.00%	2.33%	16.00%	2.00%	$0.09	$0.10	$0.04	$2.00
1985	11.00%	9.60%	4.75%	6.00%	2.33%	16.00%	2.00%	$0.09	$0.10	$0.04	$2.00
1986	11.00%	9.60%	4.75%	6.00%	2.35%	16.00%	2.00%	$0.09	$0.10	$0.04	$2.00
1987	11.00%	9.60%	4.75%	6.00%	2.35%	16.00%	2.00%	$0.09	$0.10	$0.04	$2.00
1988	9.30%	9.30%	4.75%	6.00%	2.35%	16.00%	2.00%	$0.09	$0.10	$0.04	$2.00
1989	9.30%	9.30%	4.75%	6.00%	2.35%	16.00%	2.00%	$0.09	$0.35	$0.04	$2.00
1990	9.30%	9.30%	5.00%	6.25%	2.35%	16.00%	2.00%	$0.09	$0.35	$0.04	$2.00

Year	Personal Income	Corporate Income	State Sales & Use	Combined State & Local Sales & Use	Insurance	Estate	Vehicle License Fee (VLF)	Gasoline	Cigarette	Beer	Distilled Spirits
1991	9.30%	9.30%	6.00%	7.25%	2.35%	16.00%	2.00%	$0.15	$0.35	$0.04	$2.00
1992	11.00%	9.30%	6.00%	7.25%	2.35%	16.00%	2.04%	$0.16	$0.35	$0.20	$3.30
1993	11.00%	9.30%	6.00%	7.25%	2.35%	16.00%	2.00%	$0.17	$0.35	$0.20	$3.30
1994	11.00%	9.30%	6.00%	7.25%	2.35%	16.00%	2.00%	$0.18	$0.35	$0.20	$3.30
1995	11.00%	9.30%	6.00%	7.25%	2.35%	16.00%	2.00%	$0.18	$0.37	$0.20	$3.30
1996	9.30%	9.30%	6.00%	7.25%	2.35%	16.00%	2.00%	$0.18	$0.37	$0.20	$3.30
1997	9.30%	8.84%	6.00%	7.25%	2.35%	16.00%	2.00%	$0.18	$0.37	$0.20	$3.30
1998	9.30%	8.84%	6.00%	7.25%	2.35%	16.00%	2.00%	$0.18	$0.37	$0.20	$3.30
1999	9.30%	8.84%	6.00%	7.25%	2.35%	16.00%	1.50%	$0.18	$0.87	$0.20	$3.30
2000	9.30%	8.84%	6.00%	7.25%	2.35%	16.00%	1.30%	$0.18	$0.87	$0.20	$3.30
2001	9.30%	8.84%	5.75%	7.00%	2.35%	16.00%	0.65%	$0.18	$0.87	$0.20	$3.30
2002	9.30%	8.84%	6.00%	7.25%	2.35%	16.00%	0.65%	$0.18	$0.87	$0.20	$3.30
2003	9.30%	8.84%	6.00%	7.25%	2.35%	16.00%	0.65%	$0.18	$0.87	$0.20	$3.30
2004	9.30%	8.84%	6.25%	7.25%	2.35%	16.00%	0.65%	$0.18	$0.87	$0.20	$3.30
2005	10.30%	8.84%	6.25%	7.25%	2.35%	0.00%	0.65%	$0.18	$0.87	$0.20	$3.30
2006	10.30%	8.84%	6.25%	7.25%	2.35%	0.00%	0.65%	$0.18	$0.87	$0.20	$3.30
2007	10.30%	8.84%	6.25%	7.25%	2.35%	0.00%	0.65%	$0.18	$0.87	$0.20	$3.30
2008	10.30%	8.84%	6.25%	7.25%	2.35%	0.00%	0.65%	$0.18	$0.87	$0.20	$3.30
2009	10.55%	8.84%	7.25%	8.25%	2.35%	0.00%	1.15%	$0.18	$0.87	$0.20	$3.30
2010	10.55%	8.84%	7.25%	8.25%	2.35%	0.00%	1.15%	$0.35	$0.87	$0.20	$3.30
2011	10.30%	8.84%	6.25%	7.25%	2.35%	0.00%	1.15%	$0.35	$0.87	$0.20	$3.30

Base/measure: Personal income: taxable income; Corporate income: net income; Retail sales and use: receipts from sales or lease of taxable items; Insurance: gross premiums; Estate: taxable federal estate; VLF: market value; Gasoline: gallon; Cigarette: package; Beer: gallon; Spirits: gallon.
Source: California Governor's Budget Summary (various editions), California State Board of Equalization

California's original personal income tax was steeply progressive and extraordinarily anti-growth. And, so it is again today. California's economy currently struggles with a steeply progressive and exceptionally high personal income tax rate system and a high corporate income tax rate—both of which were seen to be associated with low growth from our cross state analyses. Additionally, the operations of California's state and local government bureaucracy are rife with misaligned incentive structures, not to mention that the legislature is completely dysfunctional. All of these obstacles combine to create the anti-growth policy environment that is now plaguing the state.

Righting California's economy requires an understanding of how California's current anti-growth policies are altering the incentives to work, save, and invest in the state. It is the universal applicability of the theory of incentives across all states (and nations) that explains why even in California economic policies matter.

Earlier chapters provided the theory linking changes in economic policies to changes in economic outcomes. Chapter 3 looked at all of the states while Chapter 7 focused on California's housing market. As illustrated in our review of all 50 states, there is a strong correlation between sound pro-growth economic policies and robust economic outcomes. California's own history illustrates the same strong correlation between sound economics and prosperity. Although macroeconomists lament the fact that they have no truly controlled experiments to use to isolate the effects of different fiscal policies, the case of California comes pretty close to fitting the bill. This chapter provides a brief review of California's economic history, emphasizing the key policy changes and subsequent economic results to illustrate that California's economic prosperity is also linked to the economic policies that it implements.

> **Righting California's economy requires an understanding of how California's current anti-growth policies are altering the incentives to work, save, and invest in the state.**

California's political and economic swings from Karl Marx to Adam Smith become apparent when we compare the total tax burden (total state and local tax receipts divided by the state's personal income) in California to the total state and local tax burden in the U.S. When California's state and local tax burden was low, California prospered by just about any measure you would like to pick. And when California's state and local tax burden was high, the opposite held true as well. The present circumstances of California's economy are yet more proof of the principle that bad results follow bad policies. Exhibit 34 compares California's tax burden to the U.S. tax burden from 1960 through 2010. An inspection of Exhibit 34 shows that we should focus our review on several key periods.

Exhibit 34

Tax Burden for California and U.S.
State and Local Tax Revenues per $1,000 of Personal Income

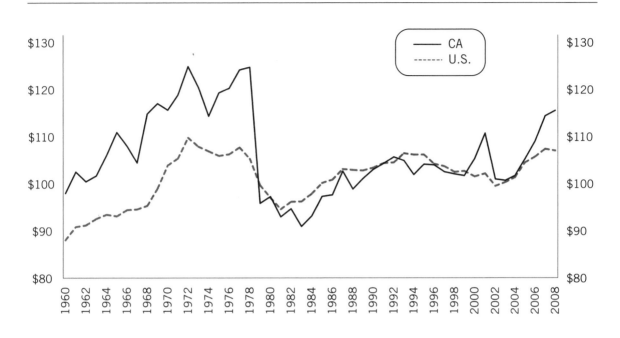

Source: Bureau of Economic Analysis, U.S. Census Bureau

The first period encompasses the 1960s on through the mid 1970s. At the outset, California's tax burden was substantially higher than the nation's tax burden and as this period progressed, California's already heavy tax burden continued to increase, rising even further above the also-rising U.S. average. Then, seemingly in a blink of an eye in the late 1970s, California's tax burden dropped dramatically back to the U.S. average where it remained for a number of years—the second period. The third period begins during the late 1980s and early 1990s, when California's previous lower-than average tax burden grew again, returning California up to the U.S. average. The fourth period began in the late 1990s and lasted through the early 2000s when the tax burden once again fell back below the U.S. average. Finally, the last period began in the mid–2000s when California's tax burden surged higher than the national average for all state and local governments and has continued to the present. Exceptionally observant readers will connect these periods with the changing economic outcomes presented in Chapter 7.

But the one problem we have identified as universal has plagued California throughout all of these periods: California's steeply progressive corporate and personal income tax system. If we had to sum up the booms and busts of California's volatile history, two words would suffice: *progressive taxes*. California's progressive income tax accentuates California's economic and tax revenue volatility. The higher California's top personal income tax rate, the greater California's volatility has been. Due to the pivotal role the progressive income tax has played in California's economic history, it is useful to first review California's progressive income tax problem.

Progressive Taxes Are Driving California Progressively Broke

Our story outline runs as follows: politicians in Sacramento inevitably paint themselves into a corner. The tax code is steeply progressive, with the highest 10 percent of income earners paying almost 75 percent of all tax revenues resulting from the income tax. This tax structure showers riches on the state during periods of prosperity, which are of course immediately spent. Then when the downturn comes—as it inevitably does—state revenues are reduced disproportionately because of the loss of high income earners. Yet since government spending is much easier to expand than it is to contract, the revenue shortfalls lead to massive deficits.

Volatile revenues—the alter ego of progressive taxes—inextricably lead to big government by increasing spending during prosperity and ratcheting up tax rates during slow times.

To close the budget deficit gap, the "solution" all too often is to hike taxes even more, which in turn serves to further discourage employment and output—and hence reduces the tax base. Because of the dynamic effects (as illustrated by the Laffer Curve), the tax hikes don't raise as much revenue as predicted, and thus budget deficits persist and continue to disappoint. At the same time, welfare rolls and other support programs expand right along with rising unemployment. The downward spiral is only arrested when the public is finally fed up and demands drastic tax relief. Yet old habits die hard; the vicious cycle resumes once again in a few years when the public has forgotten the lesson. But at each new cycle the tax and spending problems ratchet up further and further. California today may just be testing how far this vicious cycle can go.

It is this famine/feast syndrome so characteristic of economies with progressive taxes that has precipitated once again a California revolt. But the resolution is far from certain. The crisis of the late 1970s/early 1980s gave us lower property taxes following the passage of Proposition 13, the abolition of our state's inheritance tax, indexed personal income taxes and the Gann spending limit— all wonderful. Yet the crisis of the early 1990s gave us mandatory education spending levels regardless of need or student performance, personal income tax increases, increases in the gas tax, increases in the sales tax, and a disemboweling of the Gann spending limit (Proposition 111)—all horrible!

Progressive taxes, because they automatically increase taxes as a share of income as income rises, also lead to a higher overall share of output going to the government than the electorate would prefer. Tax cuts are never as popular with politicians in good times as are tax increases in bad times. Volatile revenues—the alter ego of progressive taxes—inextricably lead to big government by increasing spending during prosperity and ratcheting up tax rates during slow times. Those who argue that California's government is more liberal than its electorate miss the point: big government is a byproduct of a progressive tax code.

Progressive tax codes lead to a plethora of specific fees and taxes, many of which don't even raise enough revenue to pay for the costs of their collection. It's a shame, but true. It's always tough (but not impossible) to raise the big taxes—especially with the Proposition 13 mandated two-thirds majority vote requirement to raise taxes in California—but less visible taxes often can be snuck in under the tent late at night. During downturns, when legislators want to raise taxes for fiscal reasons, they turn to less visible taxes, often disguised as fees. As a result, we have literally thousands of taxes and fees at the state and local level here in California. While it may be impossible to compile a complete list of all state and local taxes and fees levied, you can surely get a flavor of what Californians face by reviewing Appendix A.

California's progressive income tax system has led to massive overestimates of general fund revenues during difficult economic times and massive underestimates of general fund revenues during periods of strong economic growth.

The volatility created by California's progressive tax system also makes it difficult to forecast revenues for the state. Exhibit 35 illustrates California's budgeting record. Whether it was during the actual budget process (about 12 months before the end of the fiscal year) or during the mid-year review (about six months before the end of the fiscal year), California's progressive income tax system has led to massive overestimates of general fund revenues during difficult economic times and massive underestimates of general fund revenues during periods of strong economic growth. To partially explain these gigantic goofs, in Exhibit 36 we show the shocking "V"–shape pattern of California revenue from the tax on personal income. The surges and drops in tax revenue from personal income's share of total General Fund revenues correspond with the persistent underestimating and overestimating of revenues.

Exhibit 35

California General Fund Revenue (and Transfers): Forecast as a Percent Above or Below Actual

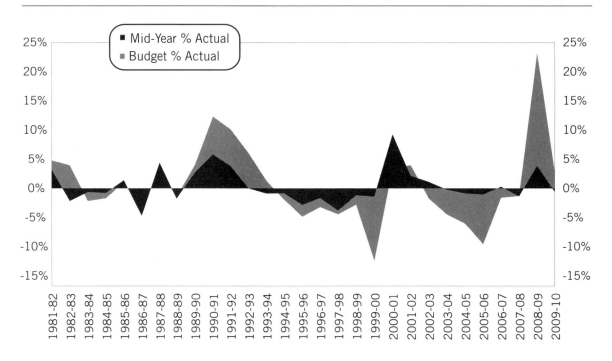

Source: California Department of Finance

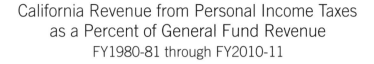

Exhibit 36

California Revenue from Personal Income Taxes
as a Percent of General Fund Revenue
FY1980-81 through FY2010-11

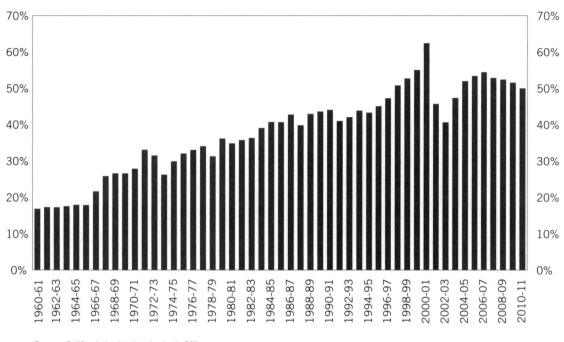

Source: California Legislative Analyst's Office

To drive home the point, consider this: the number of reported millionaires in California dropped from 44,000 in 2000 to 29,000 in 2002. And yet those original 44,000 millionaires contributed $15 billion to the state treasury in 2000, meaning that the richest 0.15 percent of the population contributed roughly 20 percent of the total income tax revenues. The last thing in the world California should ever want to do is drive these people away or to enact policies that make them poor. Make no mistake, there really are productive individuals who have moved out of California.

In fact, if we digress a little bit more, not only are millionaires important, but two components of their income are inordinately important...taxes collected on realized capital gains and exercised stock options. These two sources of tax revenue as a share of general fund revenues are plotted in the chart below. Just look at 2000. A full 24.8 percent, almost one-fourth of all general fund revenues came from these two sources alone. It is inconceivable yet true nonetheless that almost one-fourth of all general fund revenues come from taxes collected on exercised stock options and realized capital gains. Talk about a messed up system. And you wonder why tax revenues in California are so volatile?

Exhibit 37

California Revenue from Stock Options and Capital Gains as a Percent of General Fund Revenue
FY1995-06 through FY2011-12 (estimated)

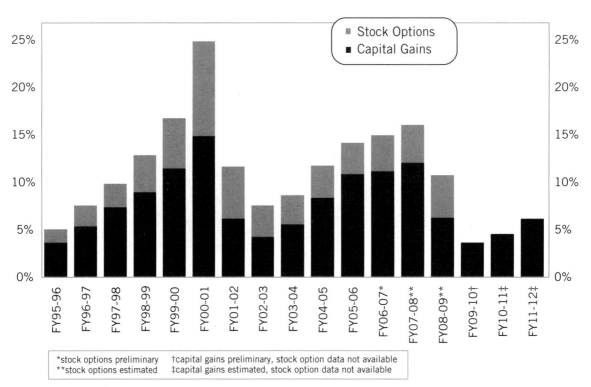

*stock options preliminary   †capital gains preliminary, stock option data not available
**stock options estimated   ‡capital gains estimated, stock option data not available

Source: California Governor's Budget Summary, various years

The policy mess in Sacramento cannot be solved without addressing California's steeply progressive income tax that encourages budget boom and bust. The Golden State applies a top marginal income tax rate of 10.3 percent, one of the highest on earnings of any state, according to the Tax Foundation. And the 10.3 percent (as of September 2011) applies to capital gains as well as ordinary income. Because federal tax deduction for state income tax payments are a preferred item on the Alternative Minimum Tax (AMT), a rising share of those who pay the 10.3 percent rate are now hit by the federal AMT. About one-third of California's income tax is no longer deductible on the federal tax return. State taxation without federal tax deductibility is one more reason for taxpayers to flee the state.

Just to mention in passing, the current 10.3 percent highest marginal tax rate was 10.55 percent last year until the surcharge lapsed. The powers that be couldn't get the surcharge renewed, although God knows they tried.

Our quick lesson leads to the obvious conclusion: If California wants to balance its budget and revitalize its economy, the progressivity of the income tax system needs to be either diminished or greatly reduced and the tax rates need to be slashed, not increased. In my opinion, relying on the vigilance of the voters to "guard the guardians" is naïve. If you don't believe me just look again at Appendix A, a partial selection of California's State, County and City Taxes and Fees. A more promising approach is to completely revamp California's tax code, replacing it with a single tax rate on two flat tax bases of personal income and business value added. By reducing the highest marginal tax rates, such a reform would immediately energize the state's most productive individuals, as well as attract more talent from outside its borders. Beyond the boost to average incomes and growth, the switch to a low rate flat tax would also allow California to reduce its overall tax burden and the volatility of its tax revenue stream. But, we will discuss this in more detail later.

Now that we've summed up the problems with California's steeply progressive income tax, we next offer a punctuated chronology of some of the major events in California's history to better understand how we got into our current fix, and to underscore our claim that pro-growth policies are the only solution. California truly is a state of exaggerated policy swings moving from Karl Marx to Adam Smith and back again in a blink of an eye.

The Gipper as Governor: Don't Let Reagan Be Reagan

From the early 1960s to the early 1970s, California, along with the aggregate of all states, increased taxes as a share of personal income by enormous amounts, see Exhibit 34. From 1960 to 1972, California increased total state and local tax receipts as a share of personal income from 10 percent to 12.7 percent, as shown in Exhibit 34. In the vernacular, that percentage increase in California's total tax burden is not "chopped liver" by any stretch of the imagination. During that same time period the sum of all states raised their tax burden from 8.9 percent to 11.1 percent. California was right at the forefront of the lemmings as they marched over the cliff. Edmund G. (Pat) Brown was governor during the 1960 to 1967 period, followed by Ronald Reagan. For those of you who weren't around back then, Pat Brown was current Governor Jerry Brown's father. I remember Pat Brown most for his editorial comment responding to my support for Prop. 13: if he were a Communist he would support Prop. 13. There you go!

To keep everything in its proper perspective, the 1960s and early 1970s were the eras of the "Go-Go" sixties, followed by the Johnson/Nixon melt-down. The mid–1970s was a period of massive tax indigestion following the tax binge. The U.S. economy was weak everywhere, but was especially bad in California.

For the country as a whole, the period 1966 through 1982 was the period when America was governed by whom I like to refer to as the four stooges…Johnson, Nixon, Ford, and Carter; the largest assemblage of bipartisan ignorance ever put on planet earth.

The stock market is probably the perfect metric to give you a flavor of just how bad that period was. In early February 1966, following President Kennedy's tax cuts and other Kennedy Administration supply side measures, the Dow Jones Industrial Average hit an intraday high of 1000. About 16½ years later in August of 1982, the Dow Jones Industrial Average hit a low of 777. That corresponds to a nominal decline of 22.3 percent in the value of America's capital stock in 16½ years.

But from early 1966 to August 1982, the U.S. price level trebled so the change in the real inflation adjusted value of the Dow Jones Industrial Average went from 1000 in February 1966 to 235 in August of 1982. That is a 76.5 percent decline in 16½ years, or slightly over a 7 percent annual average compounded decline. That really is a bear market.

From 1960 until 1978, California's tax burden and the aggregate tax burden of all states moved in lock step, with California always having a much higher tax burden. From 1960 through 1977, California remained one of the very highest taxed states in the nation—a dubious honor to be sure. In 1977, for example, California ranked as the third highest taxed state in the nation. In 1960, California had been way up there on the tax charts too. But prior to the end of the 1960s, even though California's taxes were relatively very high, they had been rising sharply from a much lower base (see Exhibit 34).

From the standpoint of how a state's economy performs, both the state's absolute tax burden and its relative tax burden should be important. Using an admittedly extreme hypothetical illustration to make our point, if California's state tax burden were twice that of other states', and yet amounted to only two pennies of tax per $1,000 of income, the relative tax burden should have only a minimal impact on how well California's economy should perform. The absolute tax burden would be so small as to dilute the relative tax effect.

In the very early 1960s California's relative tax burden was quite high, but its absolute tax burden was much less than it was in the mid–1970s. As a result of a lower absolute tax burden, California's relative tax burden should have weighed less heavily on California's economy in the early 1960s than in the mid–1970s. However, consistently increasing taxes from a low tax burden will eventually lead to a large tax burden. And, while no one appreciates President Ronald Reagan (1967–1975) more than we do, a sharply rising tax burden is what happened during his watch by the late 1960s and early 1970s.

If not the very best president ever, Ronald Reagan was surely one of the best presidents in our nation's history. In fact, in our view, Reagan's only modern challenger for greatness was John F. Kennedy. But part of Reagan's greatness was his humanity, humility, and ability to learn from his mistakes—of which he made several while serving as governor of California. Although some of Reagan's critics may bitterly point to the "Bloody Thursday" shooting at UC Berkeley or his enthusiasm for capital punishment, Reagan was in many respects a Hollywood liberal on social issues. In our view, Governor Reagan's critical mistake came when he hiked the highest tax rates on personal and on corporate income, as well as on capital gains. The top marginal rate on personal income and capital gains went from 9.3 percent to 11 percent by 1974, and the top marginal tax rate on corporate income was 9 percent by 1974. Yikes!

The savior for California in the early to mid 1960s was the pro-growth U.S. policies of the Kennedy Administration at the federal level. Kennedy not only cut tax rates like mad, but he also put in the investment tax credit, shortened lives for depreciable assets, and pushed the Kennedy Round tariff cuts into a reality. As a result, U.S. growth was enormous and the period was called the "Go-Go" sixties. California benefitted from U.S. growth. But once U.S. growth was gone, so was California.

During the late 1960s through the mid–1970s, the reader will recall, California's economy underperformed. Four of the variables we have tracked as measures of economic well-being are relative personal income growth, relative population growth, relative employment growth and housing values. Throughout our historical review we will bring in California's performance in these areas to connect the policies implemented to the economic outcomes created. During Reagan's period as Governor neither the policies nor the economic outcomes were desirable.

Exhibits 38–41 illustrate California's share of U.S. personal income, U.S. population, U.S. employment and California's housing values. As the reader can clearly see, California's economic performance in light of its rising relative tax burden and higher marginal tax rates was awful. While California's share of the national economy was growing in the early part of the 1960s, from the mid-1960s through the mid-1970s the growth in California's economy relative to the U.S. economy came to a halt. The same story holds true for California's share of national employment, population, and home values.

Exhibit 38

California's Share of U.S. Personal Income, 1960–1990

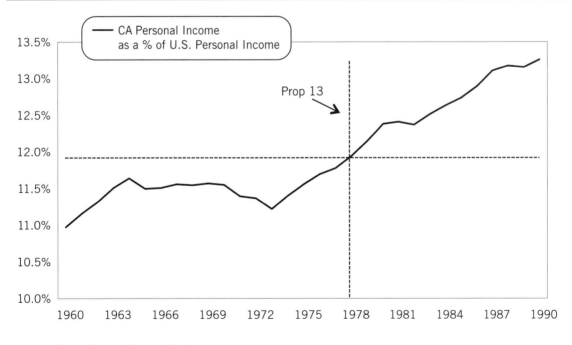

Source: Bureau of Economic Analysis

Exhibit 39

California's Share of U.S. Population, 1960–1990

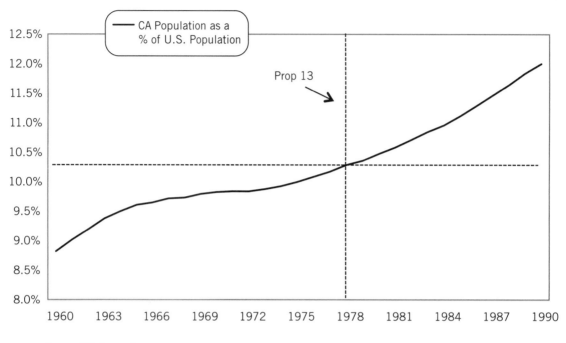

Source: U.S. Census Bureau

Exhibit 40

Excess State and Local Tax Burden vs. Excess Unemployment
California vs. U.S., 1963–1990

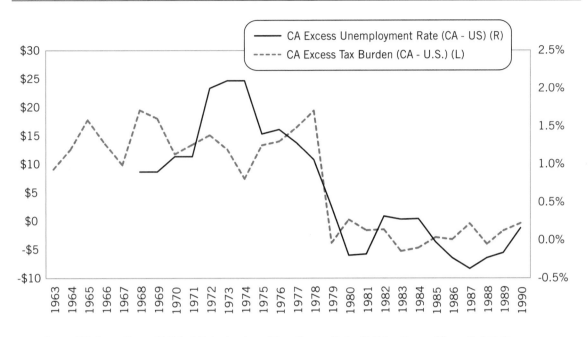

Source: U.S. Census Bureau *Statistical Abstract,* various editions; Bureau of Labor Statistics; Bureau of Economic Analysis

At the macroeconomic level, the changes in the economic variables that lead to downturns in the real estate market can be used to forecast when the downturn in the real estate market will occur. Population growth fell during the late 1960s through the mid–1970s and was followed by downturns in the real estate market.

The California Story   99

Exhibit 41

California Excess Unemployment vs. California Median Home Prices, 1968–1997

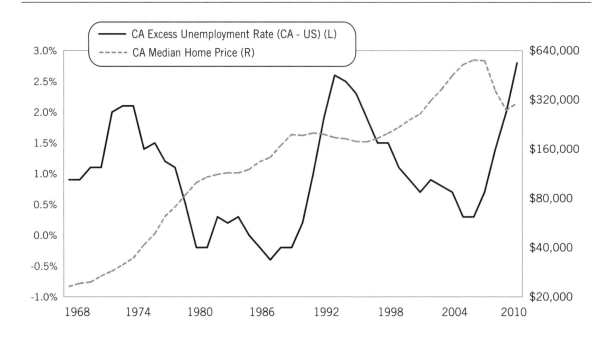

Source: U.S. Census Bureau Statistical Abstract, various editions; Bureau of Labor Statistics; California Association of Realtors

It was not just the economy that was troubled throughout the 1970s. Racial tensions, like the rest of the country, were also plaguing California during this time. They boiled over in 1965 in the Watts Riot that raged in Los Angeles for five days.

We often forget just how racially disruptive the U.S. society had been prior to President Reagan taking office. When I joined the University of Chicago faculty, you wouldn't believe how bad the riots were in the South Side of Chicago surrounding the assassination of Martin Luther King. Teenage members of the Black P. Stone Nation gang literally stopped cars to check for incendiary material as those cars entered their South Side Chicago gang territory. There was no police presence and as a result of gang inspections, no buildings were burnt in their territory. It was scary. California was no different.

Exhibit 42

Number of Major Race Riots by Administration,
(four-year periods to the present)

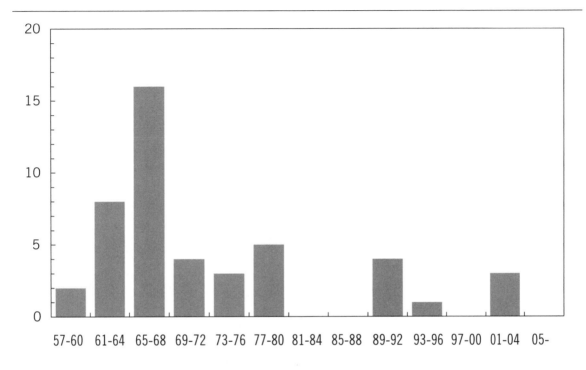

Source: The Encyclopedia of American Facts and Dates, 10th edition.
Past published research paper. Supplemented by wikipedia.com and other web sources.

And then there was pollution. Pollution was a real problem for California. It was not that long ago that a charcoal gray postcard with the caption: "Los Angeles on a clear day" was an accurate reflection of the problem facing California. The Mayor of Azusa was reputed to have claimed that "he doesn't trust air that he can't see."

Smog in Los Angeles has been documented as far back as 1943. In fact some have it that the inversions that cause pollution occurred in the Los Angeles basin before man inhabited the area. Being downstream from a herd of buffalo was pretty gross. But the problem of pollution grew along with California's population throughout the 1950s and 1960s, peaking in the late 1960s. I personally vividly remember driving down from Stanford to visit my cousins in Anaheim in 1964. I was driving on the 10 Freeway in what seemed like a dense opaque yellow-green fog. I believe that on that day there was a 100-plus car pile-up on the 10 Freeway. Pollution levels remained high throughout the 1970s but were on a steady downward path to their significantly lower levels today.

Exhibit 43

Percentage of Days Per Year in Violation of Federal Air Quality Standards in the Los Angeles Area (South Coast Air Basin)
Annual through 2005

Source: South Coast Air Basin data from the South Coast AQMD.

Throughout this period California began implementing what could be considered the most stringent environmental regulations in the country. California's laws and regulations also were at the forefront of pushing new products—such as the catalytic converter, which reduces emissions from automobiles. Pollution levels did fall dramatically throughout the 1970s and 1980s. These regulations were amazingly helpful as shown in Exhibit 43.

These same regulations, pushed way too far in later years, are at the root of later economic crises and California's current uncompetitive regulatory environment. As discussed in the next chapter, the roots of California's electricity crisis during the early 2000s can be traced back to some of these energy regulations. These regulations have also come at a great cost to Californians working and investing in the state. For example, a study commissioned by the state legislature and published by Varshney and Tootelian (2009) found that California's overall regulatory burden (both environmental and other regulations) costs "$493.0 billion which is almost five times the state's general fund budget, and almost a third of the state's gross product. The cost of regulation results in an employment loss of 3.8 million jobs which is a tenth of the state's population."[2]

While racial tensions and pollution undoubtedly have many causes and must be addressed from a multi-faceted approach, ensuring a vibrant economy is clearly a key to racial harmony and a clean environment. Putting first things first, it is crucial that federal, state, and local governments establish an environment in which the economy can flourish. It is only when there is a prosperous economy that important problems such as pollution and racial tensions can be solved in a just and permanent manner. The policies of the 1970s were creating just the opposite affect.

Then came Proposition 13.

Hiding up in the mountains
Laying low in the canyons...
Their funky exile.
"Los Angelenos"
—Billy Joel

Chapter 9

A Man's Home Is His Castle: The Legacy of Prop. 13

In 1978, a force that had been building strength for several years finally brought huge and dramatic change to the California economy. Proposition 13 is an event that earned the moniker "the tax revolt heard round the world." Proposition 13 was made law thirty years ago, June 6, 1978. On that day America was jolted by the political equivalent of a sonic boom. Political analysts often argue when the modern-day conservative movement in America was officially launched. Some say that it was Barry Goldwater's campaign in 1964. Others, say it was the election of Ronald Reagan in November 1980. In our view, modern day supply-side economics had its origins when Proposition 13 was passed. We believe that a strong case can be made that the conservative, tax-cutting tide began in 1978 when almost 60 percent of California's voters declared thumbs up on Howard Jarvis's and Paul Gann's brainchild.

This was arguably the greatest tax revolt since the Boston Tea Party and the Whiskey Rebellion. And do you remember when we postulated California as being the nation's trend setter? Well, the spirit of Proposition 13 was rapidly exported to the rest of the country. Within five years of Prop. 13's passage, nearly half the states strapped a similar straitjacket on politicians' tax raising capabilities by cutting income or property taxes, or both. In many ways, Prop. 13 presaged the improbable presidential election of Ronald Reagan, who sailed into the White House on the crest of a national anti-tax wave by promising a supply-side 30 percent income tax cut for one and all. I can personally assure you that had Prop. 13 not passed, Ronald Reagan would have been a very different president. Once again, the old maxim was proven true: as goes California, so goes the nation.

Two patriots led this tax revolt: Paul Gann and Howard Jarvis, men described by the *Los Angeles Times* as "the chief spokesmen for this expanding group of angry and disgruntled taxpayers across the state who believe they are paying too much for the cost of government." And that was the essence of the Proposition 13 revolt: after a decade-long voracious expansion in the size of the Great Society welfare state, along with years of double-digit inflation that escalated tax burdens through bracket creep and soaring asset values while erasing family purchasing power, Americans no longer believed that government was giving them anywhere near their money's worth. In the 1970s, real family tax payments rose at almost twice the pace of real family income. In California, uncapped property tax assessments were driving thousands of residents out of their homes—particularly seniors with fixed incomes who had little capacity to pay the double-digit tax rate increases on their homes.

Almost everyone of consequence in both political parties (even Reagan was originally skeptical) and almost every organized interest group in the state condemned Proposition 13 as reckless. Joel Fox, the longtime director of the Howard Jarvis Taxpayers Association writes in his book entitled, *The Legend of Proposition 13*: "Surprising to many, was that big business stood opposed. Businesses not only lent their names to the "NO on 13" campaign, they helped finance it."[1] The opponents of Prop. 13 warned voters of the doom that awaited the state if Proposition 13 passed: on June 6, 1978, San Francisco's schools and libraries would be closed; 2,500 Los Angeles policemen would be laid off; prisoners would be released into the streets for lack of funds; and 450,000 jobs would be lost in the state according to the UCLA Business School. If those claims seem familiar, UCLA's business school released a similarly shrill and preposterous prediction on the impact of President George Bush's tax cut.

On a very personal level, my godfather, Justin Dart strongly supported Proposition 13 but was outvoted by his colleagues on the Business Roundtable and therefore, by the Roundtable's rule of speaking with one voice, was forced to oppose Prop. 13 officially. Secretly however, he had his fingers crossed hoping it would pass and was egging me on all the time.

Few listened to the hysteria. Taxes were so suffocating in California that even firefighters in Los Angeles voted 2 to 1 in favor of Prop. 13.

In June 1978, Proposition 13 (commonly called the Jarvis/Gann initiative) roiled the entrenched political establishment. Proposition 13 was a constitutional amendment that:

- **Set property taxes not to exceed 1 percent of the property's fair market value;**
- **Allowed the base value to grow no more than 2 percent per year unless the property changed hands; and,**
- **Required that all new or increased special taxes at the local level receive a two-thirds vote of the electorate and that any new or increased special taxes at the local level receive a two-thirds vote at the electorate and that any new or increased tax at the state level receive a two-thirds vote of each house.**

Proposition 13 won in a landslide.

Following on Proposition 13's heels were ballot measures and legislation including an elimination of the state's inheritance tax, indexing of the state's income tax, and the elimination of the state's business inventory tax. In 1979 Proposition 4 (the Gann spending limit initiative) passed, locking the tax gains into place by requiring:

- Spending to grow no faster than the sum of population growth and inflation; and
- All surplus revenues to be returned to the taxpayers.

Contrary to the protestations of the critics, Prop. 13 ushered in a second California gold rush in the decade following its enactment. In the 10 years after the passage of Prop. 13, incomes in California grew 50 percent faster than the nation as a whole, and jobs grew at twice the pace. During the 1980s and 1990s, the high tech sector in Silicon Valley ignited the greatest burst of technological progress anywhere at any time in history.

Other states had their own Prop. 13 which also worked and surprisingly were frequently supported by Democrats. Just read the quotes from Steve Moore's paper "Timber! State Tax Rates Continue to Fall," Laffer Associates, May 29, 1997:

> An income tax cut is the single most important step we can take to make Maryland more competitive and create more jobs.
> —Democratic Governor Parris Glendening

> Even when the final and deepest phase of New York's income tax cut is implemented this year, the state's resurgent economy appears likely to generate more income tax revenue under Gov. George Pataki than it ever did under former Gov. Mario Cuomo.
> —Empire Foundation Report, April 1997

In 1964, while a first year student at the Stanford Business School, I had my first job in California as a night watchman at Shockley Transistor at 1801 Page Mill Road in Palo Alto. It was a hoot, but unfortunately I was so young and ignorant that I hadn't realized who the people were who passed by my desk. William Shockley received the Nobel Prize in Physics for his discovery of the germanium transistor when he had worked at the Bell Labs. A number of the other applied physicists there formed Texas Instruments. You could literally touch the high tech revolution. I still have and use in my office the first generation HP calculator which was given to my boss George Shultz (then director of the Office of Management and Budget) by Deputy Secretary of Defense David Packard in 1971. George gave it to me.

If the modern conservative view of Ronald Reagan is a bit fuzzy when it comes to his early years as governor, the same holds true in reverse for Jerry Brown. Now admittedly, Brown was a bit of an odd bird in social settings, but even so he was a great governor. People forget just how unpopular Proposition 13 was amongst the "elite"—we use the term lightly—before the public overwhelmingly

In the 10 years after the passage of Prop. 13, incomes in California grew 50 percent faster than the nation as a whole, and jobs grew at twice the pace.

approved it in June of 1978. As we've said, Californians were treated to all sorts of terrifying predictions of what would happen under the tax cuts and limitations of Prop. 13. In fact, noted leftist economist John Kenneth Galbraith sent me a toy fire engine to replace the real fire engines that my support for Prop. 13 would ostensibly eliminate. Ken Galbraith always stayed in character as an elongated wind instrument.

Amid the dire forecasts of financial catastrophe, Jerry Brown saw to it that the state assessor sent out tax notices the week before the election, indicating a five-fold increase in property taxes. Brown then said he had a much larger budget surplus than people had originally thought. The point, of course, was to disarm the critics who said Prop. 13 was fiscally irresponsible. With a much larger surplus, the argument that schools, libraries, and firehouses would be closed and masses of police and fireman would be laid off sounded pretty hollow.

In 1976 I was quite recognizable to the public since I had been the TV presence voicing opposition to the Cesar Chavez movement. I had also become well known for my involvement in Reagan's presidential race. Later, I also became known for all sorts of issues including Proposition 13. On the very evening when Prop. 13 passed, Jerry Brown and his chief of staff Gray Davis invited me (an outspoken proponent of the measure) to Sacramento where they held discussions over the course of three days. As a humorous illustration of Governor Brown's social awkwardness, on the way to a joint press conference, Governor Brown remarked, "Professor Laffer, I do hope you don't take this opportunity to dump all over me." His awkwardness was only exceeded by his good governance. Governor Brown made sure Prop. 13 would be implemented correctly. He was great as governor and became one of my lifelong friends. And to be quite serious, Jerry Brown wasn't a fair weather supporter of good economics.

While drumming up support for Prop. 13, I wrote a pamphlet for the United Organization of Taxpayers in March 1978—10 weeks before the vote. I predicted that the static revenue forecasts overstated the losses to the state treasury from Prop. 13 because of supply-side effects:

> Property tax revenues will fall by less than [the static forecast of] $7 billion because property values will rise and new construction activity will expand. Both of these effects will expand the tax base, and thus lead to less property tax revenue loss. In the out-years, property tax receipts will fall by far less than $7 billion annually. Take, for example, a $100,000 home, paying taxes of 3.5 percent of market. Taxes would be $3,500 per year without Jarvis. If Jarvis passes, the tax rate would fall to 1 percent of market, but tax receipts would be greater than $1,000. Using a discount rate of 10 percent, the approximate receipts would initially be $1,250, reflecting a rise in the market value of the house to $125,000.

In short order, the higher values of homes would encourage more new construction and an enlarged property base. As this process progressed, total property values would rise by far more than the 25 percent of the example.

Tax revenues elsewhere would expand absolutely. Social welfare mandated spending would fall. With property taxes lower, businesses will expand their activities within the State. This expansion will create new jobs, more investment, and higher real wages. Sales, incomes, and other forms of activity will expand. Sales taxes, income taxes, etc., all will rise. In addition, State outlays for social welfare will fall (unemployment compensation, rent subsidies, medical, etc.).

Tax revenues in future years will be reduced by less or, quite conceivably, even expanded as a result of Jarvis-Gann. When combined with the healthier economic base and, as a direct consequence, less social welfare expenditures, the State should shortly be back in a surplus condition.[2]

Indeed, history vindicated my supply-side analysis. This is clearly captured in Exhibit 44, which is Exhibit 34 reproduced for the era prior to and following Proposition 13. These figures show that the tremendous tax cut for Californians led to a substantial economic recovery relative to the rest of the nation. Exhibit 44 shows just how dramatic Proposition 13 et al has been to California's relative tax burden and how this tax burden remained low throughout the "roaring" 1980s. It was amazing! While Proposition 13 and all of the other pro-growth policies of that era did occur in and around 1978, a lot of political build-up had been apparent in California well before 1978. Without Proposition 13, there would not have been the Reagan tax revolt and Margaret Thatcher surely would not have been the Margaret Thatcher we know and love.

Exhibit 44

State and Local Tax Burden Per $1,000 of Personal Income
California vs. U.S.

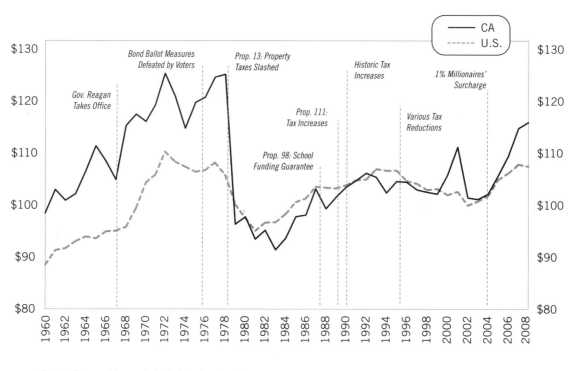

Source: Bureau of Economic Analysis, U.S. Census Bureau

In Exhibit 45, California's tax burden is directly related to the State of California's economic well-being. Exhibit 45 plots California's tax burden against the state's excess unemployment over the period 1960 through 2009. As charts of this genre go, this is a good fit. It is worth a brief tangent to review this relationship as this vacillation between good and bad economic policies is at the center of California's vacillating economic fortunes—a theme we return to again and again throughout this chapter.

With the implementation of Proposition 13, and its significant reduction in California's tax burden relative to the U.S., there was a corresponding reduction in the rate of unemployment in California relative to the U.S. California's lower relative unemployment rate persists until the historic tax increases of the mid–1990s. It is important to note that despite the higher tax rates, California failed to realize significantly higher tax revenues. Consequently, the actual tax burden from the tax increases is much higher than the burden as shown in Exhibit 45. And, as to be expected by now, once California lowered its tax burden in the late 1990s, its relative economic performance compared to the nation once again soared—measured here by the relative unemployment rate. The final period in Exhibit 45 shows that as California once again turned to tax increases to solve its budget problems, the economic consequences depressed relative economic growth. Simply put, over the broad sweep of time, California's excess unemployment is definitely correlated with California's tax burden. When one realizes just how little is included in this analysis, the relationship is much more impressive.

Exhibit 45

Excess State and Local Tax Burden vs. Excess Unemployment
California vs. U.S.

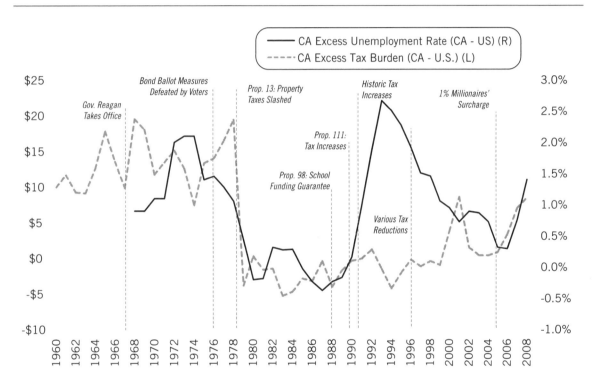

Source: U.S. Census Bureau Statistical Abstract, various editions; Bureau of Labor Statistics; Bureau of Economic Analysis

Returning to our post-Prop 13 story, the fiscal outcome also played out just as predicted. Proposition 13 passed on June 6, 1978, one month prior to the end of FY1978. State and local property tax revenues fell $5 billion, from $11 billion in FY1978 to $6 billion in FY1979, far short of the static revenue loss forecast of $7 billion. In addition, this drop was largely offset by higher revenues in every other major tax category. Total state and local total tax revenues fell by only $1.1 billion that first year. Obviously, tax revenues other than those from property taxes rose by $3.9 billion. That $3.9 billion increase is on a tax base of a little more than $25 billion. Not bad!

Looking at the bigger picture, the combined state and local tax burden per $1,000 of personal income fell from $124.57 in FY1978 to $94.93 in FY1982, a 24 percent reduction. Yet in spite of the precipitous fall in the state's average tax rate, state and local revenues did not fall proportionately. In fact, total tax revenue grew by 19 percent from $27.4 billion in FY1978 to $32.5 billion in FY1982. The tax base expanded by more than enough to offset the reduction in tax rates. "Neener neener neener," is all I have to say to you of little faith.

Economic expansion and higher property values led to healthy property tax growth over the following years, and by FY1985 property tax collections were back to their FY1978 $11 billion level. What this means is nothing short of astounding. Property tax rates were reduced by over 65 percent and yet in seven short years the property tax base rose by enough to fully offset the cut in tax rates and leave tax revenues unchanged. The disruptive shortage of funds so widely anticipated never materialized.

For Californians, Prop. 13's legacy has been to save the average homeowner in California tens of thousands of dollars in property tax payments over the past 25 years.

During the interim while property taxes were catching back up, Governor Brown, in yet another major pro-growth positive move, made sure local governments—who rely heavily on property taxes—were "made whole" by a state subvention of revenues program. In other words, the state transferred tax monies the state had collected to the cities, counties, and local districts impacted by Prop. 13. Governor Brown proved himself to be a governor's governor. And yes he was a Democrat. But not like those today. He believed in jobs, economic growth, and prosperity.

Turning our attention to spending, total state and local direct general expenditures were not slashed between FY1978 and FY1979 as skeptics had predicted; in fact, expenditures increased 1.6 percent from $36.9 billion to $37.5 billion over this period. Even better, spending on police and fire services increased 3.7 percent in FY1979. So much for a shortage of fire trucks, Dr. Galbraith! The tax reduction which had invigorated the state's economy so profoundly did not impose any significant reduction in government services.

Political aversion to heavy taxes went hand in hand with a desire to tighten the reins on spending. In November 1979, Proposition 4 placed a constitutional limit on state and local government spending. This limit, as we mentioned earlier, commonly referred to as the Gann limit, allowed spending to increase each year based on 1) the statewide population growth, and 2) inflation as measured by the percentage growth in the U.S. CPI or in California per capita personal income. Certain appropriations were not subject to the Gann spending limit, including the costs of retiring voter-approved bonds and the costs of bonds in existence when Proposition 4 was enacted. Exceptions to the limit also included appropriations required by the federal government and court mandates as well as unrestricted funds transferred to local governments or schools. In the early 1980s, Propositions 6 and 7 passed, which repealed the inheritance tax and made full indexation of the income tax permanent.

The state's balanced budgets during this period reflect the remarkable success of combining lower tax rates and increased output, employment and production with restrained spending.

For Californians, Prop. 13's legacy has been to save the average homeowner in California tens of thousands of dollars in property tax payments over the past 25 years. This is tax money that was returned to homeowners and would have fueled an even more rapid escalation in California's state and local public bureaucracies if those dollars had been sent to Sacramento and city halls. Californians intuitively understand why Proposition 13 is good for all of California as well as homeowners. That is why every major poll from 1978 to today has confirmed that a large majority of residents in California for the last 30 years continuously say that they would still vote for Prop. 13 again if it were on the ballot.

Taxpayers nationwide also owe a debt of gratitude to Howard Jarvis and Paul Gann. They helped reverse the economically disabling era of unrestrained over-taxation, over-spending, and over-regulation of government at all levels in America that dragged the nation into a malaise at the end of the 1970s. Just as important, they taught us all an enduring civics lesson that we should never forget: in America you really can fight city hall. And judging from California's wobbly performance of late, the indifference, and not so benign neglect of the political class in the state, it may be high time for another revolt heard round the world in the Golden State.

And out of good still to find
means of evil.
"Paradise Lost"
—John Milton

Chapter 10

Proposition 13: Lost, Regained, and Lost Yet Again

The great tax revolt of the late 1970s gradually faded away during the 1980s, as memories of the pre-Proposition 13 troubled economy vanished. State spending and taxes crept up. California once again had become the proverbial frog that was slowly being boiled to death.

The beginning of the end actually occurred under Governor George Deukmejian in 1988, with the passage of Proposition 98. This incredible measure required that K-12 schools and community colleges receive 41 percent of all general revenue funds. This minimum share of the budget must go to schools regardless of the state's fiscal circumstances or the impact on other programs. What Proposition 98 meant was that an additional dollar spent anywhere on any program required that an additional 69.5 cents be spent on education. When Prop. 98 first passed, times were good and the proposition didn't appear onerous. But when revenues stagnated, other state services disproportionately felt the brunt of the state's shortfall in revenues so that schools could get their automatic allotment.

In June 1990, Proposition 111 passed, which further eroded the Gann spending limit. Instead of using the lesser of inflation as measured by the U.S. Consumer Price Index or California's per capita personal income, only per capita personal income would be used to revise the limit. Spending by local governments would also have the local option of per capita personal income or an alternate growth factor that would account for the change in the assessed valuation of local commercial construction. In addition, Prop. 111 exempted from the spending limit appropriations for "qualified capital outlay projects." Thus, highway spending was removed from the Gann spending limit without lowering the limit. Virtually any and every spending category was given free rein. For all practical purposes this meant that the Gann limit was no longer operational.

On the tax side, Prop. 111 increased the state tax on gasoline and diesel fuel 5 cents per gallon, followed by 1 cent increases on the first day of each of the next four years. It also increased the truck weight tax by 40 percent and raised ethanol and methanol taxes. The increase in fuel taxes was estimated to generate $687 million during FY1991 and $970 million during FY1992.

The tax hikers were just warming up.

On July 1, 1991, the first day of the 1992 fiscal year, the '92 budget agreement took effect. The top rates on the personal income tax, the corporate tax, and capital gains tax were raised from 9.3 to 11 percent while certain credits and deductions were suspended. The AMT (Alternative Minimum Tax) on personal income was increased from 7.0 percent to 8.5 percent. The per gallon excise tax on beer was increased from 4 cents to 20 cents, while the tax on distilled spirits increased from $2.00 to $3.30 per gallon and for wine rose from 1 to 20 cents. Two weeks later, the state sales tax went up to 6 percent from 4.75 percent.[1] This sales tax increase was on top of local sales taxes.

To understand the magnitude of these hikes, consider that total state tax collections were projected to rise some $8.6 billion from FY1991 to FY1992; $2.2 billion of the projected increase was due to natural growth in the California economy, while the remaining $6.4 billion increase in tax revenues came from the tax rate increases (based on a static analysis). This represented a 15 percent increase over the total tax revenues collected in FY1990, making it the largest state tax increase in U.S. history. In terms of percentages, the Proposition 111 and subsequent tax increases were nearly four times larger than the record-breaking tax increases being proposed at the same time by President Bill Clinton for the U.S. economy.

The entire fiscal history of California is nothing other than a perpetual ride up and down the Laffer Curve. Where do you think I got the idea in the first place?

These massive tax increases were to ostensibly balance the California state budget. To us, this approach to balancing the state's budget was unjustified in terms of good economics—you don't want to kick the economy when it's already down and goodness knows the California economy was already down and falling fast to boot. After all, even if it did work, how is it good governance to balance the government's budget at the expense of every household's budget? In any event, as we illustrated in the last chapter, the actual revenues from the massive hikes fell way short of their projections. Moreover, *actual tax receipts fell* in spite of a (static) $6.4 billion tax increase on a budget in the $35 billion range. The California economy fell off a cliff as shown in Exhibit 46. And who says there's no Laffer Curve? Go figure! The entire fiscal history of California is nothing other than a perpetual ride up and down the Laffer Curve. Where do you think I got the idea in the first place?

So, once again California turned a blind eye to Adam Smith and embraced a Marxian view of the world. And, the economic results were the same as the last time California embraced a high-spending, high-tax economic path. California's rising relative tax burden and higher marginal tax rates led to (surprise!), a declining share of personal income, declining share of national employment, decreasing population growth, and the primary asset of Californians—their homes—stagnated.

Exhibit 46

California's Share of U.S. Personal Income, 1990–1995

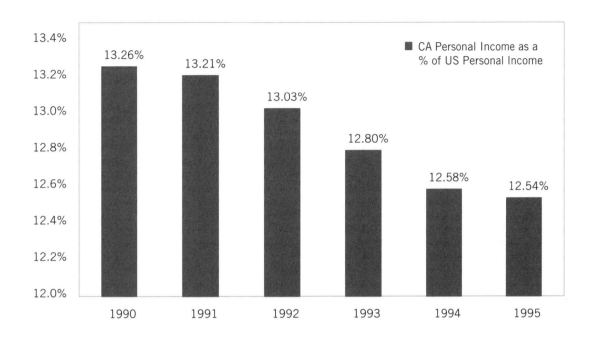

Source: Bureau of Economic Analysis

One other consequence of the bad economics of that period was the incredible bankruptcy of Orange County in 1994. Orange County's chief investment officer Robert Citron became a household name like the Swedish Match King Ivar Krueger who in an earlier era went bankrupt and then killed himself, Eisenhower's financial supporter Bernard Goldfine who gave gifts to his friend Sherman Adams, and Enron's Ken Lay. The aftermath of the bankruptcy however was a miniature version of the tax battles to follow pitting high-taxing proponents against the supply-side forces of Truth, Beauty, and the American Way of Life—by the way we won.

Exhibit 47

California's Share of U.S. Population, 1990–1995

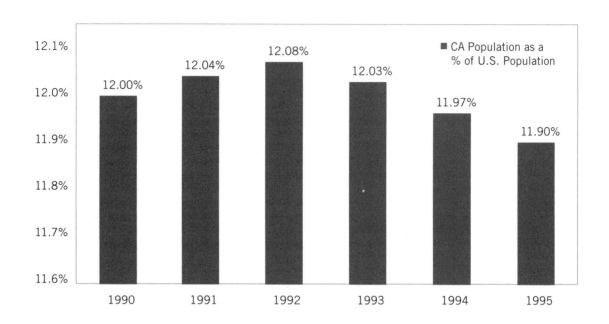

Source: U.S. Census Bureau

Exhibit 48

California's Share of U.S. Employment, 1990–1995

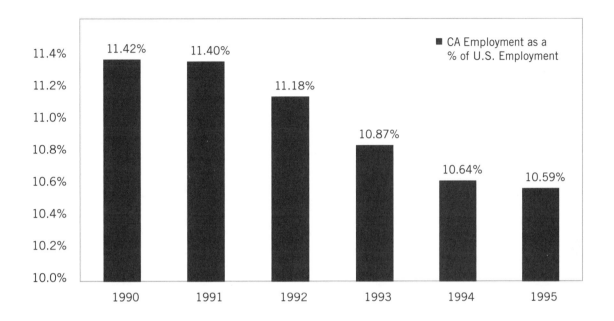

Source: Bureau of Labor Statistics

And, once again, the slowdown in population growth was followed by downturns in the real estate market.

Exhibit 49

California Excess Unemployment vs. California Median Home Price

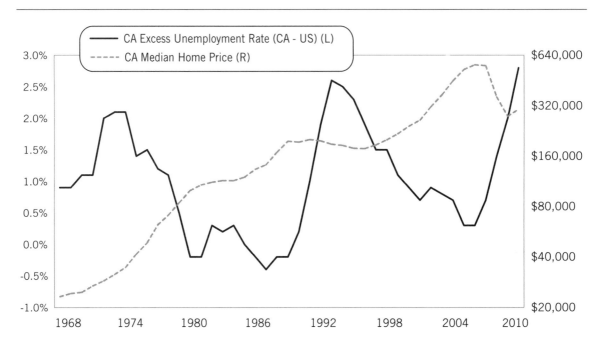

Source: U.S. Census Bureau Statistical Abstract, various editions; Bureau of Labor Statistics; California Association of Realtors

It is noteworthy that the early 1990s were, once again, a period of heightened racial tensions in California. There was the 1990 Inglewood High School riot between Latino and Black students and the 1992 Los Angeles riot in response to the acquittal of the police officers in the Rodney King case. It is our belief that none of this would have happened if the path of economic evil had not been followed. With tax increases and economic malaise, all sorts of bad things come to the fore that would otherwise be taken in stride. Darth Vader's spirit reigned supreme.

Regaining the Spirit of Proposition 13

Following years of tax rate increases during California's severe recession of 1990-1995, the 1996 tax environment began a dramatic reversal. Due to the sunset provisions of previously enacted state legislation, California's highest marginal tax rates on personal income fell from as high as 11 percent to the relatively lower rate of 9.3 percent on January 1, 1996. The tax surcharge on individuals and corporations lapsed as of January 1, 1996; and Governor Pete Wilson was also proposing serious additional tax cuts.

The news of personal income and alternative minimum tax rate reductions in California made California debt, equity, and real estate much more competitive than they had been prior to the tax rate reductions. All in all things were looking up in the Golden State; and California was on the cusp of a major turn for the better.

John Wayne was truly bigger than life. And as a person he made Orange County his home (Balboa Island just off the coast of Newport Beach) and Orange County in turn made John Wayne its symbol. At Orange County's John Wayne Airport is a huge bronze statue of The Duke carrying a rifle. On a personal note, my dream has always been to fly a direct flight from John Wayne Airport in Orange County, California to Ronald Reagan National Airport in Washington D.C. without a layover in George Bush Intercontinental Airport in Houston, Texas.

In December 1994 at the height of the economic collapse in California, Orange County declared bankruptcy following the financial debacle of Robert Citron. All the powers that circled the wagons and declared that nothing other than a .5 cent sales tax increase for 10 years could save Orange County. The battle was on to pass Measure R in a special election on June 27, 1995. The measure would require a two-thirds majority for passage because of Prop. 13.

Measure R was defeated by a vote of 61 percent opposed and 39 percent in favor in spite of being outspent 10 to 1. John Wayne would have been proud.

Within a year, the issue of Orange County's bankruptcy and indebtedness was over and done. Orange County's budget in fiscal year 1995 had been $462 million and in fiscal year 1996 it was $275 million. The problem was solved without a tax increase and a new era of prosperity for Orange County and California was about to begin.

California's strong policies were influenced heavily by improving policies at the federal level as well. In 1997, President Bill Clinton's capital gains tax reform exempted the first $500,000 of capital gains derived from the sale of a personal residence for a couple filing a joint return. This exemption could be used every two years. California followed the president's lead at the state tax level. In essence, the extension of this exemption to California homeowners allowed them to avoid paying ordinary income taxes—which is also the tax rate on capital gains—on these housing gains. For a state that has experienced rapid appreciation of home prices, this was a major tax cut for individuals.

On a personal level I can attest to the power of the elimination of the state and Federal capital gains tax on realized capital gains from the sale of a home. I owned a home in 1997 in Rancho Santa Fe, California that was valued at $1.5 million. Prior to 1997, capital gains taxes were allowed to be deferred as long as the capital gains were rolled over into another home of greater value. The basis for my home was $39,500, which was the price of my first home purchased in the South Side of Chicago where I lived when I taught at the University of Chicago in 1968. While I rolled over my capital gains in homes over the years, I still mortgaged my house to about 70 percent of current market value, which meant I had a $1 million mortgage on my house.

If I had sold that house prior to Clinton's cutting of the capital gains tax rate from 28 percent to 20 percent and exempting capital gains for home owners, I would have had a capital gain of roughly

$1.5 million and been faced with a 28 percent federal capital gains tax of $420,000 and a state capital gains tax of $150,000. But because state taxes are deductible on federal returns, I would have had an offset on my federal return of about $60,000 (39.6 x $150,000) resulting in a net tax bill of about $510,000 or a tax liability more than my total equity in the house. After Clinton's tax exemption, my tax bill for selling my house would have been zero.

California's outlook and investment opportunities became a reality in response to California's improved tax policies. The resurgence of California's economy—along with the dot com boom—was afoot.

The Spirit of Proposition 13 Lost Yet Again

Wilson's successor, Gray Davis, actually was more a victim of circumstance than a bad governor. Although he had pushed for tax hikes that (fortunately) were blocked because of Prop. 13's supermajority requirement, it was not Gray Davis' fault that some 24.8 percent of his general fund revenues in 2001, as we have repeated *ad nauseam,* came from taxes on *exercised* stock options and *realized* capital gains. (see Exhibit 37). When the stock market crashed and took Gray Davis' budget surplus with it, the catastrophe was outside of his control. Even so, in fairness we must remember that it was others who created the explosive tax code that Davis inherited. No matter what exogenous circumstances he inherited, however, Davis could have exercised more fiscal responsibility in the face of such a financial crisis.

Chapter 11

Bureaucrats Gone Wild, Politicians Gone Wilder

A regulatory mess that had been building for decades came home to roost on Gray Davis's watch. In early 2001, an electricity crisis afflicted California, hitting businesses and citizens alike.

In January 2001, Intel chief executive officer Craig Barrett referred to California as a Third World country. Some businesses even threatened to leave the state—an action that we have seen time and again as the ultimate arbiter of a state's prospects. The crisis ultimately helped push one of California's two largest utilities, Pacific Gas & Electric, into bankruptcy. Electricity shortages, like a lot of other crises, don't just appear out of nowhere. The roots of the electricity crisis can be traced back to decisions made back in the 1980s and 1990s.

Like other states, California's electricity industry once operated under a standard regulatory environment whereby the utilities produced power and sold it at a rate fixed by the California Public Utilities Commission (CPUC). The CPUC allowed the utilities to earn enough revenue for repairs and a "decent" profit. Utilities commonly were considered "safe" investments for pensioners, providing steady dividends rather than the risk of dramatic volatility in their stock prices.

Beginning in the 1980s in California, environmentalist restrictions made it much more difficult to build new electricity generation plants. Environmentalists also successfully lobbied to prohibit just about any new kind of power plant except those using natural gas, which burn more cleanly than coal or diesel plants, don't disturb wildlife as much as hydroelectric plants, and don't have the stigma of nuclear power plants.

Another factor against the development of electricity generation plants was California's pervasive NIMBY (not-in-my-backyard) attitude toward just about any kind of development. Lew Uhler, president of the National Tax Limitation Committee, cites the following as just some of the projects that have been canceled:

The Sacramento municipal utility district's Rancho Seco nuclear reactor was mothballed, despite the fact that it was still able to provide power for years… Auburn Dam, with its huge hydroelectric production potential, has remained unbuilt for more than 30 years as a result of the interference of so-called conservationists… In 1995, the California Energy Commission approved a 240-megawatt plant for San Francisco. Mayor Willie Brown and the Port Authority refused to provide the land, so the plant was never built… The San Jose City Council just turned down Calpine Corporation's major new clean-burning power plant that would produce 600 megawatts in Coyote Valley.[1]

In the early 1990s, the recession led to an underestimation of future power needs. California's recession was deeper than the national recession largely due to the record state tax increases of $7 billion a year in 1991. The result was a double-whammy to California's economy, pushing unemployment up above 10 percent. While the national economy began recovering in 1992, California's recovery was delayed until 1994, when the tax increases were being phased out. Also, the uncertainty of the deregulatory atmosphere of the mid–1990s—with the picture cloudy about who exactly would own many of the power plants—contributed to the reluctance to build more plants.

Another factor against the development of electricity generation plants was California's pervasive NIMBY (not-in-my-backyard) attitude toward just about any kind of development.

It was within this background that the deregulation of the electric utilities occurred. But those involved with electricity generation—the utilities, consumer advocates, the political parties, ambitious legislators—all had a say in the deregulation causing many adverse and unintended consequences. When the "deregulation" legislation was passed in 1996 as AB 1890, the power industry claimed that its generation capacity was 30 percent above what was needed. That proved inaccurate. Few people foresaw the massive economic upsurge that occurred in the late 1990s, which led to the high-tech industry's great demand for electricity. All that growth and all those new computers, networks, Internet sites, and chip and router factories required electricity. Demand grew by 15 percent from 1996 to 1999.

If the CPUC (California Public Utility Commission) simply had been abolished at the time, things might have been fine. But it wasn't. By law, AB 1890 immediately forced utilities to cut rates by 10 percent, a nice bait to make consumers happy. It also forced the utilities to sell off most of their generating capacity to other companies. The price controls also had a limited duration. They could cease when each of the three big utilities made adequate profits from the sale of their respective assets. These "stranded costs" were considered to be part of the investment utility investors had made over the decades. Reported Dan Weintraub, a columnist for the *Sacramento Bee*:

PG&E wasn't complaining when it gained $2.1 billion off the restructuring deal in 1998 and $2.2 billion in 1999. Even after losing $2.6 billion in 2000, the company was still ahead $1.7 billion for the entire period. Southern California Edison didn't do as well but remains about $780 million in the black for the three years combined… But when the utilities helped write this deal in 1996, they acknowledged that they were not guaranteed to come out ahead. In effect, they agreed to supply their retail customers with electricity at roughly 6 cents per kilowatt hour for four years. They figured they could get the energy for half that on the wholesale market and come out flush. For a while it looked as if they were right. Some bad judgment on their part and some foolish decisions by state regulators turned things sour.[2]

The stranded costs were paid off in June 1999 for San Diego Gas & Electric. PG&E and Edison were scheduled to do the same by March 2002. But the whole system was cancelled by the CPUC and the legislature as the crisis unfolded and price controls were restored. However, by forcing the utilities to sell production capacity, one of the seeds of the future crisis was sewn. The retail rates the utilities could charge consumers were frozen, but the wholesale prices charged by the independent power producers were not.

Following AB 1890, the CPUC retained a great amount of regulatory authority, in particular over prices, as evidenced by its refusal to let the utilities raise rates to meet costs until it allowed the up-to-46 percent hike on March 27. AB 1890 also created a new bureaucracy, the Oversight Board. The board was made up of three appointees by the governor and one each by the leaders of the Assembly and Senate. According to Steve Moore, "There really hasn't been deregulation. It's really restructuring—a changing of regulatory structures. It's hard to say we netted less regulation."[3]

In the summer of 2000, San Diego Gas & Electric was the first to be hit by the crisis. Because the utility had paid off its "stranded costs" in 1999, it could charge whatever it wished for electricity. By August, the utility more than doubled rates. Governor Davis and the legislature stepped in, reintroducing price controls retroactively to June 2000 and extending them to December 31, 2003. However, the money consumers saved will have to be paid back in future years through delayed rate increases.

During the San Diego crisis, one thing became evident: When prices went way up, people started conserving.

One of the ironies of this crisis is that until March 27, 2001, electricity prices remained frozen at essentially 1995 levels (the 1996 price cut of 10 percent was rescinded by the legislature in January 2001) despite rises in other types of energy. Several other western states saw electricity prices rise by at least 30 percent. State Senator Ray Haynes pointed out, "Tacoma Power, in Washington State, operates in a regulated environment and recently requested and received a 43 percent increase in its rates."[4] Part of that rise was because California, operating under price freezes, had little incentive to conserve, drawing more power from neighboring states than was necessary and so driving up prices elsewhere. And all across America, even throughout the globe, most energy prices—for gasoline, diesel, natural gas, etc.—rose at least 30 percent. Governor Davis himself said, "If I wanted to raise rates, I could have solved this in 20 minutes." But the needed rate hike was delayed for months—and still wasn't adequate.[5]

It soon became clear that the crisis was hitting the other utilities as well. In December, Edison customers were paying 6.5 cents per kilowatt hour (kwh), but Edison was paying independent generators 30 cents per kwh. In response, the FERC (Federal Energy Regulatory Commission) reported the Associated Press, "ordered a 'soft cap' on wholesale electricity prices of 15 cents per kilowatt hour. Suppliers offering to sell power in California at more than that price would have to file paperwork with FERC defending the higher price."[6]

The price increases were still not enough to stop the hemorrhaging of red ink at the utilities. On December 13, 2000, CPUC Commissioners Loretta Lynch and Henry Duque—two of the commission's five members—announced in a statement, "The CPUC stands ready to act to protect the financial viability of California's utilities."[7]

But things kept getting worse as they usually do when politicians and bureaucrats make business decisions.

Edison and PG&E continued bleeding money. PG&E's stock plunged from $30 to below $10, finishing at $8 on April 6, the day it declared bankruptcy. Edison's stock plunged from $25 to $6, rebounded to $15, then dropped to $7 by April 6. In the first week of January 2001, Standard & Poor's and Moody's downgraded the bonds of Edison and PG&E to junk bond status. Moody's website (www.moodys.com) wrote, "The rating action reflects the generally weak CPUC rate order, which provides a modest average interim rate increase of around 10 percent, and fails to adequately address the mismatch that the utility must pay to secure electricity in the wholesale power market."[8]

The crisis hit home on March 19, 2001, as rolling blackouts struck the state two months sooner than expected, cutting power to 1.2 million homes and businesses across the state. Additional blackouts made March 20 a dark day for many as well. These blackouts affected many more Californians than the two previous blackouts in which 670,000 people lost electricity on January 18 and 380,000 were without power on January 17. Whereas the January blackouts only hit Northern California, the March blackouts rolled across the whole state.

Water, Water, Everywhere, Nor Any Drop to Drink

Unfortunately, California's anti-market regulations are not restricted to the electricity market. For instance, California imposes a byzantine set of rules and pricing requirements on water that separate users' marginal costs from users' marginal benefits.

Economics 101 teaches us that under such a scenario the inevitable result is market inefficiencies followed by periods of shortages and surpluses—often precipitated by natural climactic variability. The continued "water crisis" that posits inevitable water shortages and laments the insufficient investment in the water infrastructure is simply the pre-ordained outcome from the same water regulations.

California consistently faces water crises and shortages. However, why anyone would describe California as having periodic water shortages is beyond us. The price of water is simply too low because government controls its distribution and price. The economics of water is the domain of politicians and bureaucrats. It's as simple as that.

Periodically, prolonged droughts will greatly diminish the water available to California. At the same time, California's population continues to grow. But just because demand grows while supplies will periodically contract doesn't warrant the moniker "shortage." If that name were appropriate then every market would always be in a perpetual state of shortage or surplus. It's price changes that keep markets in balance as Samuelson's parrot knows.

Higher priced water really would discourage waste and entice additional supplies such as desalinization. Price changes keeping demand and supply in balance are the essence of markets. California's problem is one of government interference not inherent water shortages. State and local governments have prohibited markets from doing what they do well—allocating scarce goods.

Even more to the point, California state and local governments are capable of controlling the price of water, but their ability to alter the weather is in considerable doubt. Framing the issue in terms of a shortage guarantees fuzzy thinking. One of my neighbors during the so-called shortage shouted, "How in the hell can there be a shortage? Every time I turn on my faucet water comes out just fine."

With water, California's state and local governments have already gone way too far, and by their actions, have guaranteed major trauma. We personally have nothing against alfalfa, rice, and cotton farmers—and presume the same is true for the average Californian. But, all too often during California's water crisis, government attempts to frame the issue in terms of one person's shower versus a farmer's flood irrigation. Class conflict is all but certain when the issue is framed in this manner. Government regulators, as smart and as fair as they may be, just don't hold a candle to free markets.

To minimize the damage from a prolonged history of abusive government interference in the water market, the State of California should forthwith:

- Charge all farmers, government agencies, and other water users the same price for water, no exceptions. Everyone should have the same incentive to treat water with the respect it deserves.
- The price of water should be raised such that the average price charged is initially set at five times the current average price. Such a dramatic move would clearly get people's attention. Because households are currently charged much more for water than are farmers, a higher average price, in conjunction with one price for all consumers, would still mean a relatively small increase for households.
- Grant all existing water users a credit on 70 percent of the amount of water they used last year. Consumers, therefore, would pay the same total amount they paid last year at 70 percent of last year's usage. Above that point they would pay the new market price for all

water in excess of 70 percent of last year's usage. If usage were less than 70 percent of last year's usage, then a credit would be given for their conservation at the new market price.

■ The rationale for the 70 percent credit is based solely on fairness grounds. If farmers and other users were required immediately to pay an enormous amount more for each unit of water, some would suffer tremendous hardship. Fairness requires that people be given a period of adjustment. And yet, incentives do need to be continuous both discouraging of profligacy and encouraging of efficiency. This credit is specifically designed to reduce the unfairness of a radical change in water policy and yet not interfere with the process of allocation by price.

■ Each year the credit will be reduced by 10 percentage points until it disappears in seven years. All users need to be given full information for planning purposes. Announcing the fact that the credit diminishes will make it more difficult for special interest groups to change the decision by lobbying politicians.

■ Government should under no circumstances deprive the natural environment of its water set-asides. Our forests, bays, rivers, and marshes already share the burden of drought with us and can ill-afford any additional deprivation by reducing water set-asides. These water set-asides are a small gesture reflecting the fact that other life forms share the planet with us.

■ Lastly, if water usage doesn't fall below supplies at the new higher price the price should be raised until it does. Once water usage falls below supplies and reservoirs of water are rebuilt then water prices should be adjusted continuously to balance supply and demand.

Besides having a natural superiority for fairness and efficiency, market pricing may also help California's state and local governments meet their budget obligations. In fiscal year 2008 total state and local utility revenues for water were about $9.7 billion. A five-fold increase in water prices could add billions of dollars a year to California state revenues after the seven year adjustment period. Depending upon your point of view, however, giving our government more money may be a blessing or a curse.

Of Recalls and Disappointments

By the end of Davis' tenure, out of control state spending and general fiscal frivolity, along with recurrent energy and water problems, had laid the groundwork for California's worst debt position in state history. As of December 31, 2003, the amount of California's outstanding general obligation (GO) debt was $31.7 billion, with another $22.2 billion created in 2004.[9] California's debt rating was BBB at the end of 2003, the lowest debt rating of any state and tied for the lowest credit rating any state had ever been assigned.[10]

California was once again in a budget hole, and the same group of critics who objected to Proposition 13 in the first place were blaming it for "starving the state and cities of revenues." Nonsense. In real dollars California's budget climbed from $55 billion in 1980 to more than $100 billion in 2004. After inflation, tax revenues more than doubled as of 2004 since Proposition 13 passed.

To understand the real reason California faces recurring deep budget holes, we need to re-emphasize that when Proposition 13 passed, it had a cousin designed to control state expenditures known as the Gann Amendment. The Gann Amendment was intended to limit the growth of state spending to population growth and inflation. For a while it worked and California's economy went gangbusters. If the Gann Amendment had been enforced over the decade ending in 2004, the state would not only have had a balanced budget, it would have had enough money left over to return $400 in taxes to every family in the state.[11] But over time, powerful interest groups, particularly the teachers unions, were successful in poking gaping loopholes in the Gann Amendment, and by the late 1980s and early 1990s it had been all but eviscerated, meaning spending could grow much faster than originally allowed. As with all the states today, California does not have a revenue shortfall problem. It has a chronic overspending disease. And, once again, this chronic overspending disease has taken its toll on California's economic performance.

This brings us up to the Schwarzenegger period. When Governor Arnold Schwarzenegger entered office he proclaimed that he would address California's overspending problem. To emphasize this commitment, Governor Schwarzenegger, with his budget director Donna Arduin (and now our business partner in Arduin, Laffer & Moore), came up with the clever idea of personally helping move the furniture of the first business to move back into the state. Arnold's bulging muscles lifting office furniture out of the moving van was a great symbol of a new era of a pro-business attitude for the state. He also held a gigantic "garage sale" to sell off all the excess equipment and property owned by the state but not being used: computers, desks, autos, staplers, etc. This was also a high-profile way to say to the taxpayers of California that the state was going to stop wasting money.

If the Gann Amendment had been enforced over the past decade, the state would not only have a balanced budget, it would have enough money left over to return $400 in taxes to every family in the state.

But this new ethic of fiscal restraint didn't last. Despite heavy rhetoric, debt levels remained high and California's general obligation (GO) debt was downgraded to its lowest level ever—and the lowest rating of any state government ever to boot. The yield spread between California's outstanding debt and a AAA GO debt municipal benchmark is a measure of the premium investors must receive to hold California debt versus the lowest risk municipal debt (Exhibit 50). California's Standard and Poor's debt rating is also shown. California's spread over the AAA benchmark at the time of Davis' departure was as high as it has ever been, and the spread under Schwarzenegger exceeded even that record.

Exhibit 50

California's General Obligation Debt Rating (Shaded Line) and the Yield Spread Between California GO Debt and the AAA GO Benchmark

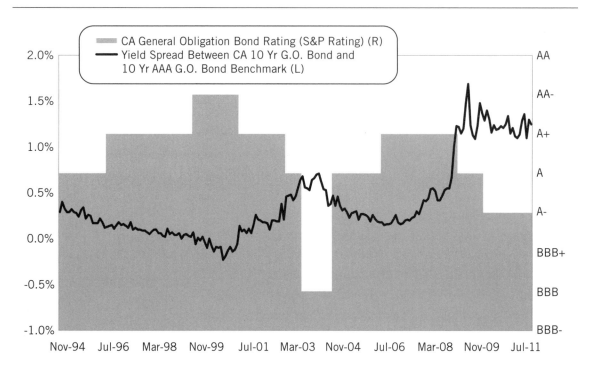

Source: Califoria State Treasurer's Office, Bloomberg

I am not exactly fickle, but it is true that in late June 2006 my family and I picked up stakes in Rancho Santa Fe, California and moved to Belle Meade, Tennessee. The move had been contemplated for several years but the actual catalyst for the move came in early 2006 when California's then-Governor Arnold Schwarzenegger made a 180° turnaround from good economics to pandering.

In November 2005, Governor Schwarzenegger called a special election and backed four seminal ballot propositions. Proposition 76 would have put a limit on state spending; Proposition 77 would have mandated unbiased redistricting of the state's political districts; yet another would have granted state teachers tenure after five years instead of two years; lastly, Proposition 75 would have required unions to get the express written consent from each union member to use his or her dues for political purposes.

For those who understand the wisdom of pro-growth policies, these measures were entirely reasonable and should have easily passed. Yet after incessant union attacks and literally millions and millions of dollars spent against his initiatives, on that day in November all hell broke loose and each of the governor's propositions went down in flames. The governor's personal popularity had been severely damaged. In order to avoid an ouster by voters in the next election, Arnold moved two giant leaps to the left, appointing liberal Democrats to key policy slots, promising to provide universal health care, turning dark green on environmental issues, fattening the budget, and cozying up to the unions.

The liberals were empowered and emboldened by their huge victory over Governor Schwarzenegger and mounted an enormous counteroffensive. Qualified for the June 2006 primary election was Rob Reiner's proposition that would have increased the highest marginal personal income tax rate by 1.7 percentage points for incomes over $400,000, raising the state's highest marginal personal income tax rate to 11 percent on incomes over $400,000 and 12 percent on incomes over $1,000,000. The proceeds of this new tax would have been used for pre-K education. The polls showed this ballot measure way ahead. There was also a ballot measure that would have imposed a very large tax increase on cigarettes. There were lots of other ballot measures in the works for California's 2006 general election, including a huge increase in the state's minimum wage.

Solving Global Warming

Then there was AB 32. Known as the California Global Warming Solutions Act of 2006, AB 32 established a comprehensive cap and trade program designed to reduce greenhouse gas (GHG) emissions in California. There were two fundamental problems with AB 32: it really wasn't a market-based solution and it would only have caused carbon emitters to leave California, not to stop emitting carbon.

Although the cap and trade system is billed as a market-based approach to managing carbon emissions, nothing could be further from the truth. Cap and trade regulations establish an aggregate constraint "cap" on the amount of carbon that can be legally emitted. Typically this constraint is benchmarked to the carbon emissions from a certain year. AB 32 establishes a carbon emissions cap that is already effective and must be achieved by 2020.

The aggregate constraint is then sub-divided into emission allowances that are allocated to manufacturers. Constrained by the overall cap, all manufacturers face a choice—comply with their emissions allocation by changing their production levels or production technologies; or purchase (trade) more emission allowances from other emission allowance holders. *The Economist* magazine had described the theoretical workings of the cap and trade, stating:

> The basic idea is that power plants and manufacturers will be allowed to emit a certain number of tons of carbon. If they exceed that amount, they must buy 'credits' from companies that pollute less than their allowance. One day the price of a ton of carbon may be as widely quoted as that of a barrel of oil."[12]

Advocates of the cap-and-trade system claim this approach is superior to a carbon tax because of its flexibility and market-based approach to the problem. As the theory goes, there is an efficient division of labor: the government establishes how much carbon may be emitted while the market sorts out who earns the right to produce the carbon emissions. The products that are in greater demand will be able to pay a higher price for the right to emit carbon. As a consequence, the manufacturers of the products in high demand will outbid other users for the right to emit carbon; while the manufacturers of the less valued products will either have an incentive to sell these rights to the manufacturers of the products in high demand or will not be able to purchase these rights in the first place. Either way, only the products that consumers value the most will end up with the right to emit carbon. In this manner, the market is allocating the scarce right to emit carbon based on its most valued use.

The fundamental economic flaw with cap-and-trade regulations in general is that at its core, cap and trade is simply a quantity constraint. Quantity constraints impact the price of the product: the greater the quantity restriction, the larger the regulation's impact on price. With quantity fixed, prices will adjust to ensure that the market clears, which creates significant price variability. Because quantity constraints have a varied impact on price, these regulations create significant price volatility in the marketplace. Depending upon the quantity level set, the price of the carbon emissions allowance could be cheap or expensive. If the quantity cap creates a significant production constraint, then the price for a carbon emissions allowance will skyrocket. On the other hand, if the cap is a minor constraint, prices will plummet.

Significant price volatility also emerges in the market because market supply and demand curves are not known to policymakers when they establish the initial cap and trade policies. The Congressional Budget Office raised these precise concerns in a 2003 paper:

> When costs and benefits are uncertain…tightening restrictions on emissions is likely to raise the incremental cost of mitigation much more quickly than it lowers the incremental benefit. As a result, the cost of guessing wrong and imposing an overly restrictive quota could be relatively high. In contrast, the cost of guessing wrong about the appropriate tax level—and perhaps failing to reduce emissions enough in any given year—will probably be relatively low.[13]

The efficacy of environmental policies is increasingly dependent on the degree to which they are applied universally. If only one-half of the earth implements pollution reducing environmental policies, total pollution emitted would decline but by far less than one-half of the decline had the whole earth implemented the same policies. Pollution of the environment is truly as global as the earth's stratosphere. Chinese pollution affects global warming from Santiago, Chile, to Vladivostok, Russia, from polar ice cap to polar ice cap. An environmental policy imposed only on one specific location will simply push polluting industries out of that location and into other locations that are more tolerant of polluting. Under this scenario, while the earth's atmosphere may be little impacted, production in the specific location may well be devastated.

Applying this insight to AB 32, this policy will be ineffective in controlling global warming because economic activity will simply leave California. The point here is simply that failure to achieve universality in a global warming policy greatly reduces its effectiveness and yet does not

It is simply not California's role, nor within California's ability, to impact an issue as grandiose as global warming. Doing so creates all costs for the state with absolutely no benefit.

significantly reduces its costs. Put another way, California does not make decisions for either the entire U.S. or the entire world. It is simply not California's role, nor within California's ability, to impact an issue as grandiose as global warming. Doing so creates all costs for the state with absolutely no benefit.

California Education:
High Spending + Big Salaries = Bottom Performance?

Then there is the dire state of California's education system. California's math and reading scores lag the national average,[14] yet teachers in California are actually paid higher salaries than the U.S. average ($60,600 in California compared to $49,600 for the U.S. average).[15] Importantly, this is a 22 percent salary premium for California teachers whereas the median household income in California over this same time period was only 12 percent higher. Therefore, higher salaries/cost of living cannot explain the higher teacher salaries in California. Taxpayers are simply spending more per teacher. Although California's teachers are paid more, total spending per student is slightly below the national average—$11,683 per student in California compared to $12,110 per student for the U.S. average and median incomes are still 12 percent higher than the national average.

Because California spends less per student, a tempting answer to California's low test scores is to raise expenditures per pupil. California's budget crisis notwithstanding, there simply is no relationship between total education expenditures per student and outcomes. In fact, if anything, the relationship goes the other way. Those who spend more per pupil have lower test scores.

Exhibit 51

2007-08 Expenditures per Pupil by State vs. 2007-08 Average SAT Scores by State

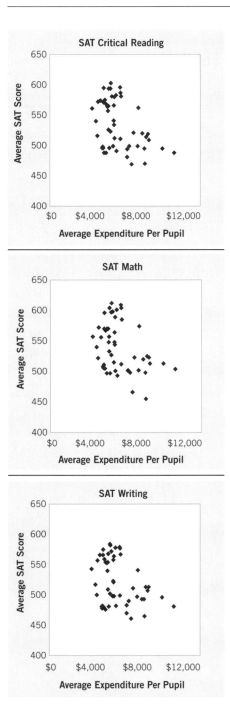

The figure above relates total expenditures per pupil in 2007-08 in each state plus the District of Columbia to the average (mean) SAT scores for that state in 2007–08. If there were a strong positive relationship between expenditures and education achievement, then there would be an upward sloping to the right pattern in the dots in each one of these charts. This would illustrate that as a state spent more money per student, the educational achievement of the students (in this case measured by how well college bound students perform, on average, on the SATs) would rise. As is evident in the figure, neither the critical reading SAT scores, math SAT scores, or writing SAT scores form an upward sloping to the right pattern. With my high powered spectacles I'll be darned if the relationship doesn't look like it goes a little bit the other way. Simply put, there is no positive relationship between how much a state spends and how well the average student performs on the SATs.

The National Assessment of Educational Progress (NAEP) is another measure of student performance. The table below shows the difference between California students' performance and the national average on the NAEP test, also known as "The Nation's Report Card." In the four subject categories and test years below, California student performance has never exceeded the national average.

Exhibit 52

Difference Between California State Average Score (out of 500) and U.S. Average Score (out of 500)

Positive Means California Schools are Better than National Average,
Negative Implies California Schools Worse

Category	1992	1994	1996	1998	2000	2002	2003	2005	2007	2009
4th Grade Math	-12		-15		-13		-8	-8	-10	-8
8th Grade Math	-7		-9		-13		-11	-10	-11	-13
4th Grade Reading	-15	-17		-13		-13	-12	-12	-12	-11
8th Grade Reading				-11		-14	-12	-12	-12	-11
4th Grade Science*					-18			-14		
8th Grade Science*			-12		-20			-13		
4th Grade Writing						-8				
8th Grade Writing				-9		-9			-8	

* Science tests use 1996 test specifications
Source: The National Assessment of Educational Progress (NAEP). Also known as "the Nation's Report Card," is the only nationally representative and continuing assessment of what America's students know and can do in various subject areas. Data reported only in years survey conducted.

Exhibit 53

Compilation Ranking of States:
Fourth and Eighth Grade Reading and Math Scores, 2009

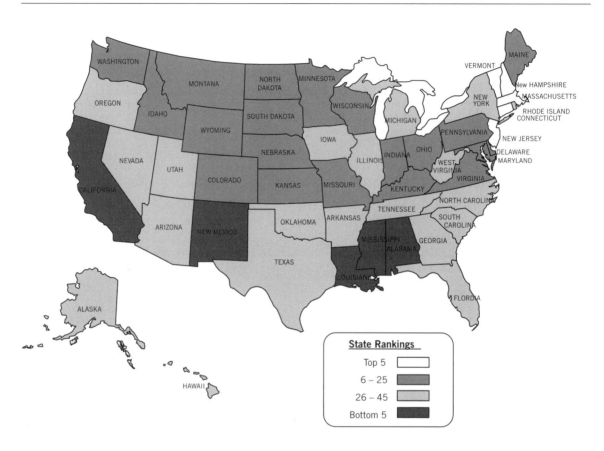

State Rankings

Top 5

6 – 25

26 – 45

Bottom 5

Source: Laffer Associates, National Assessment of Educational Progress (NAEP)

The map above provides another perspective on California's poor education performance compared to other U.S. states. The ranking for each state is based on the average fourth grade and eighth grade math and reading scores. To create one score we added the ranking in each category together to create a compilation ranking across all four categories. As the map illustrates, California's combined rank is among the five worst in the country (actually California is fourth from the bottom) with test scores as bad as New Mexico, Louisiana, Alabama, and Mississippi. It also significantly lags the performance of all of its neighbors let alone the top scorers of New Jersey, Connecticut, Vermont, New Hampshire and Massachusetts.

California's school system is in a sad state, and taxpayers and students deserve better. As if we need to write it, but California needs to reform its educational system now. Merit pay for teachers, abolish tenure for teachers, prohibit the California Teachers Association from engaging as a union in political activities, support voucher plans, reinvigorate charter schools, and measure the performance of teachers and students. This is the least we owe to the next generation of Californians.

From Governator to Girly Man

Far from taking a firm stance against all of these attacks on the state's economy, Governor Arnold Schwarzenegger pirouetted. Just read the words he spoke in his State of the State address on January 5, 2006, you can then understand why I hadn't felt so bad since I was in the White House when President Richard Nixon gave his famous 1971 Camp David speech. Yikes! Schwarzenegger stated:

> Our systems are at the breaking point now. We will need more roads, more hospitals, more schools, more nurses, more teachers, more police and fire, more water, more energy, more ports…more, more, more…

He went on to say:

> Yes, things will be tight, but funding our future is the fiscally responsible thing to do. Not to do so is to abandon the people…Let me give you an idea of where we would invest the money over the next ten years:

> 1. Transportation. Traffic does not have to keep getting worse. It can get better. If we add 1,200 miles of new highway and HOV lanes in congested areas, and add 600 miles of mass transit, we can actually reduce traffic delays in the next ten years, even as our population grows. At the same time this investment in transportation will create 150,000 new jobs for our state. I say build it.

> 2. Air Quality. Congestion on our roads and at our ports pollutes our air. Pollution decreases our productivity and increases our health care costs. When one in six children in the Central Valley goes to school with an inhaler, it's time to consider clean air as part of our critical infrastructure. We have the technology to clean our air. I say build it.

> 3. K-12 Education. In the next ten years, a quarter of a million more students will be attending our schools. To meet this need, our plan over the next decade proposes constructing more than 2,000 small schools and 40,000 classrooms and modernizing another 140,000. I say build it.

> 4. Higher Education. California's system of colleges and universities is an enormous asset that fuels our innovation economy. In the next ten years, we must prepare for

more than half a million new students. To meet the infrastructure needs of higher education, we need new classrooms, libraries and science labs in hundreds of new buildings on our campuses. I say build it.

5. Water and Flood Control. We have done little to expand our water supply in nearly fifty years. We must build more storage capacity, expand our delivery network and strengthen our levees. The Strategic Growth Plan increases our water supply to serve an additional 8.5 million people, supports our agricultural industry and doubles the amount of flood protection in the Sacramento area, better shielding us from a Katrina-type disaster here at home. I say build it.

6. Public Safety. Local jails and state prisons are so overcrowded that criminals are being let out on the street because we have no room to lock them up. Our proposal provides for two new prisons, a new crime lab, emergency response facilities and space for 83,000 prisoners over the next ten years. We must keep the people safe. I say build it.

7. Courts. Our courts are as congested as our roads and our prisons, but something even more basic to our democracy is at stake—justice. Justice delayed is justice denied. The Strategic Growth Plan includes 101 new courts, 56 renovations and 44 expansions, so that justice will not be denied at home. I say build it.

And then to cap things off:

The economy has bounced back, so it is now time for those who often work the hardest and earn the least to benefit from California's growth. Let us increase the minimum wage by one dollar an hour, with half starting this year. And I ask you to pass this measure immediately so that I can sign it without delay.[16]

While the governor's State of the State address is just a speech, his actual January 2006 budget proposal breathed life into the beast. He estimated that his infrastructure initiatives would cost something around $222 billion over 10 years. That figure is approximately two and one half times that year's general fund expenditure and doubles that year's total expenditures. To be sure, he expected much of this infrastructure spending to be funded federally and also a large part to overlap with spending that would have occurred naturally. But, after all is said and done, there was a lot of additional spending left over for the state to shoulder, and he proposed sizeable bond issues to fund it.

Not withstanding Governor Schwarzenegger's proposals, the last thing California needed was more spending or more government. The state was already suffocating under a load that includes literally hundreds of different government agencies and commissions, shown in Appendix A.

Now can you understand why I left California?

In the first paragraph of my February 17, 2006 paper "California Who Are You?" which explained just why I was leaving California, I wrote: "From the birth of Proposition 13 to the recall of Gray Davis and beyond, I have been intimately involved with the happenings in my state. I've always done my best to forecast—cool, calm and collected—the good times and the bad. I'm afraid I now bring to you bad tidings. California is embarking on a radical path of tax increases and budget-busting spending programs. The Golden State is becoming one of the most oppressive, intrusive, anti-wealth states in the nation—if we're not there already."

The tragedy of all this is that we should know from tons of circumstantial evidence that a state—any state, including California, cannot spend and tax its way to prosperity. And the charts we have been tracking illustrate that during the Davis/Schwarzenegger period, California's tax and expenditure burden rose, top marginal personal income tax rates increased, and its relative economic performance suffered.

In fairness to Governor Schwarzenegger, when he first took office he appeared to try to do what was right. In the November 2005 Special Election, there were four propositions that constituted the core of the governor's reform agenda (out of a total of eight initiatives on the ballot):

1. Proposition 74 would have required teacher tenure to be granted after five years on the job instead of the then current two years. Defeated 55.2 percent to 44.8 percent.

2. Proposition 75 would have required members of public employee unions to annually sign a document if they want some of their wages used for political activity by the unions. Defeated 53.6 percent to 46.4 percent.

3. Proposition 76 was intended to significantly reform the budget process by creating a spending formula, building a rainy day fund, and giving the governor emergency powers in a budget crisis. Defeated 62.3 percent to 37.7 percent.

4. Proposition 77, of which I was a co-sponsor, would have removed legislative district redrawing powers from legislators and give the authority to a panel of retired judges. Defeated 59.8 percent to 40.2 percent.

Because of the Unions' huge campaign against both Schwarzenegger and his four propositions, the Governator ended up having an unfavorable rating of 54 percent and a favorable rating of 38 percent. For a man who desperately craves public (and private) adulation as he does, the pressure was unbearable and he became a "Girly Man" as shown by his speech above. What really turns my stomach however is that it was primarily the same California Teachers Association that spent all that money to defeat good economics all the while they were shirking their jobs to educate our children.

Jerry Brown is once again governor and the moving vans are going the other direction again and the garage sales are being held by the latest wave of out-migrants who can't afford all of the state's crazy laws, regulations, and taxes. And yet, the quality of government services continues to decline not despite the burdensome regulations and high taxes but because of the burdensome regulations and high taxes.

"Extreme justice is extreme injustice"—Cicero

California's prison system is another California system that is as we write, in a state of crisis. A 2011 Supreme Court decision ruled that "If a prison deprives prisoners of basic sustenance, including adequate medical care, the courts have a responsibility to remedy the resulting Eighth Amendment violation."[17] In practical terms, by a 5-4 decision the Supreme Court "…ordered California to release tens of thousands of inmates or take other steps to ease overcrowding in its prisons to prevent 'needless suffering and death.'"[18]

Corrections and Rehabilitation expenditures represent around 10 percent of the state General Fund budget or around $9 billion in expenditures a year.[19] If California were able to reduce its per prison costs to the U.S. average, the state could save $2.2 billion or a 23 percent reduction in Governor Brown's proposed FY2011-12 budget. Bringing the state prison population down to the national average—in addition to per prisoner costs—would create even greater budgetary savings. California has too many prisoners and spends too much on them.

California's higher per prison costs illustrate that, based on the current "production technologies", California is an inefficient producer of corrections services. Allysia Finley, in an April 30, 2011 *Wall Street Journal* op-ed describes one such inefficiency. Due to the power of the corrections officers union, Finley advises potential Harvard University students to consider enrolling in the California Department of Corrections and Rehabilitation Academy:

> a brochure from the California Department of Corrections and Rehabilitations boasts that it "has been called 'the greatest entry-level job in California'—and for good reason. Our officers earn a great salary, and a retirement package you just can't find in private industry. We even pay you to attend our academy." That's right—instead of paying more than $200,000 to attend Harvard, you could earn $3,050 a month at cadet academy.

It gets better:

> Training only takes four months, and upon graduating you can look forward to a job with great health, dental and vision benefits and a starting base salary between $45,288 and $65,364. By comparison, Harvard grads can expect to earn $49,897 fresh out of college and $124,759 after 20 years.
>
> As a California prison guard, you can make six figures in overtime and bonuses alone. While Harvard-educated lawyers and consultants often have to work long hours with little recompense besides Chinese take-out, prison guards receive time-and-a-half whenever they work more than 40 hours a week. One sergeant with a base salary of $81,683 collected $114,334 in overtime and $8,648 in bonuses last year, and he's not even the highest paid.[20]

California's tight budget precludes significant increases in correctional spending to comply with the Supreme Court's ruling. Exhibit 54 illustrates that additional spending is not required. As of FY2007, using the latest comparable data available from the Department of Justice, California spent $347 per Californian on corrections expenditures, which is 54.2 percent higher than the national average. Exhibit 55 illustrates, total correctional expenditures per prisoner per day is also higher than the national average, 38 percent higher. Consequently, California's high cost prison system is due to both a higher prison population per capita and higher expenditures per prisoner.

With such high labor costs it is no wonder that California's prison costs are so high. Because the state corrections department is no longer an efficient producer of correction services, California's taxpayers should find more efficient private producers.

While budgetary savings are important, maintaining public safety and discouraging illegal activity are important as well—perhaps more so. Justice budgetary savings are only valuable if the state provides the same (or better) justice services following the budget cuts.

Exhibit 54

Per Capita State and Local Corrections Expenditures
All 50 States, FY2007[21]

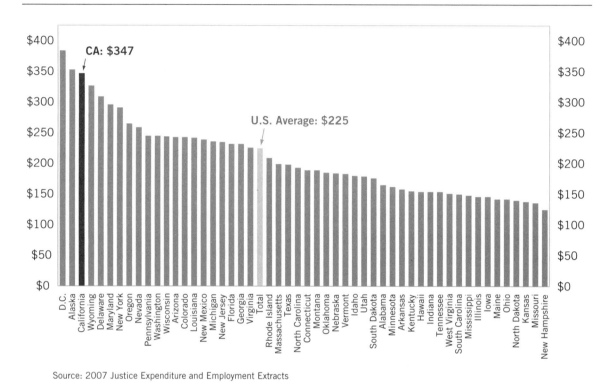

Source: 2007 Justice Expenditure and Employment Extracts

California should end the monopolistic power of the prison guard unions, carefully evaluate which crimes require prison and which do not, use financial penalties more and prison less, outsource as much as economically feasible, and lastly make sure that prison sentences are not over used. Prison is primarily needed to protect society from dangerous criminals, not to punish those criminals who pose no threat to society.

Exhibit 55

Total Correction Costs Per Prisoner Per Day Relative to the National Average
All 50 States, FY2007[22]

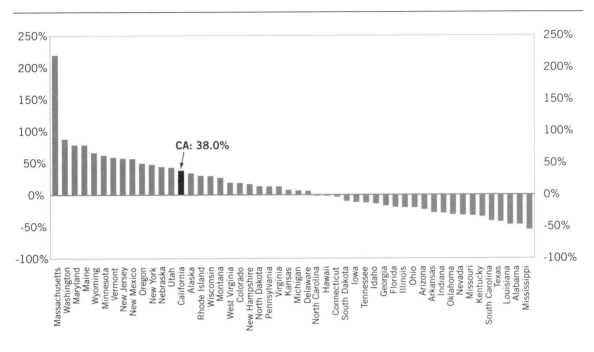

Source: 2007 Justice Expenditure and Employment Extracts

Concluding Thoughts

As our brief history of California shows, economic theory actually works in the real world. Large tax cuts lead to rising employment, income, home values, population, and tax revenues. Large tax increases have the opposite effect. If Governor Brown wants to solve California's recurring budget crises, he should create an environment conducive to economic growth and prosperity.

What is needed is a true pro-growth tax code that eliminates the boom and bust revenue cycle and creates the largest incentives for firms and workers to come to California. California's regulatory structure must be overhauled so that the regulations achieve their intended purposes without all of the collateral damage created by the current regulatory structure. It is time for Governor Brown to implement his flat tax!

This brings us to our recommendations that will reignite the California dream—the topic of our next chapter.

You know I'm thinkin' about movin' somewhere else
But I can't because I love America too much
Especially California, yeah.
"1040 Blues"
—Robert Cray

Chapter 12

Primum Primorum: A Low Rate Flat Tax for California's State and Local Governments

California's tax codes have been wreaking havoc on the state's finances since they were first introduced in 1936 with a whopping 15 percent highest marginal tax rate. During good times, revenues have poured in and they've been spent, often on frivolities. Then come the bad times and revenue shortfalls that led to cuts in essential services, enormously inefficient disruptions in long-term projects, and tax increases that only exacerbate the crises. The first and foremost job to bring California back to prosperity is a total overhaul of California's tax code.

In every discussion of restoring prosperity to a state, it's essential to remember that the key ingredient of any state's prosperity is the state of the overall U.S. economy. My guess is that some 85 to 90 percent of the year to year changes in a state's total economic performance is attributable to the U.S. economy. State and local economic policies are at best responsible for some 10 to 15 percent of a state's performance on a year to year basis. But over longer time horizons, state and local economic policies aggregate while the impact of the U.S. economy tends to offset. It is easy to underestimate just how important state and local economic policies are to both the overall health of the country and the economic health of the specific state in question.

California's highest corporate income tax rate is 8.84 percent (25 percent above the national average of 7.1 percent); its highest personal income tax rate stands at 10.3 percent (among the highest in the nation); its top tax rate on capital gains is also 10.3 percent. And it was only about a year ago that the highest marginal personal income tax rate and capital gains tax rate were 10.55 percent due to the 0.25 percent surcharge added to each income tax bracket retroactive to January 1, 2009. This surcharge expired December 31, 2010. In addition to these sky-high income tax rates, Californians face tax rates among the highest in the nation in almost every other major tax category. High tax rates have left California with a total state and local tax burden of 10.50 percent of personal income (eighth highest in the nation). Property tax rates which are the exception, are relatively low primarily because of Proposition 13, which was passed in 1978. But because of California's favored location, property values are high, thereby reducing some of the advantage of low property tax rates. There is a curve that illustrates this principle.

A highly progressive tax structure such as California's means that the most successful and productive of the state's residents and businesses are the ones who are taxed the most on the margin. And they are the ones who make the decision whether to locate in California or, if they are already here, whether or not to stay. They are also the primary employers of other people. Their opinions and actions are far more important to the economy than is their share of income. Their political weight however, is still only one person, one vote.

With this in mind, juxtapose California's high tax rates with the fact that there are nine states in the U.S. without a state personal earned income tax at all—including the biggies of Florida and Texas, and California's neighbors, Nevada, Washington, and Oregon. You can see why California once again is facing the very serious prospect of a brain drain. It is a wonder that California has any entrepreneurs or venture capitalists left.

Census Bureau data show that California went from losing nearly 450,000 people to other states during the extraordinarily high tax year of 1994 alone (Exhibit 56), to losing only slightly more than 40,000 people in 2001 back to losing around 100,000 people in 2010 when the surcharges mentioned were in effect. The consequences of these population inflows and outflows and their potential effects on state revenues should not be ignored.

In 2008 the highest income 0.3 percent of California's population (those filers with an adjusted gross income over $1 million) paid 31.1 percent of all personal income taxes—by far the state's most important source of revenue.[1] The top 4.13 percent (those filers with an adjusted gross income over $200,000) paid 61.3 of the state's personal income taxes and earned 34.5 percent of all income. California can ill afford to tax the wealthy to the point where they choose to leave the state. And, California's progressive income tax system, beyond being the root cause of California's excessively volatile tax revenues, provides a strong incentive for the wealthy residents (those residents that the state is dependent upon for its revenue base) to leave the state. These wealthy residents, many of whom are baby boomers approaching retirement age, are mobile and could decide to become ex-Californians in a heartbeat.

Exhibit 56

California: Net Domestic Migration, 1993–2010

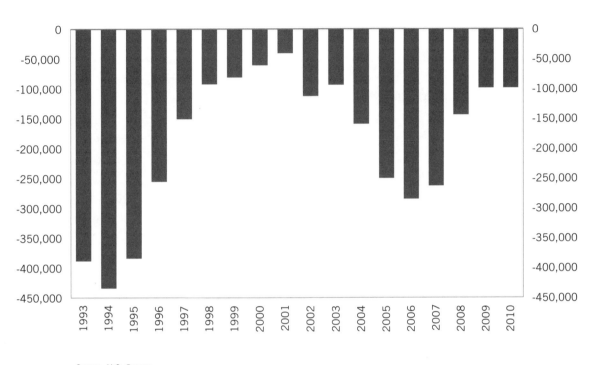

Source: U.S. Census

These same incentives to relocate apply equally if not more so to the corporate tax as they do to the personal income tax. One of the major costs of a business is the tax bill that business has to pay. If California's government raises taxes on businesses, especially during bad economic times, the cost of doing business rises *pari passu*. It won't take long for these businesses to realize that most states have a more business-friendly environment than does California. In fact, there is nary a state with as high a corporate income tax rate within 2,500 miles of California—and that includes by boat to Hawaii.

But high tax rates aren't the only costs taxpayers have to pay when they pay their taxes. The costs taxpayers actually incur are far greater than the net sums the government collects in taxes. There are a whole slew of other costs from accountants and lawyers and tax filing firms to record-keeping and personal filing costs that also have to be paid. Beginning with the tax collection process and extending through the benefit disbursement process, there are inherent costs associated with the government's vast tax collection infrastructure. These costs can be and often are quite large and do just as much damage dollar for dollar as the actual taxes paid. The only difference between these costs and actual taxes are that with these costs, the government collects nothing.

Before individuals and businesses pay their tax liability, they must first spend time collecting records, organizing files, and wading through the tax code to determine exactly what their tax liability is. Individuals will often purchase products and services, such as tax software or hire an accountant, to assist them in determining their tax liability. These are tax compliance outlays. Taxpayers must also pay the administrative costs of the IRS, which are needed to run the IRS for tax collection purposes. Still there is more.

Businesses, large and small, hire teams of accountants, lawyers, and tax professionals to track, measure, and pay their taxes. This tax infrastructure is also used to optimize the tax liability of the business. Individuals and businesses change their behavior in response to tax policies, hiring tax experts to discover ways to minimize their tax liabilities. The efficiency costs from both legal tax avoidance and illegal tax evasion are difficult to quantify, but could be the highest costs of all.

A study we did with John Childs created a comprehensive estimate of the total administrative costs, time costs, and direct tax compliance costs created by the complex U.S. federal income tax code.[2] One can only imagine what the full burden of government on the well-being of society might be. Our analysis estimated that U.S. taxpayers pay $431.1 billion annually, or 30 percent of total income taxes collected, just to comply with and administer the U.S. income tax system.

The revenue crises caused by California's progressive tax system, which historically have lasted upwards of four or five years and are exceptionally deep, are usually precipitated by U.S. business cycles and then are exaggerated in California because California has the single worst tax system in the U.S. The time has come to consider a low rate flat tax on personal income and a business value added in California.

It's shocking how far off California's tax revenue forecasts can be from what actually occurs—see Exhibit 35 in Chapter 8. With revenue estimates this far off the mark and having runs in the same direction for as long as they have, it is no wonder that California's legislature and governor can't govern rationally. Unfortunately, politicians are only human like the rest of us.

It is tax revenue volatility resulting from a highly progressive tax structure that is the root cause of California's recurring fiscal crises. Tax revenue volatility is the stepchild of a steeply progressive tax code and business cycles. High tax rates, even without considering revenue volatility, irreparably damage the state's secular growth potential. Having two ornery stepchildren is a real bummer.

Previous opportunities to reform California's tax system came and went unheeded, and the state has once again reached fiscal crisis. Today, California's tax structure is characterized by top marginal tax rates among the highest in the nation in most every tax category, and these tax rates are applied to a small tax base. And California relies more heavily than most states on the volatile revenue stream from highly progressive personal and corporate income taxes.

Forgive my being so repetitious, but I find it both astounding and such a perfect representation of what California is that in FY2001, income taxes collected solely from exercised stock options and realized capital gains accounted for 24 percent of all state general fund revenues. Overall, California's state government relied on the personal income tax for 44.9 percent of its total tax revenue between

FY2001 and FY2010, while this figure is 30.9 percent for all of the states on an equal weighted basis and 34.6 percent on an income weighted basis. Similarly, California's state government relied on the corporate income tax for 8.8 percent of its total tax revenue between FY2001 and FY2010, while this figure is 5.6 percent for all of the states on an equal weighted basis and 5.9 percent on an income weighted basis. And, not only does the income tax shoulder a heavier load in California than elsewhere, the burden in California is highly skewed toward its most productive income earners. A casual review of our last few chapters would show that a more ill-conceived tax code is hard to imagine.

California fails miserably in reaching the ideal of having the lowest possible tax rates on the largest possible tax base.

Theory Put into Practice

Our central proposal to restore prosperity to California is for California to adopt a low rate flat tax. There are two types of incentives in this world; positive and negative incentives. By way of illustration: If you scold a dog, you know where the dog won't be—it won't be where you gave it the scolding; but you have no idea where the dog will be. The dog is going to run, but you can't tell in which direction it is going to run. Negative incentives tell you what not to do.

On the other hand, if you feed a dog you know exactly where the dog will be—the dog is going to be right where you gave it the hamburger. If you want to attract people to do something, you want to use positive incentives. If you want to repel people from doing something, you want to use negative incentives. This is classic behavioral dynamics: positive and negative, pleasure and pain, scolding and praising, reward and punishment, taxing and subsidizing.

This is classic behavioral dynamics: positive and negative, pleasure and pain, scolding and praising, reward and punishment, taxing and subsidizing.

Taxes are like scolding. You know exactly what people will try not to do. They will try not to report taxable income. But you don't know how they won't report the taxable income. They'll use evasion, avoidance. They'll use the underground economy; they will use tax loopholes; they might even go out of business and become unemployed; or they might get up and move to a neighboring state. They will do all they can to avoid reporting taxable income. People don't like taxes. So the whole theory behind a low rate flat tax, very simply, is that the best tax has the lowest possible tax rate on the broadest possible tax base. The best tax provides people with the least incentives to evade, avoid, and otherwise not report taxable income and symmetrically provides people with the fewest places to which they can escape to avoid the tax.

You should recognize my proposal here for California because it is very similar to the federal proposal made by our current governor, Jerry Brown, for the entire country when he ran for president in 1992. In fact Governor Brown and I developed that proposal together. The low rate flat tax he proposed for the U.S. had a tax rate of 13 percent. It was a flat tax rate for one and all. The flat tax addresses the problems we have today. And those problems are simply highly volatile revenues and extreme disincentives to production.

The California Flat Rate Tax

Without reforming its tax codes, California will never break out of its fiscal crisis. Spending controls by themselves won't work. A quick review of the history of the Gann spending limit and Governor Reagan's failed attempt to get spending controls with Proposition 1 exemplifies this point starkly. You can't expect politicians to sit idly by and not spend rainy day funds that to make a real difference would presently have to be $75 billion or more. And given the content of character of the political class, term-limited politicians won't pass billions of unspent dollars on to their successors. It just ain't going to happen. No sooner was the Gann spending limit actually effective than Proposition 111 passed, rendering the Gann spending limit totally ineffective. Governor Reagan's Proposition 1 never passed. The best form of spending control is the simplest form of spending control: don't give government the extra money during good times and don't shortchange essential programs during tough times. The case for a flat tax is nowhere more compelling than it is in California today. Moreover, California does have a constitutionally required balanced budget that to some degree does limit spending.

I am proposing a revenue-neutral single low rate flat tax with two tax bases upon which the single low tax rate would be applied. One tax base would be personal unadjusted gross income with a couple of deductions. The other tax base is business net sales or value added. Now, for those of you who know your macroeconomics, these two tax bases are double counting gross state product. All accounting systems have a debit and a credit. Value added is the sum total of all expenditures which is gross state product. And of course total income is also gross state product. All money that is spent is all money that is earned. The business value added is the spending side of gross state product and personal income is the income side of gross state product. Our proposal would tax gross state product twice, but at half the rate. The low rate and broad base provides the least incentive to evade, avoid, or otherwise not report taxable income and the broadest possible tax base reduces places for people to hide income to avoid taxation.

A California flat tax is just as promising today as it was when I first presented it for California back in 1990 and for the U.S. in 1983.[3] California needs a complete tax overhaul—not higher tax rates. Raising taxes, especially during trying economic conditions, makes no sense. Whoever heard of an economy taxing itself into prosperity? No one! It's senseless to put California's fiscal house in order by putting California's citizens' houses in the red. The citizens are, in fact, the reason why state and local governments exist.

Also, putting a company out of business helps no one because not only is the company worse off, the state doesn't even get to collect taxes. And, the state is probably also liable for paying income assistance to the company's former employees and their families. It's a lose/lose situation. Encouraging a person or business to move to another state through higher taxation is squandering opportunity. Yet now, once again, California is levying a large tax burden on already-suffering residents and businesses.

Excessive taxation is detrimental to everyone: labor and capital, poor and rich, men and women, and old and young. It is an equal opportunity tormentor. In the short run it means higher taxes on labor or capital and lower after-tax earnings. In the longer run, mobile factors "vote with their feet" and move away from the state, leaving immobile factors (such as low-wage workers and land and buildings) to suffer the tax burden. The research of the past chapters demonstrated that states with high tax burdens and/or high marginal tax rates on personal and corporate income, on balance, experienced relative income and population declines, falling relative employment and decreasing housing values.[3] Overall tax burden in addition to high marginal tax rates is also a prosperity killer.

To find a solution for our future, we reach back into our past for the criteria for judging the efficacy of a state's tax system. These were summarized well in the 19th century by Henry George, who said that the best tax by which public revenues can be raised is evidently that which will closest conform to the following conditions:

1. That it bear as lightly as possible upon production—so as least to check the increase of the general fund from which taxes must be paid and the community maintained.

2. That it be easily and cheaply collected, and fall as directly as may be upon the ultimate payers—so as to take from the people as little as possible in addition to what it yields the government.

3. That it be certain—so as to give the least opportunity for tyranny or corruption on the part of officials, and the least temptation to law-breaking and evasion on the part of the taxpayers.

4. That it bear equally—so as to give no citizen an advantage or put any at a disadvantage, as compared with others.[4]

We propose here a true complete economic low rate flat tax to replace *all* the various state and local taxes currently in effect here in California. Many of these current taxes raise little revenue relative to their economic cost in terms of incentives, record keeping, and collection. This complete flat tax would eliminate much of the inefficiency from California's tax system by both broadening the tax base and significantly lowering the highest marginal tax rates. By having the largest possible tax base combined with the lowest possible tax rate, people are provided the least opportunity to avoid paying taxes and the lowest incentive to do so. Reduced incentives to avoid or evade taxes result in a reduction in the associated costs of monitoring these activities. In addition, lower tax rates go hand in hand with greater incentives to work and produce. To summarize the strengths of this proposal:

- Fairness: Everyone will pay the same tax rate. This means that today's modest income earners will have their taxes reduced considerably. The elimination of regressive taxes such as payroll taxes, sales taxes, excise taxes, gas taxes and property taxes will more than offset the elimination of the progressive income and capital gains taxes.

- Simplicity: The straightforward calculation of the tax base and the application of a single tax rate simplify the entire tax system. This means that the additional costs taxpayers have had to pay to comply with the tax code will be greatly reduced.

- Transparency: By having only one source of revenue with a single tax rate, everyone will know exactly what taxes are. There will be no hidden taxes whatsoever. And, politicians will be less tempted to abuse our tax codes for political or personal gain. Democracy will have a chance to function properly because people will be fully informed.

- Completeness: By eliminating all other state and local taxes and replacing them with the single low tax rate on the broadened tax base, revenues will be assured for the appropriate level of all state and local government spending.

- Efficiency: The reduction of marginal tax rates coupled with the broadening of the tax base will minimize many of the distortions that make the current tax system counterproductive. The economy would undergo substantial expansion, resulting in an increase in revenues for state and local governments and increased prosperity for private Californians.

- Stability: From the day the flat tax is enacted and beyond, state and local governments would not only get more revenues, but the revenue stream would be far more stable from year to year.

California's fiscal crisis is the consequence of its hodge-podge of taxes. As of September 2011, we have a projected general fund deficit in the state of over $20 billion. The late *New York Times* columnist Bill Safire used to refer to these numbers as "MEGO" numbers, which stood for My Eyes Glaze Over. Discussions to balance California's budget include raising existing taxes. I can assure you, given the state of California, you really don't want to raise taxes. With California's unemployment rate among the highest in the nation, it makes no sense to raise taxes on the last three guys working here in the state. And for those who are currently working and who don't pay taxes, you're never going to catch them by continuing our current tax system. They already know how to game the system. Higher tax rates don't make anyone's life any better and the government won't get any more money. It makes no sense to raise taxes on a business that is already in trouble. A business that is having a hard time making it now will be pushed under with higher taxes. It is these businesses that create employment.

People and businesses vote with their feet—it is intuitive. Suppose you have two locations, A and B. If you raise taxes in B and you lower them in A, producers and manufacturers are going to move from B to A. We found that out in California in the early to mid–1990s when taxes were raised dramatically in the state. California became an economic super nova. We lost population to our neighboring states and we were sending out solar systems of economies to neighboring states. It was terrible! It didn't work. The revenues never came.

One of my neighbors from Palos Verdes back then suggested that we have an old neighborhood reunion. For convenience sake, we should hold it in Phoenix, Arizona.

The taxes California would collect from a tax increase would come from the very people the state governs. Frankly it makes no sense to make the citizens go bankrupt while making the state solvent. You've got to remember there is no tooth fairy; economics is double entry bookkeeping. For every dollar the state collects, there is someone who loses that dollar and who also has a budget to balance just like everyone else. So, you've got a situation here where you either lose people (they lose their jobs or they leave the state) or you put one fiscal system out of order by trying to put the state's fiscal situation in order. Yikes! Efficiency is the only answer.

In California we have a tax code that costs a lot more than the taxes government collects by setting anti-growth incentives everywhere. This counterproductive tax code is both Republican and Democrat—it's political.

In fiscal year 2012, California is right back where it was in the early 1990s and early 2000s—the state faces large and continual budget deficits and a depleted rainy day fund. Cities, counties, and the local districts have huge fiscal problems as well. One proposal to help the state's finances is to do away with subventions to the cities, counties, and local districts. For the state to stop sharing revenues with them is like a poor guy stealing from an even poorer guy—it's a catastrophic situation.

The lessons learned from our analysis of the states is that a low rate flat tax will in short order result in a lot more tax revenue. And, that revenue will be raised at far lower cost to both taxpayers and state government.

A Brief Comment on Sin Taxes

There are some taxes that admittedly do provide revenues, but were not implemented to raise revenues. These are called sin taxes such as the taxes on alcohol, tobacco, firearms, speeding tickets, fines by judges, etc… All of these sin taxes exists not so much to raise revenues as to discourage certain behavior. The reason you have a speeding ticket is to discourage people from speeding. It's not supposed to be a major revenue source for government. Given their different function, we do not eliminate all sin taxes from the tax base. The taxes to be replaced, thus, are all state and local taxes (and many of the fees as well) save sin taxes.

Two Low Rate Flat Taxes

One tax base is personal unadjusted gross income and the other is business net sales or value added. For the value added tax base the corporation or business would report revenues during the time period being taxed, and then subtract from those revenues the purchases the business has made from other tax paying businesses. That's the tax base. That difference is business value added, and is the tax base upon which they would pay a low rate tax. Because all purchases from other businesses are deductible, businesses would be able to expense capital purchases 100 percent in the year of purchase. If a business buys a piece of capital equipment, that capital equipment is 100 percent deductible in the year of purchase.

In the first few years, 100 percent expensing of capital purchases in the year of purchase will have the effect of leaving a lot of un-depreciated capital on the books of firms. Therefore, during a transition period this proposal would allow businesses to continue their depreciation of previously acquired capital over time, setting the tax rate a little higher than it otherwise would be and then phasing out the higher tax rate.

However, once fully implemented, there would never be an issue of loss carry forwards or other such complications. Every company would pay its share of the tax burden based upon its use of California's precious natural resources. The distortions inherent in our current tax codes that discriminate against successful companies by taxing profits, and as a result subsidize inefficient companies, would be gone.

On the individual side, total personal income from all sources would be the tax base. A single tax rate would be applied across the board from the first dollar to the last dollar on that base. While there are other complications for special circumstances such as those for gamblers, independent contractors, transfer payments, government output, etc., these don't materially affect the principal. Both the business tax base and the personal tax base are each approximately equal to gross state product.

Just a Few Deductions Allowed

Some of the flat tax proposals authored by extraordinarily competent people like Steve Forbes and Dick Armey are less comprehensive than our flat tax proposal. In most cases these other flat tax proposals focus on a subset of taxes such as the income tax. In addition, they usually aren't single rate taxes because they allow for generous exemptions. They have deductions, individual exemptions and exclusions. The moniker of a flat tax was so *de rigueur* that one politician actually proposed a flat tax which had five different tax rates! There you go.

From our perspective, there is no benefit of a tax deduction or an exemption to someone who has no income. At best, tax deductions help the more affluent of the poor, not the poorest of the poor. Tax deductions cause a deadweight revenue loss across all individuals who get those tax deductions. And to make up for the lost revenues, there has to be much higher tax rates at higher income levels—just where high tax rates do the most harm. There should be one and only one tax rate on all income from dollar one to the last.

Mortgage Deductions

For a tax system with a single rate, calculation of the precise tax base is crucial. And some so-called deductions are far from giveaways but are required by good economics. Our guiding light should be economics not linguistics. Thus, deductions that comport with good economics should be allowed while those that don't make sense should be trashed.

For example, interest payments by individuals, especially mortgage interest, should be tax deductible. The logic is straightforward. Imagine a person who borrows $100,000 at 10 percent and then lends that $100,000 at 10 percent. That person has done nothing of any economic consequence. That person has merely been a conduit for a loan and should not pay taxes on that transaction! Therefore, to have no tax liability, the tax base has to be zero, which means that either interest income should not be taxable, or if interest income is taxable, interest expense must be deductible.

A second example answers which is correct. If a person borrows $100,000 at 10 percent and then lends $100,000 at 20 percent, that person should, of course, be liable for taxation. He's acting as a financial intermediary, a bank, an insurance company, a savings and loan, a mutual savings bank, and should be liable for taxation just like anyone else. There is value added on the transaction. Therefore all interest income should be taxable and all interest expense should be deductible.

It doesn't matter the purposes to which those loans were put. From the standpoint of pure economic theory and good practical politics and economics, all interest income in the system should be taxable and all interest expense should be deductible. Thus on the individual tax return, as well as on business tax returns, all interest expense should be deductible. The tax code should have interest expense as a deduction on the individual level. By the way, because all interest income is taxable the interest deductions are offset 100 percent by interest income. Interest paid is the same as interest received.

Charitable Contributions

Some supposedly charitable contributions clearly should not be deductible. If you send your kids to private school, and the private school says wink, wink, wink, instead of charging you tuition, how about making a contribution to the school and we'll put your children on scholarships. The contribution to the school that you make substitutes for the tuition you should have paid with after-tax dollars and should not be deductible.

But obviously there are other charitable deductions that should be deductible. When a person gives altruistically and has no personal benefit whatsoever, and that person gives charitable contributions that give no benefit to the contributor, of course those charitable contributions should be deductible. It is often difficult to tell which charitable contributions should be deductible for the individual. Even though some of them might not be 100 percent proper, we have stayed with all charitable contributions being tax deductible. Charitable deductions aren't large enough to make a major difference to the tax rate and yet are jealously guarded by their proponents.

Rent on One's Primary Residence

There is one other deduction we would allow. In this world of ours, if you own a home, you have tax benefits, and those benefits are not because you can deduct mortgage interest. The benefit you have from owning your own home is that you are able to rent that home from yourself with pre-tax dollars. If you decide you like your neighbor's home, and your neighbor likes your home, and you both switch homes i.e. you rent your neighbor's home from him, and he rents your home from you, you would have a significant tax consequence. You would have to pay the rent to your next door neighbor in after-tax dollars and your neighbor would have to pay the rent to you in after-tax dollars. If your neighbor lives in his own home and you live in your home, however, you won't have any tax consequences.

Now, there are some people who would like to tax the imputed rental value of owner occupied homes, which is probably correct economics. However, we would not tax the imputed rental value of owner occupied homes. It would set a whole new precedent and it would be difficult to administer. There is a real discrimination in our society between homeowners—people who rent the home from themselves—and people who rent their primary residence and who do not own homes. On grounds of equity, our view would be to allow rent on one's primary residence to be deductible. People who rent should not pay more taxes per square foot than people who own their own homes, and therefore we would make as a deduction on the personal income tax for the rent on your primary residence.

All Other Taxes Eliminated

So those are the deductions. We would make interest expense deductible, charitable contributions tax deductible, and rent on your primary residence deductible if you're a renter. With those deductions in mind, our low rate flat tax would replace all state and local taxes except for sin taxes. There would be no state income tax. There would be no state business profits tax. There would be no state payroll taxes either employer or employee. There would be no state gas tax. There would be no state tax on capital gains. There would be no state tax on exercised stock options. There would be no state property tax. We would get rid of all property taxes. There would be no state sales tax—we would get rid of all state sales taxes; those accruing to the state and those accruing to cities, counties, and local districts. We would eliminate all taxes, entirely in the state of California, 100 percent. The only taxes we would keep are the sin taxes. And to replace all taxes, we would have two low rate flat taxes on the tax bases we described. Those taxes would be on personal unadjusted gross income and business value added, along with those deductions we mentioned.

A Look at the Numbers

Our preferred flat tax structure would encompass all local taxes as well as all state taxes. This includes the state personal income tax, state corporate income tax, state sales tax, local sales tax, local property taxes, the vehicle tax, as well as the hundreds and hundreds of small tax sources listed in Appendix A that burden the state with a complex tax system but raises very little revenue for the state.

To get a sense of what the statically revenue neutral flat rate tax would be today, we calculate the necessary flat rate tax base from 2000 through 2008—a period containing good economic times and bad. But first, several data distortions must be considered.

For instance, the progressivity of California's tax system causes revenue surges during strong economic periods that are disproportionate to the growth in income. During recessions California's progressive tax system causes revenues to crash further than the accompanying income decline. The transitions between economic booms and busts introduce biases because the growth pattern of tax revenues will not change with the same timing as the growth pattern of economic activity. For instance, Chapter 8 illustrated that the peak in the tax revenue surge from capital gains and stock options occurred in FY2001—the calendar year when all three major stock indices tanked. The different timing of tax revenue declines compared to declines in the economy partially explain why tax revenues were peaking while the economy was declining.

On grounds of equity and fairness between homeowners and renters, our view would be to allow rent on one's primary residence to be deductible.

However, alternative timing is not the only distortion. Part of the explanation for peaking capital gains and stock option revenues during FY2001 is the differences between California's fiscal year, which runs from July 1 through June 30, and a calendar year. National and state economic data are based on a calendar year. California's budgets and expenditures are based on the July through June fiscal year. Income taxes are also collected on a calendar year basis. Consequently, comparing annual economic data with annual budget data contains distortions because the period being evaluated is not the same.

To adjust for these distortions, we smooth the relevant tax revenue and income data across the entire 2000 through 2008 period. Using the smoothed values addresses many, though not all, of these distortions and provides the relevant statically revenue neutral tax rate that would provide California with sufficient revenues over the entire business cycle.

The total tax base that needs to be replaced is presented in Exhibit 57. To replace all state and local taxes in 2008 we would need to raise around $185 billion with some $69 billion of that total for local government. In total, over the 2000 through 2008 period, average annual state and local tax revenues were $145.1 billion—slightly lower in 2000, slightly higher by 2008. Of this total, around $3.3 billion was raised through excise taxes, fees, and other sin taxes and would not be replaced by the proposed flat tax. Consequently a total of $141.8 billion in revenue, on average, would need to be replaced by the flat tax over this nine-year period in order for the flat tax to raise the same amount of revenues on a static basis during the same period. On a dynamic basis, the flat tax would raise a lot more revenues than does the current tax system.

Exhibit 57

California State and Local Tax Revenues to be Replaced
Average Values Over the 2000 through 2008 Period (billions $)

	Average Revenues 2000–2008
Total Tax Revenues	145.05
Tobacco Tax	1.10
Alcohol Tax	0.35
Pari-mutuels Tax	0.04
Fines and other "Sin Taxes"	1.79
California State and Local Tax Revenues to be replaced	**141.77**

The $141.8 billion would be raised by levying the state flat income tax against the two proposed tax bases: personal income and business value added. There are some slight differences between the personal income and business value added tax bases worth reviewing up front. The personal income tax base is the income earned by all individuals in California—the Bureau of Economic Analysis' measure of personal income. Business value added, on the other hand, is based on the total value of goods and services produced in the economy, or total income of the economy (GDP). Theoretically speaking, GDP is larger than the income people receive (personal income) due to: 1) depreciation; and, 2) the difference between profits earned by companies and profits paid out by companies. For the purpose of estimating the size of the tax base, both of these measures also need to be adjusted to remove non-market transactions that will not be taxed under the flat tax proposal.

There are three major adjustments to the government's measure of personal income that need to be made. First, as measured by the Bureau of Economic Analysis, personal income does not include capital gains. Capital gains would be considered income under the low rate flat rate and therefore need to be added back into the personal income tax base. The Franchise Tax Board provides estimates of total capital gains realized in California over the relevant time frame.[5]

Second, estimates for the three primary deductions—charitable contributions, mortgage interest, and rent on one's primary residence—need to be deducted from the tax base. Lastly, personal income as measured by the Bureau of Economic Analysis adds in the value of certain non-market transactions (e.g. the amount of rent that homeowners implicitly pay themselves for living in their own homes). For obvious reasons, the value of these non-market transactions will not be subject to the personal income tax. Consequently, we need to subtract them from the value of California's income for the purposes of establishing the personal income tax base.

The California data are estimated by applying California's proportion of total personal income to total U.S. charitable contributions and mortgage payments from the IRS, and, total U.S. transfer payments, total U.S. imputed income, and tenant occupied housing output from the Bureau of Economic Analysis. Exhibit 58 presents the average values of these calculations from 2000–2008.

Exhibit 58

Estimated California Personal Income Tax Base
Average Values Over the 2000 through 2008 Period (billions $)

		Average Value 2000–2008
	Personal Income	1,343.40
+	Capital Gains	82.50
-	Charitable Contributions	21.50
-	Mortgage Interest Payments	50.10
-	Imputed Income	103.40
-	Rental Payment on Tenant Occupied Housing	35.30
=	**Tax Base for Personal Income**	**1,215.60**

The tax base for business value added is simply the total net output of all businesses in California subtracting out all depreciation currently on the books, and then removing all non market transactions that are included in GDP but would not be subject to the tax. The national estimates of these data from the Bureau of Economic Analysis are allocated to California based on California's share of national GDP. Exhibit 59 presents the average values of these calculations from 2000–2008.

Exhibit 59

California Business Value Added Tax Base
Average Values Over the 2000 through 2008 Period
(billions $)

	Average Value 2000–2008
Gross Domestic Product	1,594.70
- Depreciation	108.10
- Imputations	238.60
= **Tax Base for Business Value Added**	**1,248.00**

The appropriate single tax rate is obtained by dividing targeted revenues by the total tax base. To raise the targeted level of state and local revenue, the required single tax rate on the personal income tax base and the business value added tax base would have to have been an average of 5.8 percent over this time period to raise the same amount of revenues. Therefore, a 5.8 percent tax rate would be more than enough to achieve the necessary state and local tax revenues. And, this is a high estimate. The tax base will be larger once the depreciation that is currently on the books of California's businesses is completely written off—$108.1 billion larger, on average, during the 2000 through 2008 period. This implies that once the depreciation is written off, the flat tax rate can be further reduced to an even lower 5.5 percent.

Exhibit 60

California Flat Tax Calculations
Average Values Over the 2000 through 2008 Period
(billions $ unless otherwise noted)

	Average Value 2000–2008
Personal Income Tax Base	1,215.60
Business Value Added Tax Base	1,248.00
Total Tax Base	2,463.60
Targeted State and Local Tax Revenue	141.77
Flat Tax Rate	**5.80%**

If the flat rate tax were implemented, all the distortions in California's current tax system would be gone. Our view is that this final reform should be put through in a constitutional amendment form. Could you imagine what would happen if California had a flat rate tax of 5.8 percent, that's it, on all your income. Nothing else, no sales taxes, no gas taxes, no payroll taxes, no income taxes, no corporate taxes—just the flat tax, which is revenue neutral.

The flat tax proposal is designed to minimize the disincentives induced by tax rates and yet still provide the requisite amount of revenues to provide the necessary services. This revenue-neutral proposal will, by definition, raise the same amount of revenue as the current system. But, in truth, California has everything to gain from its implementation. The broad-based, low rate tax minimizes distortions and maximizes efficiency gains. The state's competitive environment would increase and California's economic activity and California-based asset values would increase. Tax revenues would soon exceed the most optimistic projections. The longer this new tax system is in place, the greater will be these gains.

Other practical considerations, including the allocation of revenues between the state governments to local governments, will need to be addressed. What the flat rate tax achieves, however, is a very stable, steady source of revenues for both state and local governments. That way the government can plan on programs so that they don't have to cut way back on critical programs in one year and expand them squanderously the next year, which is exactly what is currently happening. We want to provide a stable, steady revenue source that moves a little bit with personal income, but it doesn't have the huge yo-yo effect that we have from the hodge-podge of taxes that we've put into the system. This is the proposal I'd like to make. It is the single most important reform California could make to achieve the prosperity its citizens so deserve.

There are lots of issues and problems with a proposal like this. Our view is it should be set into the constitution, so you have that single tax rate and we can know exactly what should be done every year. The state and local governments get a percentage of total revenues. By the way, everything we tell you about the state government, on having more revenues going forward and having less during the boom years, would have been true in spades about cities, counties, and local districts. They are suffering terribly, as you know, in California. The flat rate tax would have provided the local governments with very stable, steady revenue so the risk of school teachers or police being fired would be minimized. It would create a much more stable situation.

The key to good tax reform is to not just look at how you can solve the budget problem this week, this month, this year, but to set into place a system that will not cause California's state and local governments to have the same crisis every decade. An ounce of prevention they say is worth a pound of cure. Our current crisis is exactly the same crisis we had in 1992 to 1995, and again in 2001 to 2003. If you remember from the previous chapter, it is the exact same problem that, our hero, Ronald Reagan faced when he was governor. The only solution to eliminating the revenue crises is to eliminate the unsustainable revenue surges. The solution is a low rate flat tax!

Tax Amnesty

Once a low rate flat tax is set in stone it would make lots of sense to have a statewide tax amnesty program to allow those people who made judgments in error, some many years ago, to reenter the legitimate economy. On a personal level it doesn't make a lot of sense for laws to prohibit people from not breaking the law. Our tax laws and the penalties for breaking them, especially but not exclusively criminal prosecution, are wonderful when it comes to discouraging tax evasion. But for whatever reasons the tax codes themselves, even with the threat of penalties and criminal prosecution, led to widespread tax evasion in California. With our low rate flat tax the very reasons for evasion would be removed but the prospects for prosecution would force scofflaws to remain underground. A tax amnesty program would quickly bring these tax evaders above ground.

There would be a substantial one time revenue surge for state and local governments, but even on an on-going annual basis revenue would be higher and tax law enforcement could be more concentrated on the remaining tax cheats. Thus we wholeheartedly recommend a tax amnesty program along with the low rate flat tax.

Enterprise Zones

A low rate flat tax code is also easily modified to provide enterprise zones for the very poorest and underprivileged segments of California society. By lowering the tax rates in depressed regions, jobs will move to where they are needed the most thus partially countering the lack of economic opportunities. This enterprise zone proposal more than anything else could help restore prosperity where it is most desperately needed. In the words of President Kennedy, "The best form of welfare is still a good high-paying job."

Global Warming Cooling California's Economy

Californians have a real proclivity to support activist government policies in all sorts of areas. If not thought through carefully, then activist policy ventures can lead to wholesale disaster. Fortunately the low rate flat tax is extraordinarily flexible and capable of adapting to changes in political proclivities. One arena where California has been especially activist is with regards to global warming. Whether global warming is manmade or curable by economic policies or even whether global warming actually exists is beside the point. Californians want their government to tax hydrocarbons.

To assure that the tax on hydrocarbons does no harm those taxes can easily be incorporated into the low rate flat tax framework by considering a tax on hydrocarbons as a sin tax. Thus the single low tax rates will be reduced by the static revenue generated by the carbon tax. It will be a 100 percent tax offset. That's it. The system remains fully intact and the sin tax on carbon is in place.

The low rate flat tax is the crucial policy initiative to achieve prosperity. Without a low rate flat tax, it is hard for us to envision a thriving, energetic, pro-growth California society. In our next chapter, we will discuss political reforms that we believe will provide the means by which the economic reforms can be achieved. And lastly there are a number of important reforms that would greatly facilitate prosperity which work in close coordination with a low rate flat tax.

To take full advantage of the low rate flat tax which addresses the issues of the highest marginal corporate tax rate, the highest marginal capital gains tax rate, the highest marginal personal income tax rate, and in conjunction with the state's constitutionally required balanced budget as a spending constraint, there is also the need to deal with the state's average tax burden.

We would suggest that the single tax rate be reduced by 15 percent from its initial static revenue rate (about 5.8 percent) over its first decade in effect. In this way California can avail itself of all the growth benefits resulting from a lower total tax burden. And in case you forgot, the low rate flat tax in conjunction with the lowered overall tax burden will provide plenty of tax revenues for the state to function as well if not better than other states.

This is the brass ring and California should go for it.

And its blow, boys, blow,
For Californi-o,
On the banks of the Sacramento.
"Iron Men & Wooden Ships"
—Frank Shay

Chapter 13

Politics (pol-i-tiks): poly meaning many; tics meaning blood sucking insects

If you are feeling somewhat bewildered by state government economic policies given the perverse results we have shown in earlier chapters, join the club. But there are reasons why so many states pursue counterproductive policies. Most of these reasons boil down to a simple concept called the agency problem. State government policy makers—whether elected or appointed—don't bear the bad consequences of their actions, yet they often are rewarded in the short run politically even when the results turn out bad. Quite simply, when it comes to state government, incentives are not properly aligned with the public interest. To get a visual of what I am driving at, review Appendix A: A Partial Selection of California's State, County, and City Taxes and Fees and Appendix B: A Partial List of California Commissions. No rational, well-ranged system could ever devise this type of dysfunction.

Even the political consequences of bad behavior are muted and impeded almost to the point of being non-existent by the huge amorphous nature of the omnipresent government of the state of California. Each state senator, for example, represents almost a million Californians; each state assembly person, almost half a million. How is it possible for them to be in touch with their constituents? They can't be.

Who in God's name could keep track of the performance of each of those commissioners on all those commissions? And even if you did follow and evaluate each of those commissioners' performance, *how* would you go about doing something about it if you didn't like what they did? The task even on a small scale is inconceivably difficult. Inertia of those things that didn't work and the misaligned incentives that create momentum for more dysfunctional apparati are the inevitable consequences of a broken political system. To redress these problems, we propose the following policies for the State of California:

1.) Merit pay for politicians and functionaries
2.) Four states versus one
3.) Sunset provision of all commissions
4.) Redistricting reform
5.) Reform of political contributions
6.) Open primaries

The political reform proposals are conceptually on a very different level than are our other strictly economic proposals. Political reforms are intended to improve the means by which the ends are achieved. If democracy is allowed to work, our belief is that good solutions will emerge.

You Pay for What You Get

One of Jackie Mason's stock political jokes about Congress goes something like, "If we want them to be successful, put them on commission and don't pay them until they show a profit."[1] For California, aligning the incentives of politicians and government employees is no joke—it is political necessity.

A fundamental tenet of economics is that incentives matter. And, California has proved the validity of this tenet over and over again. The state's response to the 1994 Northridge earthquake is the quintessential example of the power of incentives.

Among the devastation following the 1994 earthquake were two bridges on the Santa Monica Freeway that collapsed and four others that were so badly damaged that they needed to be replaced.[2] Repairing this crucial transportation infrastructure was estimated to take between nine months and two years, with a cost of $1 million to $3 million a day.[3] Assuming a 250-day work year, at $3 million a day, the total cost could have been as high as $1.5 billion. Instead the entire process took only two months and ultimately saved the state $12 million and the local economy an additional $74 million compared to projections.

Eggers (1997) summarizes how Governor Wilson's administration leveraged the power of incentives to create a positive outcome for all Californians:

> To speed up the process, Governor Pete Wilson gave Caltrans, the state transportation agency, extraordinary authority to shorten normal contracting processes. This allowed the agency to advertise the jobs for less than the required two weeks before bid opening and to accept bids from only five prequalified contractors for each job. In addition, the agency offered substantial performance incentives and penalties: a $200,000 per day bonus for completing the project ahead of schedule and a $200,000 a day penalty for each day the project was behind schedule.

> Due to the streamlined contracting process, repair work began the day after the January 17 earthquake. The financial incentives, meanwhile, resulted in the overpasses

being replaced in a little over two months, 74 days ahead of the June 24 deadline. To complete the project so early, the contractor used up to 400 workers a day and kept crews on the job 24 hours a day. The $13.8 million the contractor received in performance bonuses were more than offset by the estimated $74 million in savings to the local economy and $12 million in contract administration savings thanks to the shortened schedule.[4]

The successful government response to the Northridge earthquake can be replicated across California. The key is to apply the Northridge earthquake's lesson and properly align the incentives.

Reform of Public Employee Union Dues for Political Activity

Starting with government workers and their union *representatives*, the interest of public unions will often trump the interest of the public and government workers themselves. Public employee unions can mandate the use of members' dues for political activity, whether the employee agrees with the union's political stance or not. The "Public Employee Voluntary Political Contributions Act," was a failed attempt to address this problem. Submitted by Lew Uhler of the National Tax Limitation Committee, this act would have required public employee union members each year to give written permission for the unions to use their dues for political activities.

Public employees often find their dues are used to support political candidates or ballot measures with which they don't agree. The measure's supporters feel it is fundamentally unfair to force public employees to give money to political activities and candidates they do not support. Because public money is involved, the public has the right to give the power to public employees to approve the use of their dues for political activities. The initiative will give more freedom to individual union members to decide if their hard earned money should be used for political stands.

Merit Pay for Politicians and Government Workers

More broadly, organizations need incentives to be aligned throughout the entire organization—from the chairman of the board to the intern working his first job in the mailroom. If aligned properly, all employees will have a strong incentive to ensure the mission of the organization is pursued as efficiently as possible. Private organizations are constantly striving to discover and rediscover the optimal incentive structures throughout the organization and an entire management consulting industry exists to help firms create the optimal structure.

But, at the most fundamental level, creating the proper incentive structure is easy to see. Imagine you need to invest your retirement nest egg in one of two companies. In company A, the board of directors and officers of the corporation receive low salaries but large stock options that only have value if the company generates high and sustainable long-term profits. In other words, the board of directors and officers only receive a high payment for their services if they generate strong long-term growth for the shareholders. Company B, on the other hand, pays its board of directors and officers very high salaries regardless of the company's performance and has no stock incentive plans.

Clearly the board of directors and officers of company A have stronger incentives to ensure that company A generates stronger long-term profit growth than the board of directors and officers of company B. Company A is clearly the better investment for your retirement nest egg than company B. As we like to say, you should never fly in an airplane where the pilot has a parachute and you do not—the incentives just don't make sense.

What is true for investing is just as true for political leadership. California's political leadership has the same incentives as the board of directors and officers for company B above—they have no skin in the game. The political leadership does not bear any costs for their mistakes nor any benefits for their good decisions.

If a legislator works to implement pro-growth economic policies that encourage strong state GDP growth, rapid growth in employment, rising state incomes and rising property values, his pay does not change. Similarly, if a legislator works to implement policies that will lead to a stagnating economy, declining employment, declining real incomes, falling property values, his pay still does not change. When coupled with the gerrymandered districts (discussed in detail below) legislators have an incentive to serve special interests that fund their next re-election campaign rather than the general interest.

The quality of government services are degrading in California because the incentives of the system ensure that a high cost, low quality service will be provided, not because the quality of government workers is poor.

Rather than receive a fixed salary regardless of performance, all political leaders should receive a much smaller salary, with the remainder of their compensation dependent upon how well California performs. The performance metrics should depend upon key well-being metrics for Californians including average (or median) state income growth, corporate profitability growth, and employment growth. The growth metrics should be on a relative basis to ensure that California's leadership is not penalized for bad decisions at the national level or other "black swan" events outside of their control. This system is far from perfect, but it is one helluva lot better than what we have.

These same principles also apply to government workers. The quality of government services are degrading in California because the incentives of the system ensure that a high cost, low quality service will be provided not because the quality of government workers is poor. Great people badly incented results in tragedy, while modestly able people with the right incentives have no limits to what they are able to achieve. *Per ardua ad astra.*

Of All the Speaks I Talks, English Are Me Goodest

California's faltering education system exemplifies this problem. As discussed in the previous chapter, California's education system is badly in need of reform. Throwing money at the education problem in California has been shown time and again not to be the answer. Instead of increasing education expenditures, California should apply Governor Wilson's solution to the Northridge earthquake disaster to California's education disaster—properly align the incentives. In the case of the rebuilding effort following the Northridge earthquake, the Wilson Administration aligned the incentives of the contractors with the needs of California motorists—the rebuilding of California's transportation infrastructure in as timely a manner as possible without sacrificing quality. The solution worked, and the Santa Monica Freeway was back in action sooner than anyone could have imagined. The same could be true for education.

There is large and growing academic and policy literature that documents the benefits California can reap from an incentives-based education reform program. These necessary reforms do not require any additional education funds but will lead to increased education performance in California by changing the incentives on the supply side (teachers and the education establishment) and the demand side (parents and students).

Merit Pay for Teachers

If companies earned profits the way teachers earn salary increases, then the oldest retail companies (perhaps Macy's, founded in 1858 or Sears Holdings Company, founded in 1893) would be the only retailers in America. Recent innovators, such as Wal-Mart and eBay, would have been unable to revolutionize the industry. Or, take the computer industry. IBM would still be a computer hardware company, and the revolution started by Microsoft and Apple could never have occurred. In the automobile industry, GM would dominate the automobile market selling large gas-guzzling cars because the competition from foreign car makers would never have occurred—to the detriment of consumers and the environment. In short, our economy would be unable to progress.

It is not that teachers do not care about outcomes; they do. Nor is it that teachers do not work hard; they do. But, incentives matter. The current education system in California, like in most of America, does not reward education innovation. It should not be surprising that, in such a system, there is no innovation in the education system. In my opinion teachers are truly the chosen people. Their devotion to their students and their ideals are unmatched anywhere else in our society. And yet the California Teachers Association has been able to coerce teachers into producing an inferior product at exorbitant cost.

Instituting merit pay and measurable objective criteria of performance encourages the best teachers to remain teachers, encourages teachers to consistently find new and better ways to educate students, creates a repertoire of success case studies that other teachers can leverage in their classrooms, and encourages those teachers whose talents lie elsewhere to pursue other careers.

Change Teacher Tenure Rules

Merit pay provides a carrot, or a positive incentive, that encourages teachers to perform better. California's school system currently uses positive reinforcement to encourage the wrong behavior. These are the incentives that arise due to California's teacher tenure system and with it the inability to fire underperforming teachers. Both of these policies need to change.

Tenure rules eliminate the incentives for teachers to continue improving because the penalty for not doing so is eliminated. Workers throughout California's private sector thrive at companies for many years without tenure. In fact, their security is improved as workers are continually incented to perform or risk losing their job. The results are constant innovation and improvements. In 2005, Proposition 74 would have further increased the ability of California to reward good teachers and weed out ineffective teachers, in part, by raising the tenure requirement to five years. While Proposition 74 was an improvement over the current two-year tenure requirements, optimally the state should eliminate the tenure system all together. Teachers, like other workers in California, should have to justify their employment by providing valuable services that exceed the costs of acquiring these services.

The flip side of the tenure rules is the ability to let underperforming teachers go. Proposition 74 would have addressed this issue by allowing teachers to be dismissed if they receive two consecutive negative evaluations. Yearly evaluations are currently the law. Creating consequences for teachers from negative evaluations strengthens the incentives created by eliminating teacher tenure and will help ensure that these reforms succeed.

Disband the Teachers Unions

In the private sector, unions place firms at a competitive disadvantage. So long as a labor market is competitive, workers generally get paid their marginal product. This is not due to the employer's sense of benevolence or fair play—of course not! But if a particular worker annually adds $50,000 to the firm's bottom line, while his total cost to the firm is only $45,000, there's in essence $5,000 lying on the street, waiting for a rival firm to bend over and pick it up.

Unions don't change these fundamental facts. Although they might serve to reduce transactions costs when negotiating arrangements between employers and huge pools of workers, unions typically achieve deals (through threats of strikes or worse) that force a firm to pay more total compensation (in the form of wages, health insurance, etc.) than is justified by the employee's marginal product. Also, unions tend to negotiate counterproductive or excessive work rules, vacation time, sick leave, health benefits, pension benefits, etc. They also tend to become very political, enforcing their ends via political means. This erodes the firm's profits and leaves it vulnerable to other firms who can operate with lower costs and thus steal away its customers. This outcome doesn't help anybody, especially the workers in the unionized firm. Just look at what is going on with Boeing in its effort to build a plant in South Carolina. The union is trying to stop them by using the National Labor Relations Board— that's precisely why unions are fading away as global competition intensifies.

These forces are muted when it comes to the government sector. Moe (2011) illustrates that teachers unions create precisely these types of adverse influences on the education system across the country (including California):

> They shape the schools from the bottom up, through collective bargaining activities so broad in scope that virtually every aspect of school organization bears the distinctive imprint of union design. They also shape the schools from the top down, through political activities that give them unrivaled influence over the laws and regulations imposed on public education by government, and that allow them to block or weaken governmental reforms they find threatening. In combining bottom-up and top-down influence, and in combining them as potently as they do, the teachers unions are unique among all actors in the educational arena. It is difficult to overstate how extensive a role they play in making America's schools what they are—and in preventing them from being something different.[5]

The consequences from the bottom-up and top-down influence cannot be understated. While he acknowledges that

> The teachers unions are not solely responsible for that [declining performance in U.S. schools] failure. But as the single most powerful group in American education by many orders of magnitude, they have played an integral role in it. Through their bottom-up power in collective bargaining, they have burdened the schools with perverse organizations that are literally not designed for effective education. Through their top-down power in the political process, they have blocked or weakened sensible reforms that attempt to bring change and improvement. The combination is devastating, creating a vise-like grip in which the nation's schools are systematically squeezed—and shaped to their organizational core—by the special interests of the adults who work in them.[6]

Researchers find the same dysfunctional influence in California as for the nation as a whole. With respect to California's schools, the customers (i.e., families that already pay for the public education system via their property taxes, income taxes, sales taxes, etc.) cannot switch brand allegiance easily if the "product" becomes too expensive or if the quality becomes too low.

The teachers unions are skewing the work environments and taxpayer expenditures toward the benefit of their members—the *raison d'etre* of the unions. For instance, teachers with 20 years of tenure in the current system benefit from the tenure based pay system. Reforming these policies toward merit based pay is not in their self interest. Consequently, the teachers union should be expected to oppose such reforms. And, they do.

These perverse incentives even persist throughout California's current budget crisis. A 2011 *Wall Street Journal Notable and Quotable* quoted economist Eric A. Hanushek who wrote on July 13:

> What is the worst way one could think of to deal with the school district budget problems? Of all the options, reducing the length of the school year must be the absolute worst—at least from the perspective of the students. But California, always proud of being a leader, has written into law that this is the preferred option if districts face budgetary shortfalls...
>
> This year, the new Governor, Jerry Brown, set out to deal with the budget honestly, including putting in place contingency spending reductions if revenues did not come in at the level anticipated in the budget. This action leads to uncertainty in school district budgets, because there is a reasonable chance that the state may reduce funding midyear. And here is where the California legislature showed the kind of leadership that makes a mockery of the idea that school policy is about the kids. At the behest of the California Teachers Association, the legislature declared that to deal with the fiscal situation, none of the thousand school districts in California is permitted to lay off any teachers. What can it do? By this legislation, it can eliminate up to seven days from the school year (as long as the local union agrees to that action).[7]

Blanket diktats from up high rarely make sense, and in this case the legislature has clearly put the interests of the labor unions ahead of the interests of the kids. The union problem in California's public schools is made worse because the schools are public entities. As such, public schools cannot go out of business no matter how financially unstable or how poorly the service is provided. The inefficiencies that the teachers unions create become embedded into the school system and are reflected in the higher costs/lower quality outcomes that are emblematic of California's current school system. These inefficiencies will only be eradicated when the teachers union is fully eliminated.

Reform and Consolidate California's School Districts

Each and every one of the 1,131 local school districts in California operates as a de facto local monopolist.[8] Basic Econ 101 principles predict that local monopolists' produce less efficient services, at higher costs and with fewer innovations. And, this is precisely what has been occurring across California's 1,131 local school monopolies.

Instead of continuing to support, or even further empower, the dysfunctional local monopolies, education reforms should introduce competition into California's school system. The new competitive landscape should permit school districts to compete across the artificial school boundaries that currently exist and encourage district consolidation that would lower costs—especially administrative costs—and allow school districts to leverage complimentary assets that may currently reside in other districts.

Empower Parents with School Vouchers

All of the previous reforms were directed at remedying the inefficiencies with California's education suppliers. The current system also creates inefficiencies for the demanders of education services in California—California's families.

When Californians purchase groceries, they go to the grocery store, pick out the items they want, and directly pay the grocer. The same holds true for purchases of computers, televisions, and furniture. However, when Californians want to purchase education services through the public school system, the process works very differently. The local government collects property taxes from the family, which is sent to Sacramento. In Sacramento property tax collections from across California are combined together, mixed with other tax revenues, and sent back to the local districts for further redistribution to the specific school the family wants to attend. This convoluted system creates a very large wedge between the supplier of education services (the schools) and the purchaser of those services (the families with school age children).

A school voucher system reduces this wedge and more closely connects the providers of education services to the users of education services. Empirical studies support these theoretical claims. According to the Foundation for Educational Choice:

> Studies conducted since the late 1990s convincingly show that school choice is an effective intervention and public policy for boosting student achievement and graduation rates. Nine studies using a method called "random assignment," the gold standard in the social sciences, have found statistically significant gains in academic achievement from school vouchers; one study found improved graduation rates. No such study has ever found negative effects. One study's findings were inconclusive. Random assignment methods allow researchers to isolate the effects of vouchers from other student characteristics. Students who applied for vouchers were entered into random lotteries to determine who would receive vouchers and who would remain in public schools; this allowed researchers to track very similar "treatment" and "control" groups, just like in medical trials.[9]

Importantly, school choice programs should include public and private schooling opportunities in urban as well as middle class and affluent school districts. According to Lance T. Izumi, Koret Senior Fellow and director of Education Studies at the Pacific Research Institute, "There is a misconception that we should limit school choice only to low-income children because low student performance, it is believed, is confined largely to children from low-income families. The reality is that student underperformance is rampant in middle-class and affluent communities across the country. Many middle-class students perform poorly on national and state tests and are too often unprepared for college. In California, for example, significant percentages of students in hundreds of middle-class schools fail to achieve proficiency in the core subjects on state exams. And with middle-class families hit hard by high mortgage payments and falling housing values, they are in desperate need of school choice options such as the highly popular universal school-choice voucher program in Sweden. In 2011, Indiana enacted the largest school-choice voucher program in the nation that would eventually give vouchers to up to 600,000 low and middle-income children. California should do likewise."

One State, Two States, Three States, Four!

With apologies to Dr. Seuss, a children's book on California could easily begin "One State, Two State, Red State, Blue State". The simple fact is that California is just too large. California is significantly more geographically and ethnically diverse than any other state. To the detriment of all Californians, and all Americans, the benefits from California's diversity are currently being diminished due to its sheer size. California should be two states, or three states, or even four.

At nearly 37 million people, California is far and away the largest state: nearly 50 percent larger than its closest rival, Texas. If it were a country, California's GDP would rank eighth in the world… just behind Italy and ahead of Brazil and Spain.

And, California's unity as one state does not reflect any natural connection. In fact, California's existence violates the principles used from the Founding Fathers through the establishment of the lower-48 states that "all states should be created equal".[10] Two things were different about California when it applied for statehood that led to the violation of this principle: power and distance.

Immediately following the Mexican war and California becoming a possession of the United States, gold was discovered in California. Because of the Gold Rush, California's economy and economic power became an immediate force: an economic powerhouse that was on the other side of the continent no less. Stein (2008) citing Senator Seward in 1850 summarizes the issue succinctly:

> [California] is practically further removed from us than England. We cannot reach her by railroad, nor by unbroken steam navigation. We can send no armies over the prairie, the mountain, and the desert….Let her only seize our domains within her borders, and our commerce in her ports, and she will have at once revenues and credits adequate to all her necessities. Besides, are we so moderate, and has the world become so just, that we have no rivals and no enemies to lend their sympathies and aid to compass the dismemberment of our empire?[11]

Back in 1850 California was rich in resources, including gold, good ports and all of the natural advantages that make California such an economic leader today. California is big today because when it was becoming a state, California was powerful. It could simply dictate the terms of its accession into the country. Save Texas, no other state had such a strong bargaining position as California. From its very founding, California violated the principles of state equality and has always been a lumbering giant whose sheer size now towers over most state. But size alone is not reason enough to warrant a break up of the state

Exhibit 61

California's Size Relative to the East Coast

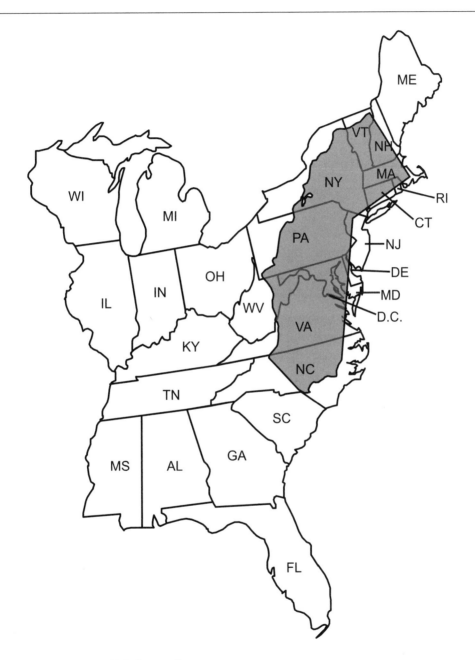

Source: U.S. Census Bureau

Nor should the current design of "50 united states" be seen as a pre-ordained conclusion. Trinklein (2010) documents dozens of states that were proposed, yet never came to be.[12] As some examples presented by Trinklein, imagine the shape of the U.S. map had the following state proposals not faltered:

- **Absaroka:** A proposed state designed around the Mt. Rushmore attraction, which would have been a squarish state drawn from south-eastern Montana, western South Dakota and northeastern Wyoming;
- **Acadia:** A proposed division of Maine would have split Maine into two due to extreme cultural differences between the north (hearty mountain folk) and the south (wealthy "summertime" residents);
- **Jacinto:** Named for the seminal battle of San Jacinto that helped bring Texas, Arizona, New Mexico, Utah, Nevada and (yes) California into the United States, Jacinto was one of several proposals to split Texas into multiple states this time along an east-west split; and,
- **Lincoln:** Idaho also has extreme differences in culture that goes back to its founding; in response to these differences a proposal in 1907 would have realigned the entire Northwest creating the state of Lincoln out of northern Idaho and eastern Washington (and a bit of Oregon)— southern Idaho and eastern Oregon would have become Idaho and the Cascade Mountains would have become the eastern borders of Washington and Oregon.

The proposal for a state of Lincoln illustrates that not only is there no divine truth to the shapes of the current states, in many instances these shapes just don't make sense. In fact, other proposals have attempted to break up (in some way shape or form) many other states including Massachusetts, Maryland, Illinois, New York, Florida, Tennessee, Kentucky, North Carolina, Alabama, Pennsylvania, Oklahoma, Kansas and New Jersey. And, lest you think dividing up California is a new idea, Trinklein notes a proposal by Southern Californians to break California into two in 1859 to separate the gold-rush settlers in Northern California from the Spanish influenced Southern California. If successful, Southern California would today be called Colorado.

Another proposal, this time in 1957, would have turned Northern California into the state of Shasta over the issue of water rights. The proposal to split California into two states today, proposed by Riverside County Supervisor Jeff Stone, follows in this tradition.[13] The Stone proposal is based on claims that the state's fiscal policies are unrepresentative and unfair to residents in the south and eastern parts of the state; and the state's policies lead to significantly lower state services for residents in the south and eastern parts of the state.

There simply is no justification for not breaking up California based on the argument that because it exists in its current form today, it must persist in that form. Whether California remains as one state should be based on practical considerations of efficiency in governing. And, on those criteria California as one state fails miserably.

One look at California's lurches from one fiscal catastrophe to another show beyond a shadow of a doubt that the state is too big. It simply cannot be governed. The state has to be divided into more manageable smaller units. Just like AT&T and the trusts of old, California needs to be divided into several states to ensure responsive government accountable to the electorate. While a few people would be hurt, the vast majority of Californians and non-Californians would be better off.

California unfairly dominates the selection process of both political parties. The state also has undue influence in the House of Representatives. This excessive influence helps explain why there are so many military bases and government contracts in California. California is like a "black hole." It is so big it pulls everything into its orbit.

On the other hand, Californians are under-represented in Washington D.C. In the U.S. Senate, California has the same representation as Wyoming, the state with the smallest population in the nation at less than 550 thousand people. And yet, Wyoming has two senators—the same as California with nearly 37 million people. California has 16 counties with more people each than the whole state of Wyoming.

Nevertheless, equal Senate representation sets up a situation of incredible inequities in the national Senate to the extreme detriment of the citizens of California and the nation. In Wyoming, there are two senators or one senator for every 272 thousand people. Kentucky and Louisiana, the two median population states, also are represented by two senators; the people living in these states have one senator per 2.2 million people.

In comparison, Californians have one senator per *18.5 million people*. Compared to tiny Wyoming, each Californian has 1/100 of the Senate representation as each Wyomingite. Compared to the median states, each Californian still only has slightly more than 1/10 of the Senate representation. Forming several states out of California would go a long way toward solving these disparate "influence" problems.

And, California's lumbering size does not just impact federal politics.

Political scientists commonly describe the states as being the "laboratories" of democracy that bring government closer to the people. But within California, major political factions tend to get lost in the shuffle. For instance, the state government, always with its eye to the voter-rich south, exploits the water resources of the north. Hispanics, who could have a real say if Southern California were a state on its own, have become so diluted in California as it now exists to have less power than their demographics would foretell.

The idealistic notion of state government as a place where the citizens oversee their tax dollars at work is a sham in California. It makes no more sense to raise the sales tax in Los Angeles to pay for earthquake damage in San Francisco than it does to raise the sales tax in New York, Cleveland, or Baton Rouge for the same purpose. The state as a unit is unwieldy and gawky, but most of all it is unfair. And California is unfair to virtually everyone in and out of the state.

Yes, it is true that, once elected, the power held by the governor of California would be diminished if California became two or more states. California's current governor, Jerry Brown, for personal reasons alone should oppose any break-up of California. But the Constitution of our country did not envision two presidents—the real one and the governor of California. The separation of powers and states rights should not be treated loosely. Such power, as is currently vested in California's governor and California's legislature, is potentially dangerous.

Ronald Reagan once quipped that if the pilgrims had landed in California the East Coast would still be unsettled. Well, he was about right. If California were placed over the East Coast from top to bottom it would cover ten states, the District of Columbia, and more than half of Virginia.

Even within California the government has become so big and out-of-touch that it has become the playground of super stars and the super-rich.

Even within California the government has become so big and out-of-touch that it has become the playground of super stars and the super-rich. Normal people just do not have any effect in the media market of Hollywood-style campaigns. Grassroots advocacy is what state and local governments should be all about. One Washington D.C. is enough for any country.

The imperious government of California is far from the vision held by our ancestors. Why, even back at the founding of this country when our Founding Fathers deemed the original thirteen states appropriate, there were only 3.5 million people in America total. There are currently two metropolitan areas in California with more population than the entire country had in 1780.

While breaking up can be hard to do, the benefits from splitting are often worth the effort. Such is the case with California. Splitting California into two, three, or four addresses many of these issues. The disproportionate power of California in the U.S. House would be immediately reduced, while its representation in the Senate increased. At the state level, Californians of today could create a state government that provides more representation and that jettisons the ungovernable aspects of the current California statehouse.

Too Many Cooks Spoil the Soup

Referring back to Appendices A and B, each one of the hundreds upon hundreds of commissions, school districts, and local governments (commissions) represent an independent fiefdom. While some fiefdoms may be quite small, the commissions' authority over those areas covered by its fiefdom is absolute. The potential economic damage from these commissions is great should they over-reach their intended authority or continue to exist long after the problem they were designed to address is resolved. The sheer number of commissions in California makes it a near certainty that many of California's current commissions have either over-reached their intended authority or outlived their intended purpose.

To correct for this problem, no commission should ever be created without a sunset provision. The sunset provision should clearly delineate the purpose of the commission and the commission's authorized timeframe of operations. Before the sunset date arrives for any commission, the state legislature and governor should be empowered to renew the commission's charter as is, or amend it to reflect the current needs of Californians.

For the hundreds of commissions that already exist, California should implement a sweeping five-year sunset provision for each and every commission in the state. The state legislature would then be responsible to review the purpose, operations, and effectiveness of all of these commissions over this timeframe. All commissions that are abiding by their stated purpose and whose purpose is still valuable to Californians should be renewed—with an appropriate sunset provision attached. All commissions that do not meet these criteria should have their charter's amended, or for those commissions that have outlived their purpose, should be wound down.

California's description as "the ungovernable state" is foreboding. Unfortunately, it is also accurate. Anti-democratic political and budgetary rules, gerrymandered districts, and over-empowered politicians and bureaucrats are thwarting the democratic process in California. They also make pro-growth economic reforms and sensible budget policies impossible to implement. Comprehensive solutions to California's ills must include reforms to the political process that revitalizes California's democratic process. In California, the highest priority is redefining California's political districting process.

Redistricting California's Uncompetitive Districts

During a statewide election, it has not been unusual in California politics for no legislative seat to change party hands. *Washington Post* political columnist David Broder called this "Soviet-style conformity."[14] The explanation for the lack of political competitiveness is the current redistricting process prior to the recent reforms that is commonly called "gerrymandering."

The term gerrymandering comes from early American political history when Massachusetts Governor Elbridge Gerry (later vice president of the United States under James Madison) helped create election districts in odd shapes so that his political allies could easily be elected to office. One district was said to look like a salamander. Combining the governor's name with the end portion of the word salamander produced the now well-known political term, gerrymander.

California's current districting process has perfected Governor Gerry's political contortions. The 23rd House of Representatives district, known as the Ribbon of Shame, follows the California coastline for 200 miles from Monterey to Oxnard, becoming extremely thin at spots—no wider than a football field. Some say at high tide this district is cut in two!

California's elected officials did what they could to snuff out competition with the current district lines. Democracy thrives with a competition of ideas. Districts gerrymandered to the point that elections are no longer competitive thwarts the competition of ideas. The result is the partisan political process we have seen in California where the incentive to effectively govern is all but removed.

The best method for creating truly competitive districts is to remove the district drawing power from legislators and give it to a panel of retired judges. Those retired judges should be required to:

- **Pledge not to run for an office for which they draw the district lines; and,**
- **Maintain geographic boundaries of cities and counties within districts as much as practicable.**

This solution was put before the voters under the "Voter Empowerment Act," in 2005 by Ted Costa and me, which was unfortunately defeated by voters by a 59.8 percent to 40.2 percent margin. Despite its defeat, changing the districting process and creating competitive political districts are necessary first steps to righting California's political process.

However, we are happy to report that other recent reforms in California have moved the state in the right direction. Passed in 2008, Proposition 11 changed the redistricting process of the geographic boundaries of the state's 120 legislative districts and four Board of Equalization districts. As opposed to the California state legislature establishing these boundaries, Proposition 11 tasked a new, 14-member commission made up of five Democrats, five Republicans, and four Unaffiliated.

Proposition 11 also requires the commission to take into account "communities of interest" that is defined as "a contiguous population which shares common social and economic interests that should be included within a single district for purposes of its effective and fair representation. Examples of such shared interests are those common to an urban area, an industrial area, or an agricultural area, and those common to areas in which the people share similar living standards, use the same transportation facilities, have similar work opportunities, or have access to the same media of communication relevant to the election process." Proposition 20, passed in 2010, empowers the commission to redraw U.S. congressional districts.

Passed in 2010, Proposition 14 is an additional reform requiring an open primary where all candidates run in a single primary election regardless of party affiliation. The two candidates that receive the most votes will then face one another in the general election. Proposition 14, in combination with Proposition 11 and Proposition 20, should help to meaningfully impact the competitiveness of elections in California.

As with many beneficial reforms (e.g., the Gann spending limit), the gains created by Propositions 11 and 14 can be lost if these gains are not vigilantly protected. Additionally, the true test of these Propositions will be revealed if they are effective at rolling back the gerrymandered districts and make California's elections competitive once again. If these political reforms prove to be insufficient to empower Californians once again, then additional reforms closer to the Costa and Laffer proposals should be implemented.

Preserving the Two-thirds Vote for Tax Increases

Proposition 13 required that state tax increases be approved by a two-thirds vote of the legislature or passed by a two-thirds vote of the people. In 1997, the California Supreme Court ruled that fees passed by the legislature to mitigate past, actual and anticipated future problems related to business products could be passed with a simple majority vote. The case dealt with fees applied to paint manufacturers who had once used lead in their paints, lead which was subsequently found to be detrimental to children's health. The ruling by the court opened the door for more fees to be passed without a two-thirds vote—fees that often were disguised taxes.

Several recent initiatives have impacted the two-thirds majority requirement. First, spending legislation no longer needs a two-thirds majority to pass thanks to Proposition 25—a slight negative for sound budget control. However, Proposition 26 extends the two-thirds majority for passage of certain state and local fees. This means some fees will now be treated like taxes—a positive taxpayer protection against California's current trend of burdening its citizens with higher and higher costs. The net impact of these reforms are likely positive strengthening the two-thirds requirement as ultimately higher spending must be financed by taxes or fees.

The danger going forward arises due to the erroneous claims that California's two-thirds majority requirement for tax increases is part of the problem creating California's political dysfunction. In fact, it is just the opposite—California's two-thirds majority requirement for tax increases creates a crucial protection for taxpayers. Just imagine what California's top marginal income tax rate might be without it—Delaware's top rate of 19.8 percent back in the 1970s could look small in comparison. California's two-thirds majority requirement for tax increases should not only be maintained but the loopholes that have crept in should be closed thereby strengthening the taxpayer protections.

Adopt Open Primaries

As a final process reform, California should implement an open primary system. While not unique to California, primary elections in California reward those politicians that appeal to the political extremes. The candidates in the subsequent general election tend to represent more extreme positions. An economic theory known as Public Choice associated with James Buchanan and Gordon Tullock illustrates why this is the expected result.

Public choice uses economic principles to increase our understanding regarding the observed political outcomes. In terms of elections, candidates win elections by appealing to the median voter of that election. Imagine an election with five people voting. If we lined the voters up based on their political

The general election is subsequently between two candidates that while may appeal to the median voters of their respective primaries, do not necessarily represent the median voters of the district.

philosophy from left to right, then the politician who obtains the vote of the third person in this line—the median voter—wins the election.

A median voter in a closed primary tends to have more extreme political positions than the median voter for the entire population. However, candidates do not win the current primaries by appealing to the median voter of the district. Candidates win elections by appealing to the median voter of the primary. Consequently, the system rewards those politicians with more extreme positions compared to the district's median voter. The general election is subsequently between two candidates that, while may be appealing to the median voters of their respective primaries, do not necessarily represent the median voters of the district.

Regardless who wins the general election the district is, consequently, represented by a candidate more aligned with the extremes of one of the political parties. Aggregating this result across all of California's districts, the state legislature becomes more representative of the political extremes as opposed to the median voter. When coupled with California's gerrymandered districts, the results are the political paralysis that afflicts California. Adopting an open primary system would reverse these trends.

Under an open primary system, any voter, regardless of his or her party affiliation, could vote for any candidate regardless of his or her party affiliation. The primary would become *open* to all registered voters. The two candidates that receive the most votes in the primary, regardless of their party affiliation, would face each other in the general election.

The advantage of the open primary system is that to garner the most votes, candidates will have an incentive to appeal to the median voter of the district not just the median voter of the party. The result will be a general election that has a greater likelihood of representing the median voter of the district and consequently the election results world have a greater chance of representing the views of the district.

Eureka!
—Archimedes
California State Motto

Chapter 14

Ideas for Reform

A California Flat Tax

- **Replace the current state and local tax systems with a single revenue-neutral flat tax rate of 5.8 percent on personal unadjusted gross income**

    - Fairness

    Everyone will pay the same tax rate. This means that today's modest income earners will have their taxes reduced considerably. The elimination of regressive taxes such as payroll taxes, sales taxes, excise taxes, gas taxes, and property taxes will more than offset the elimination of the progressive income and capital gains taxes.

    - Simplicity

    The straightforward calculation of the tax base and the application of a single tax rate will simplify the entire tax system. This means that the additional costs taxpayers have had to pay to comply with the tax code will be greatly reduced.

    - Transparency

    By having only one source of revenue with a single tax rate, everyone will know exactly what taxes are. Politicians will be less tempted to abuse our tax codes for political or personal gain. Democracy will have a chance to function properly because people will be fully informed.

  ○ Completeness

By eliminating all other state and local taxes and replacing them with the single low tax rate on the broadened tax base, revenues will be assured for the appropriate level of all state and local government spending.

  ○ Efficiency

The reduction of marginal tax rates coupled with the broadening of the tax base will minimize many of the distortions that make the current tax system counterproductive. The economy would undergo substantial expansion, resulting in an increase in revenues for state and local governments and increased prosperity for Californians.

  ○ Stability

From the day the flat tax is enacted and beyond, state and local governments would not only get more revenues, but the revenue stream would be far more stable from year to year.

- **Replace the current state corporate tax with a business value added tax of 5.8 percent**

Ends the distortions inherent in the current tax code that discriminates against successful companies by taxing their profits and subsidizing inefficient companies.

- **Maintain the mortgage rate deduction**

The mortgage deduction is consistent with good economics. Interest payments on mortgages do not have any economic consequence and therefore should not be taxable.

- **Maintain charitable deductions**

Proper charitable deductions should continue. When a person gives altruistically and for no personal benefit, that contribution should be deductible.

- **Maintain certain "sin taxes"**

These taxes exists not to raise revenues but to discourage certain behavior. A speeding ticket, for example, is designed to discourage people from speeding. A carbon tax could also be considered a sin tax. Given their function, we should not eliminate all sin taxes from the tax base.

- **Offer tax amnesty**

Once a low flat tax rate is in place, there should be a tax amnesty program to allow people who made judgments in error—some many years ago—to re-enter the legitimate economy. The low rate flat tax eliminates the reasons for tax evasion but the prospects for prosecution would force scofflaws to remain underground. A tax amnesty program would quickly bring these tax evaders above ground.

- **Establish enterprise zones**

Establish enterprise zones for the poorest areas of California. By lowering the tax rates in depressed regions, jobs will move to where they are needed the most and thus partially counteracting the lack of economic opportunities.

Added Boon

- **Allow renters to deduct the rent of their primary residence**

This is a fairness issue. Homeowners are able to "rent" their own home at pre-tax dollars while renters pay with after-tax dollars. There is a great discrimination in our society between homeowners and renters—people who rent should not pay more taxes per square foot of living space than those who own homes.

State Government Reforms

- **Reform public employee union dues for political activities**

It is fundamentally unfair to force public employees to give money to political activities and candidates that they do not support. Because taxpayer money is involved, the public has the right to give power to public employees to approve the use of their dues for political activities.

- **Provide merit pay for politicians and government workers**

Politicians should have modest base salaries, with the remainder of their compensation depending on how well California performs. The performance measures should be based on key well-being factors for Californians, including average (or median) state income growth, corporate profitability growth, and employment growth.

- **Establish sunset provisions for all commissions**

The number of commissions in California makes it a near certainty that many of the commissions have either over-reached their intended authority or outlived their intended purpose. To correct the problem, no commission should be created without a sunset provision. For the hundreds of commissions that already exist, California should implement a sweeping five-year sunset provision for every commission in the state.

- **Reform district lines**

California's elected officials have snuffed out competition with the current district lines. Democracy thrives with a competition of ideas. Changing the districting process and creating competitive political districts are necessary first steps to righting California's political process.

- **Adopt open primaries**

An open primary system provides an incentive for candidates to appeal to the median voter of the district, not just the median voter of the party. The result will be a general election that has a greater likelihood of representing the views of the district.

- **Preserve the two-thirds vote for tax increases**

California two-thirds majority requirement for tax increases should not only be maintained but the loopholes that have crept in should be closed thereby strengthening taxpayer protections.

Out of the Box

- **Break California up into two to four states**

California needs to be divided into several states to ensure responsive government accountable to the electorate. It will provide greater representation and jettisons the ungovernable aspects of the current California statehouse.

Education Reforms

- **Empower parents with school vouchers**

A school voucher system introduces competition to California schools and more closely connects the providers of education services to the users of education.

- **Merit pay for teachers**

The current education system in California, like in most of America, does not reward innovation. Instituting merit pay and measurable objective criteria of performance encourages the best teachers to remain teachers and to consistently find new and better ways to educate students.

- **Change teacher tenure rules**

Tenure rules eliminate the incentives for teachers to continue improving because the penalty for not doing so is eliminated. In addition, removing teachers who receive poor evaluations strengthens the incentives created by eliminating teacher tenure and ensure that these reforms succeed.

- **Reform and consolidate California school districts**

Allow school districts to compete across the artificial school boundaries that currently exist and encourage district consolidation that would lower costs—especially administrative costs—and allow school districts to leverage complimentary assets that may currently reside in other districts.

Extra Credit

• Disband the teachers unions

The inefficiencies that the teachers union creates become embedded into the school systems and are reflected in higher costs and low quality outcomes that are emblematic of California's school system. These problems will only be eradicated when the teachers union is fully eliminated.

Appendix A

A Partial Selection of California's State, County, and City Taxes, and Fees

abandoned vehicle fees
activity fee
additional assessmenls on fish and game fines
admission tax
aircraft jel fuel tax
alcoholic beverage taxes and fees
animal licenses
animal shelter fees and charges
architecture public building fees
ballast water management fee
beverage container redemption fees
breast cancer research cigarette stamp tax
building construction filing fees
business license tax
cable, city cable fee
cable. franchise fee
California children and families first cig. stamp tax
California State University fees
California tire fee
candidate filing fees
childhood lead poisoning prevention fee
cigarette and tobacco products surtax
cigarette tax
city and county sales tax
construction permits
corporation tax
county clerk - miscellaneous fees
county transportation tax
court fees
court filing fees and surcharges
delinquent fees
disposal fee
district transactions and use tax
division of real estate examination fees

division of real estate license fees
domestic corporation fees
duck stamps
eating places licenses
electric, CA public benefit fee
electric, city tax
electric, franchise fee
electric, state regulatory fee
electric, underground surcharge
electric, user utility fee (UUT)
electrical energy surcharge
elevator and boiler inspection lees
employer's payroll tax
employment agency filing fees
employment agency license fees
engineering fees, inspection, and others
environmental fee
estate, inheritance, and gift tax
explosive permit fees
facility free and tiered permit fees
farmers market and ag. commission fees
filing financing statements
fines and forfeitures
fingerprint ID card fees
fish and game violation fines
foreign corporation fees
franchises tax
garbage truck inspection fees
general fees - Secretary of State
general fish and game licenses tags permits
general fish and game taxes
generator fee
genetic disease testing fees
golf course fees

guardianship fees
hazardous material fees
hazardous waste control fees
health and dental fees
highway carrier uniform business license tax
horse racing (pari-mutuel) license fees
industrial homework fees
insurance company examination fees
insurance company license fees and penalties
insurance department fees, general
insurance department fees, Prop. 103
insurance fraud assessment, auto
insurance fraud assessment, general
insurance fraud assessment, workers comp.
insurance gross premium tax
integrated waste management fee
interest, penalties. and delinquent taxes
interstate user lax
library fines and fees
liquor license fee
local revenue fund state sales tax
penalties on trafllc violations
penalty assessments
penalty assessments on fish and game fines
personal income tax
phone booth permits
phone, California high cost fund-A (CHCF-A)
phone, California high cost fund-B (CHCF-B)
phone, California relay svc. and comm. df. surcharge (DOTP)
phone, California teleconnect fund surcharge (CTF)
phone, city and county utility taxes
phone, emergency telephone users surcharge tax
phone, rate surcharge
phone, service provider number portability
phone, state regulatory fee (PUCURA)
phone, universal helpline telephone service surcharge (UL TS)
plan checking fees
private rail car tax
private railroad car tax
proceeds frorn estates of deceased persons
public administrator fees
public safety fund sales tax
quarterty public utility commission fees
real property transfer tax
recording fees
renewal fees
retail sales and tax
retail sales, and use tax realignment
revenue - abandoned property
sale of real and personal property
sales of documents
marriage licenses secured and unsecured property tax
motor vehicle fuel tax (diesel)

motor vehicle fuel tax (gasoline)
motor vehicle license (in. lieu) fees
motor vehicle registration
museum hall and art commission fees
natural gas surcharge
new motor vehicle dealer license fee
notary public license fees
occupational lead poisoning prevention fee
off-highway vehicle fees
oil spill response fee
oil spill response. prevention. and admin. fees
open space cancellation fee
other property tax
other regulatory fees
other regulatory licenses and permits
other regulatory taxes
opera and civic auditorium fees
parental fees underground
parking lot revenues
parking permits
parking violations
parks and recreation fees
pay patients board charges
penalties and interest on personal income tax
penalties on public utility commission quarterly
sewer service charges and connection fees
solid waste collection
special district taxes
state beach and park service fees
state disaster relief tax
state energy surcharge
state tax
street and curb permit
street sweeping fee
subdivision filing fees
teacher credential fees
teacher examination fees
telecommunications tax
timber yield tax
towing fees
traffic violations
trailer coach license (In-lieu) fees
transient lodging tax
storage tank maintenance fee
uninsured motorist fees
voter approved indebtedness property tax
waste water system maintenance
water service charges
water high elevation charge
water special facility charge
zoning and subdivision fees

Appendix B

A Partial List of California Commissions

1	Access for Infants & Mothers (AIM)
2	Accountancy, California Board of (CBA)
3	Acupuncture Board (ACUPUNCTURE)
4	Administrative Hearings, Office of (OAH)
5	Administrative Law, Office of (OAL)
6	African American Museum, California (CAAM)
7	Aging, California Commission on (CCOA)
8	Aging, Department of (AGING)
9	Agricultural Labor Relations Board (ALRB)
10	AIDS, Office of (OA)
11	Air Resources Board (ARB, CARB)
12	Alcohol & Drug Programs, Department of (ADP)
13	Alcoholic Beverage Control Appeals Board (ABCAB)
14	Alcoholic Beverage Control, Department of (ABC)
15	Apprenticeship Council (CAC)
16	Apprenticeship Standards, Division of (DAS)
17	Arbitration Certification Program (ACP)
18	Architect, Division of the State (DSA)
19	Architects Board, California (CAB)
20	Archives, California State (Secretary of State) (ARCHIVES)
21	Arts Council (CAC)
22	Asian Pacific Islander Legislative Caucus (API)
23	Assembly Democratic Caucus (ASMDC)
24	Assembly Republican Caucus
25	Assembly, California State
26	Athletic Commission, California (CSAC)
27	Attorney General (Department of Justice) (AG)
28	Audits, Bureau of State (State Auditor) (BSA)
29	Automotive Repair, Bureau of (BAR)
30	Baldwin Hills Conservancy (BHC)
31	Bank on California
32	Bar of California, State (CALBAR)
33	Barbering and Cosmetology, Board of (BBC)
34	Behavioral Sciences, Board of (BBS)
35	Binational Border Health, California Office of (COBBH)
36	Biodiversity Council, California (CBC)
37	Blind, Office of Services to the (OSB)
38	Boating & Waterways, California Department of (DBW)
39	Boating and Waterways Commission, California
40	Building Standards Commission (BSC)
41	Business Investment Services, California (Business)
42	Business, Transportation, & Housing Agency (BTH)
43	Business.ca.gov (GoED)
44	CA.Gov (CA.gov)
45	Cal EMA (CAL EMA)
46	CAL FIRE (CAL FIRE)
47	Cal/EPA (CALEPA)
48	Cal-Atlas (Cal-Atlas)
49	CalCareNet
50	CALFED Bay-Delta Program (CALFED)
51	CalFresh (CalFresh)
52	CalGOLD (CALGOLD)

53	California Channel (CalChannel)
54	CalJOBS (CALJOBS)
55	CalPERS (CALPERS)
56	CalRecycle (CALRECYCLE)
57	CalSTRS
58	Caltrans (DOT,CALTRANS)
59	Caltrans, District 10 (DOT,CALTRANS)
60	Caltrans, District 11 (DOT,CALTRANS)
61	Caltrans, District 2 (DOT,CALTRANS)
62	Caltrans, District 7 (DOT,CALTRANS)
63	Caltrans, District 8 (DOT,CALTRANS)
64	CalVet Loans (CALVET)
65	CalWORKS (CALWORKS)
66	Career Resource Network (CALCRN)
67	Cemetery & Funeral Bureau (CFB)
68	Central Valley Flood Protection Board (CVFPB)
69	Child Abuse Prevention, Office of
70	Child Support Services, Department of (CDCSS)
71	Chiropractic Examiners, Board of (BCE)
72	Citizens Compensation Commission, California
73	Citizens Redistricting Commission (CRC)
74	Climate Change Portal, California
75	Coachella Valley Mountains Conservancy (CVMC)
76	Coastal Commission, California
77	Coastal Conservancy, State (SCC)
78	Colorado River Board of California (CRB)
79	Community Services & Development, Department of (CSD)
80	Compensation Insurance Fund, State (SCIF)
81	Conservation Corps, California (CCC)
82	Conservation, Department of (DOC)
83	Consumer Affairs, Department of (DCA)
84	Consumer Services Agency, State and (SCSA)
85	Contractors State License Board (CSLB)

86	Controller's Office, California State (SCO)
87	Cool California (CoolCal)
88	Corporations, Department of (CORP)
89	Correctional Health Care Services (DCHCS)
90	Corrections & Rehabilitation, Department of (CDCR)
91	Corrections Standards Authority (CSA)
92	Counties, California State Association of (CSAC)
93	Court Reporters Board of California
94	Courts of Appeal, California (COURTS)
95	Courts, California
96	Cyber Safety for Children
97	Deaf Access, Office of
98	Delta Conservancy
99	Delta Protection Commission
100	Delta Stewardship Council
101	Dental Board of California (DBC)
102	Dental Hygiene Committee of California (DHCC)
103	Denti-Cal (DENTI-CAL)
104	Department of Motor Vehicles (DMV)
105	Developmental Disabilities, State Council on (SCDD)
106	Developmental Services, Department of (DDS)
107	Disability Insurance, State (EDD)
108	Disabled Veterans Business Enterprise Advisory Council (DVBE)
109	Earthquake Authority, California
110	Economic & Employment Enforcement Coalition (EEEC)
111	Economic Strategy Panel, California
112	Education Audit Appeals Panel (EAAP)
113	Education, California State Board of
114	Education, Department of (CDE)
115	eHealth Initiative, California
116	Elections (Secretary of State) (SOS)
117	Electronic & Appliance Repair, Bureau of (BEAR)
118	Emergency Communications Office (911), California

119	Emergency Food Assistance Program (EFAP)
120	Emergency Management Agency, California (Cal EMA)
121	Emergency Medical Services Authority (EMSA)
122	Employment Development Department (EDD)
123	Employment Training Panel (ETP)
124	Energy Commission, California (ENERGY)
125	Environment Resources Evaluation System, California (CERES)
126	Environmental Health Hazard Assessment, Office of (OEHHA)
127	Environmental Protection Agency (CALEPA)
128	Equalization, Board of (BOE)
129	eServices Office (ESERVICES)
130	Experience Unlimited (EDD)
131	Exposition & State Fair, California (CAL EXPO)
132	Fair Employment & Housing Commission (FEHC)
133	Fair Employment & Housing, Department of (DFEH)
134	Fair Political Practices Commission (FPPC)
135	Fair, California State (BIG FUN)
136	Film Commission, California (CFC)
137	Finance, Department of (DOF)
138	Financial Institutions, Department of (DFI)
139	Fire Marshal, Office of the State (OSFM)
140	Firearms, Bureau of (DOJ)
141	First 5 California (First 5)
142	Fish & Game Commission (FGC)
143	Fish & Game, Department of (DFG)
144	Fleet & Asset Management, Office of (OFAM)
145	Flex Your Power (FYP)
146	Food & Agriculture, Department of (CDFA)
147	Forestry & Fire Protection, Board of (BOF)
148	Forestry & Fire Protection, California Department of (CAL FIRE)
149	Franchise Tax Board (FTB)
150	Gambling Control Commission (CGCC)

#	Entry		#	Entry		#	Entry
151	Gang & Youth Violence Policy, Governor's Office of (OGYVP)		179	Housing Finance Agency (CALHFA)		213	Library, California State (CSL)
152	General Services, Department of (DGS)		180	Independent Living Council, California State (CALSILC)		214	Lieutenant Governor, Office of (LTG)
153	Geospatial Clearinghouse (CALATLAS)		181	Industrial Relations, Department of (DIR)		215	Little Hoover Commission (LHC)
154	GIS (Geographic Information Systems) Council, California (CGC)		182	Industrial Welfare Commission (IWC)		216	Lottery Commission (Lotto)
155	Governor, Office of the (GO)		183	Information Security, Office of (OIS)		217	Lottery, State (LOTTERY)
156	Governor's Committee for Employment of Disabled Persons (GCEPD)		184	Infrastructure and Economic Development Bank (I-Bank) (IBANK)		218	Managed Health Care, Department of (DMHC)
157	Governor's Mentoring Partnership (GMP)		185	Inspector General, Office of the (OIG)		219	Managed Risk Medical Insurance Board (MRMIB)
158	Governors Office of Econonomic Development (GoED)		186	Insurance Commissioner (CDI)		220	Mediation & Conciliation Service, State (CMCS)
159	Governor's Office of Planning & Research (OPR)		187	Insurance, Department of (CDI)		221	Medi-Cal (MEDI-CAL)
160	Guide Dogs for the Blind, Board of (BGDB)		188	Judicial Council of California		222	Medical Assistance Commission (CMAC)
161	Habeas Corpus Resource Center (HCRC)		189	Judicial Performance, Commission on (CJP)		223	Medical Board of California (MBC)
162	Health and Human Services Agency (CHHS)		190	Justice, Department of (Attorney General) (DOJ)		224	Mental Health Services Oversight and Accountability Commission (MHSOAC)
163	Health and Safety & Workers' Compensation, Commission on (CHSWC)		191	Juvenile Justice, Division of		225	Mental Health, Department of (DMH)
			192	Juvenile Parole Board (JPB)			
164	Health Benefit Exchange, California (HBEX)		193	Labor and Workforce Development Agency (LWDA)		226	Mentally Ill Offenders, Council on (COMIO)
165	Health Care Reform, California		194	Labor Market Information Division (LMID)		227	Military Department (California National Guard) (MIL)
166	Health Care Services, Department of (DHCS)		195	Labor Standards Enforcement, Division of (DLSE)		228	Military Museum, California State (CSMM)
167	Health Information Integrity, California Office of (CALOHI)		196	Labor Statistics and Research, Division of (DLSR)		229	Mine Reclamation, Office of
						230	Mining & Geology Board (SMGB)
168	Health Planning and Development, Office of Statewide (OSHPD)		197	Lands Commission, California State (SLC)		231	Missing & Unidentified Persons Unit (DOJ)
169	Healthy Families Program		198	Landscape Architects Technical Committee (LATC)		232	Motor Vehicles, Department of (DMV)
170	Hearing Aid Dispensers Bureau		199	Latino Legislative Caucus (LLC)		233	Museum for History, Women and the Arts, California
171	High-Speed Rail Authority (CAHSRA)		200	Law Enforcement Agencies		234	Museum, the California (Museum)
			201	Law Revision Committee (CLRC)			
172	Highway Patrol, California (CHP)		202	Learn California		235	MyCali Youth Portal (MYCALI)
173	Historic Preservation, Office of (OHP)		203	Legislative Analyst's Office (LAO)		236	National Guard, California (CALGUARD)
			204	Legislative Black Caucus (ASM)			
174	Historical and Cultural Endowment, California		205	12/14/11		237	Native American Heritage Commission (NAHC)
			206	Legislative Environmental Caucus			
175	Historical Resources Commission, State (SHRC)		207	Legislative Information (Counsel) (LEGINFO)		238	Natural Resources Agency
						239	Naturopathic Medicine Committee
176	Home Furnishings and Thermal Insulation, Bureau of (BEARHFTI)		208	Legislative Lesbian, Gay, Bisexual, & Transgender Caucus (LGBT)		240	New Motor Vehicle Board (NMVB)
177	Horse Racing Board, California (CHRB)		209	Legislative Outdoor Sporting Caucus		241	Occupational Safety & Health, California Office of (DOSH)
			210	Legislative Rural Caucus			
178	Housing & Community Development, Department of (HCD)		211	Legislative Women's Caucus		242	Occupational Safety and Health Appeals Board (DIR, OSHAB)
			212	Legislature, California State (LEGISLATURE)		243	Occupational Safety and Health Standards Board (OSHSB)
						244	Occupational Therapy, California Board of (BOT)

245	Ocean & Coastal Environmental Access Network, California (Cal OCEAN)
246	Ocean Protection Council (COPC)
247	Off-Highway Motor Vehicle Recreation (OHMVR)
248	Office of Statewide Health Planning & Development (OSHPD)
249	Oil, Gas & Geothermal Resources
250	Optometry, Board of
251	Osteopathic Medical Board of California (OMBC)
252	Paid Family Leave Insurance Program (PFL)
253	Parks and Recreation Commission
254	Parks, California State (PARKS)
255	Parole Hearings, Board of (CDCR, BOPH)
256	Patient Advocate, Office of the (OPA)
257	Peace Officer Standards & Training, Commission on (POST)
258	Personnel Administration, Department of (DPA)
259	Personnel Board, State (SPB)
260	Pesticide Regulation, Deptartment of (CDPR)
261	Pharmacy, Board of
262	Physical Therapy Board of California (PTBC)
263	Physician Assistant Committee (PAC)
264	Pilot Commissioners, Board of (BOPC)
265	Podiatric Medicine, Board of (BPM)
266	Postsecondary Education Commission, California (CPEC)
267	Pre-Existing Condition Insurance Plan (PCIP)
268	Prison Health Care Services (CPHCS)
269	Prison Industry Authority (CALPIA)
270	Privacy Protection, Office of (OPP)
271	Private Postsecondary Education, Bureau for (BPPE)
272	Procurement Division (PD)
273	Professional Engineers, Land Surveyors, & Geologists, Board for
274	Professional Fiduciaries Bureau
275	Psychology, Board of
276	Public Employees Retirement System, California (CalPERS)

277	Public Employment Relations Board, California (PERB)
278	Public Health, California Department of (CDPH)
279	Public Infrastructure Advisory Commission (PIAC)
280	Public Safety Communications, Office of (PSCO)
281	Public School Construction, Office of (OPSC)
282	Public Utilities Commission, California (CPUC)
283	Publishing, Office of State (OSP)
284	Railroad Museum, California State (CSRMF)
285	Real Estate Appraisers, Office of (OREA)
286	Real Estate, Department of (DRE)
287	Regenerative Medicine, California Institute for (CIRM)
288	Registered Nursing, Board of (RN)
289	Registrar of Charitable Trusts (AG)
290	Rehabilitation, Department of (DOR)
291	Reporting Transparency
292	Research Bureau, California (CRB)
293	Resources Recycling and Recovery, Department of (CalRecycle) (CALRECYCLE)
294	Respiratory Care Board of California (RCB)
295	Risk and Insurance Management, Office of (ORIM)
296	Sacramento-San Joaquin Delta Conservancy
297	Safe at Home Program (Secretary of State)
298	San Diego River Conservancy (SDRC)
299	San Francisco Bay Conservation & Development Commission (BCDC)
300	San Gabriel & Lower Los Angeles Rivers & Mountains Conservancy (RMC)
301	San Joaquin River Conservancy (SJRC)
302	Santa Monica Mountains Conservancy (SMMC)
303	Save Our Water (SOW)
304	School Finder, California (CDE)
305	Science Center, California
306	Secretary of State (SOS)

307	Security and Investigative Services, Bureau of (BSIS)
308	Seismic Safety Commission (SSC)
309	Self Insurance Plans (DIR, SIP)
310	Senate Majority Caucus
311	Senate Office of Research (SOR)
312	Senate Republican Caucus
313	Senate, California State
314	Sierra Nevada Conservancy
315	Small Business & Disabled Veteran Business Enterprise Certification Program
316	Small Business Development Centers (SBDC)
317	Smart Growth Caucus (SGC)
318	Smog Check Information Center (BAR)
319	Social Services Adoptions Branch, Department of (CDSS)
320	Social Services, Department of (CDSS)
321	Speech-Language Pathology and Audiology Board
322	Standardized Testing and Reporting (STAR, CDE)
323	State Mandates, Commission on (CSM)
324	Status of Women, Commission on (CCW)
325	Structural Pest Control Board
326	Student Aid Commission (CSAC)
327	Summer School for the Arts, California State (CSSSA)
328	Superintendent of Public Instruction, State (CDE)
329	Superior Courts, California (COURTS)
330	Supreme Court of California (COURTS)
331	Systems Integration, Office of (OSI)
332	Tahoe Conservancy, California
333	Take Charge California (TAKE CHARGE, DCA)
334	Tax Service Center (TAXES)
335	Teach California
336	Teacher Credentialing, Commission on (CTC)
337	Teachers' Retirement System, California (CalSTRS)
338	Technology Agency, California (Technology Agency)

339	Technology Services, Office of (OTECH)	351	Unemployment Insurance Program (EDD, UI)	362	Water Resources Control Board (WRCB)
340	Telephone Medical Advice Services Bureau (DCA, TMAS)	352	Uniform Custom Cost Accounting Commission (SCO)	363	Water Resources, Department of (DWR)
341	Tourism Industry, California (for Industry Professionals)	353	University of California	364	Welcome Centers, California (CWC)
342	Toxic Substances Control, Department of (DTSC)	354	University, California State (CALSTATE, CSU)	365	Welfare to Work Division (CDSS)
343	Traffic Safety, Office of (OTS)			366	Wildlife Conservation Board (WCB)
344	Transportation Commission (CATC)	355	Veterans Affairs, Department of (CDVA)	367	Women, Infants, & Children Program (WIC)
345	Transportation, Department of (DOT,CALTRANS)	356	Veterans Board, The California	368	Women's Health, Office of (OWH)
346	Travel and Tourism Commission, California (VisitCalifornia)	357	Veterinary Medical Board, California (VMB)	369	Worker's Compensation Appeals Board (DIR, WCAB)
347	Treasurer's Office, State (STO)	358	Victim Compensation and Government Claims Board (VCGCB)	370	Workers' Compensation, Division of (DIR, DWC)
348	Trustees, Board of (California State University)	359	Vocational Nursing and Psychiatric Technicians, Board of (BVNPT)	371	Worker's Occupational Safety & Health Training & Education Program (WOSHTEP)
349	Unclaimed Property (SCO)	360	Volunteers, California		
350	Unemployment Insurance Appeals Board (CUIAB)	361	Voter Registration - Secretary of State (SOS)	372	Workforce Investment Board (CWIB)

http://www.ca.gov/CaSearch/Agencies.aspx

Endnotes

Introduction

1   "Tombstone Script," http://www.script-o-rama.com/movie_scripts/t/tombstone-script-transcript-val-kilmer.html.html
2   Bureau of Economic Analysis. GDP by State Current Dollars. http://www.bea.gov/iTable/iTable.cfm?reqid=70&step=1&isuri=1&acrdn=1 World Bank. GDP (Current US$). 2009 GDP http://data.worldbank.org/indicator/NY.GDP.MKTP.CD/countries?display=default
3   *CIA World Factbook*. Population. https://www.cia.gov/library/publications/the-world-factbook/rankorder/2119rank.html.

Chapter 1

1   Samuelson, Paul A. and Nordhaus, William D. (2010) *Economics*, Chapter 4, Supply and Demand: Elasticity and Applications, McGraw Hill, 19th Edition; http://books.google.com/books?id=gzqXdHXxxeAC&pg=PA83&lpg=PA83&dq=samuelson+parrot+supply&source=bl&ots=y6m6BKx5IZ&sig=Abk2G4cR9DUkAbol3lqXGbA_93s&hl=en&ei=Ll4wToSVJ8HOgAeGtvmxAQ&sa=X&oi=book_result&ct=result&resnum=1&ved=0CEEQ6AEwAA#v=onepage&q&f=false
2   Bureau of Economic Analysis Table 1.1.5. Gross Domestic Product. http://bea.gov/iTable/iTable.cfm?ReqID=9&step=1. Bureau of Economic Analysis Table 3.1. Government Current Receipts and Expenditures. http://bea.gov/iTable/iTable.cfm?ReqID=9&step=1
3   IRS. http://www.irs.gov/publications/p15/ar02.html#en_US_2011_publink1000202364
4   The Tax Foundation. U.S. Federal Individual Income Tax Rates History, 1913-2011. http://www.taxfoundation.org/taxdata/show/151.html
5   California Employer's Guide. http://www.edd.ca.gov/pdf_pub_ctr/de44.pdf
6   The Tax Foundation. State Individual Income Tax Rates, 2010-2011. http://www.taxfoundation.org/taxdata/show/228.html. The state income tax payments are generally deductible on the federal tax return unless a person qualifies for the alternative minimum tax (AMT).
7   Kennedy, John. "Address to the Economic Club of New York," 14 December 1962. http://www.jfklibrary.org/Asset-Viewer/Archives/JFKWHA-148.aspx
8   Friedman, Milton. *Free To Choose: A Personal Statement*. (New York, Harcourt)
9   Laffer, Arthur B., Ph.D., Wayne H. Winegarden, Ph.D., and John Childs. *The Economic Burden Caused by Tax Code Complexity*. The Laffer Center. http://www.laffercenter.com/wp-content/uploads/2011/06/2011-Laffer-TaxCodeComplexity.pdf.

Chapter 2

1 George, Henry *Progress and Poverty* (1879; repr., New York: Cosimo, Inc., 2005), 291, http://books.google.com/ books?id=3Ex_yT6hJtEC&pg=PA291&lpg=PA291&dq=george+horse+%22badly+placed%22+%22progress+and+poverty%22&source=bl&ots=QQyGLCSVyM&sig=Sn_v3rUD0Md4I7jN042F8MF97i8&hl=en&ei=_40xTuLmJcyatweeytiQDQ&sa=X&oi=book_result&ct=result&resnum=1&ved=0CBkQ6AEwAA#v=onepage&q&f=false.

2 Siddhartha Mukherjee M.D., *The Emperor of All Maladies: A Biography of Cancer* (New York: Scribner, 2010).

3 Laffer, Arthur B., Ph.D., Wayne H. Winegarden, Ph.D., and John Childs. *The Economic Burden Caused by Tax Code Complexity*. The Laffer Center. http://www.laffercenter.com/wp-content/uploads/2011/06/2011-Laffer-TaxCodeComplexity.pdf.

4 McGuire Woods. 2011 State Death Tax Chart. http://www.mcguirewoods.com/news-resources/publications/taxation/state_death_tax_chart.pdf

5 Laffer, Arthur B., and Stephen Moore. "Boeing and the Union Berlin Wall." *Wall Street Journal*, May 13, 2011. http://online.wsj.com/article/SB10001424052748703730804576317140858893466.html.

Chapter 3

1 Tennessee and New Hampshire impose an income tax on un-earned income.

2 Numbers may not add up due to rounding.

3 We only went as far back as 1971 because we needed data from 1961 to calculate our 10-year growth rates. 50 years worth of data—one fully half century—was our time limit on case study data.

4 The personal income data are from the Bureau of Economic Analysis Regional Accounts, http://www.bea.gov/regional/index.htm.

5 Laffer, Arthur B. and Stephen Moore (2011) "Boeing and the Union Berlin Wall," *The Wall Street Journal*, May 13.

6 Vedder, Richard (2010) "Right-to-Work Laws: Liberty, Prosperity, and Quality of Life," *Cato Journal*, Vol. 30, No. 1, pp. 171-180.

7 Reed, W. Robert (2003) "How right-to-work laws affect wages," *Journal of Labor Research*, Vol. 24, No. 4, pp. 713-730."

8 I've always loved Henry George's reference to horses when it comes to taxation and politics. John Connally said that the biggest deficit problem in Washington D.C. is the deficit of horses heads. And he's right.

9 Prante, Gerald (2008) "Tax Foundation State and Local Tax Burden Estimates for 2008: An In-Depth Analysis and Methodological Overview", *Tax Foundation Working Paper No. 4*, August 7; http://www.taxfoundation.org/files/wp4.pdf.

10 Erblich, Christopher E. (1994) "To Bury Transfer Taxes Without Further Adieu," *Seton Hall Law Review*. Vol. 24, pp. 1931-1968.

11 Cataldo, Anthony J. and Arline A. Savage (2001) "US Individual Federal Income Taxation: Historical, Contemporary, and Prospective Policy Issues," Oxford: Elsevier Science, p. 146.

12 Saxton, Jim and Mac Thornberry (1998) "The Economics of the Estate Tax," Joint Economic Committee, United States Congress, December.

13 Holtz-Eakin, Douglas and Donald Marples (2001) "Estate Taxes, Labor Supply, and Economic Efficiency," American Council for Capital Formation Center for Policy Research, January.

14 Saxton, Jim (2006) "Costs and Consequences of the Federal Estate Tax," Joint Economic Committee, United States Congress, May.

15 Wagner, Richard E. (1993) "Federal Transfer Taxation: A Study in Social Cost," The Center for the Study of Taxation.

16 http://www.americansforprosperity.org/escaping-ohios-death-tax.
http://www.census.gov/govs/qtax/index.html.

Chapter 7

1 For those of you who enjoy economics *per se* this accelerator principle was used by Lloyd Metzler and Ragnar Nurkse along with the Keynesian multiplier to achieve a perpetual self-generating business cycle model.

2 Source: California Association of Realtors. http://www.car.org/marketdata/data/housingdata/

3 A more comprehensive analysis of housing affordability would include interest rates and the actual required payment on the home. For the purposes here, a more simplified affordability metric illustrates the key point of changes in income and housing prices in California relative to the U.S. overall without introducing these added complexities.

Chapter 8

1 Doerr, David R. (1997) "Conformity: The Impossible Dream" *Cal-Tax Digest*, March; http://www.caltax.org/MEMBER/digest/mar97/mar97-3.htm.

2 Varshney, Sanjay B. and Dennis Tootelian (2009) "Cost of State Regulations on California Small Business Study," Varshney and Associates, September.

Chapter 9

1 Fox, Joel. *The Legend of Proposition 13: The Great California Tax Revolt*, Xlibris.

2 Laffer, Arthur B. (1978), "Revitalizing California's Economy: A Discussion of the Impact of Proposition 13," United Organization of Taxpayers, March 22.

Chapter 10

1 Table 33 on page 86 does not show this 4.75% state sales tax rate because this rate was only in effect from January 1, 1991 to July 14, 1991. The state sales tax rate was 5% from December 1, 1989 to December 31, 1990.

Chapter 11

1   Uhler, Lewis K. (2001) "We have done everything possible to limit supply: We're paying for years of wrongheaded policy," *The Orange County Register*, January 7.

2   Weintraub, Daniel (2001) "Are California utilities victims or bandits in suits?" *The Sacramento Bee*, February 20.

3   John Seiler. "The Electricity Crisis and California's Economy." *Laffer Associates*, April 6, 2001.

4   Seiler, John (2001) "The Electricity Crisis and California's Economy," Laffer Associates, April 6.

5   Davis, Gray "Coy, Pete (2001) "Commentary: How to Do Deregulation Right," Businessweek, March 26.

6   Jansen, Bart (2000) "Overhaul ordered by FERC," *The Associated Press*, December 16.

7   California Public Utilities Commission (2000), "CPUC President Lynch and Commissioner Duque Statement," December 13.

8   Moody's Investor Services Global Credit Research (2001), "Moody's Lowers the Senior Unsecured Debt Rating of PG&E Corporation…" January 5. http://www.moodys.com/research/MOODYS-LOWERS-THE-SENIOR-UNSECURED-DEBT-RATING-OF-PGE-CORPORATION--PR_42405.

9   Taken from Schedule 11 of the "FY2004-05 Governor's Budget Summary."

10 Also rated BBB were Alaska in the 1960s and Massachusetts in the early 1990s. Source: "The State of California's Bonds." Bernstein Municipal Bond Research, November 2003.

11 Hood, John (2003) "Moore on America's Tax Revolt," *Carolina Journal*, June 16. http://www.carolinajournal.com/issues/display_story.html?id=822.

12 "How an American carbon-trading system should work". (2007) *Economist.com*, Jan 22nd.

13 (2003) Addressing the Uncertain Prospect of Climate Change. *Congressional Budget Office: Economic and Budget Issue Brief* April 25.

14 "State Education Data Profiles" NCES; http://nces.ed.gov/programs/stateprofiles/sresult.asp?mode=short&s1=06.

15 U.S. Department of Education, National Center for Education Statistics, Schools and Staffing Survey (SASS), "Public School Teacher Data File," 2007-08.

16 Schwarzenegger, Arnold (2006) "Governor Schwarzenegger's 2006 State of the State Address…" California Governor's Office, January 5. http://gov.ca.gov/news.php?id=358

17 OCTOBER TERM, 2010 SUPREME COURT OF THE UNITED STATES, BROWN, GOVERNOR OF CALIFORNIA, ET AL. v. PLATA ET AL. APPEAL FROM THE UNITED STATES DISTRICT COURTS FOR THE EASTERN AND NORTHERN DISTRICTS OF CALIFORNIA No. 09–1233. Argued November 30, 2010—Decided May 23, 2011

18 Vicini, James (2011) "Supreme Court orders California prisoner release" *Reuters*, May 23; http://www.reuters.com/article/2011/05/23/us-california-prisons-court-idUSTRE74M3DQ20110523.

19 In the 2010-11 budget total Corrections and Rehabilitation expenditures were $9.3 billion out of a General Fund budget of $92.2 billion.

20 Finley, Allysia (2011) "California Prison Academy: Better Than a Harvard Degree: Prison guards can retire at the age of 55 and earn 85 percent of their final year's salary for the rest of their lives. They also continue to receive medical benefits." *Wall Street Journal,* http://online.wsj.com/article/SB10001424052748704132204576285471510530398.html.

21 Justice Expenditure and Employment Extracts, 2007; http://bjs.ojp.usdoj.gov/index. cfm?ty=pbdetail&iid=2315.
22 Justice Expenditure and Employment Extracts, 2007; http://bjs.ojp.usdoj.gov/index. cfm?ty=tp&tid=11.

Chapter 12

1 California Franchise Tax Board, "2009 Annual Report." http://www.ftb.ca.gov/aboutFTB/ Tax_Statistics/2009.shtml.
2 Laffer, Arthur B., Winegarden, Wayne H. and Childs, John (2011) "The Economic Burden Caused by Tax Code Complexity" *The Laffer Center for Supply-side Economics*, April.
3 Arthur B. Laffer, "The Complete Flat Tax," *Laffer Associates*, February 22, 1984. and Arthur B. Laffer, "A Proposal for California Complete Flat Tax," *Laffer Associates*, October 1, 1990.
4 George, Henry (1998) *Progress and Poverty*, New York: Robert Schalkenbach Foundation.
5 http://www.ftb.ca.gov/aboutFTB/Tax_Statistics/Rev_Est_Exhibits_0511.pdf.

Chapter 13

1 For a biography of Jackie Mason, see http://www.playbill.com/celebritybuzz/whoswho/ biography/6553.
2 Cooper, James D. et al (1994) "The Northridge Earthquake: Progress Made, Lessons Learned in Seismic-Resistant Bridge Design" *U.S. Department of Transportation: Public Roads*, Vol. 58, No. 1; http://www.fhwa.dot.gov/publications/publicroads/94summer/p94su26.cfm
3 Eggers, William D. (1997) "Performance Based Contracting: Designing State of the Art Contract Administration and Monitoring Systems" *Reason Foundation* May 1; http://reason. org/news/show/performance-based-contracting.
4 Eggers, William D. (1997) "Performance Based Contracting: Designing State of the Art Contract Administration and Monitoring Systems" *Reason Foundation* May 1; http://reason. org/news/show/performance-based-contracting.
5 Moe, Terry M. (2011) "Special Interest: Teachers Unions and America's Public Schools" *Brookings Institution Press*.
6 Ibid.
7 Hanushek, Eric as quoted in (2011) "Notable & Quotable" *Wall Street Journal*. July 18, 2011.
8 http://california.educationbug.org/school-districts/
9 (2011) "The ABCs of School Choice" *The Foundation for Education Choice;* http://www. edchoice.org/CMSModules/EdChoice/FileLibrary/625/The-ABCs-of-School-Chocie---2011-Edition.pdf.
10 Stein, Mark (2008) *How the States Got Their Shape*, HarperCollins Publisher.
11 Seward, William H. (1850) "Speech of William H. Seward," *Appendix to the Congressional Globe*. Washington: United States Senate, March 11; cited from Stein, Mark (2008) *How the States Got Their Shape*, HarperCollins Publisher.

12 Trinklein Michael J. (2010) "Lost States: True Stories of Texlahoma, Transylvania, and Other States That Never Made It" *Quick Books.*

13 Johnson, Charles (2011) "California Split" *The Wall Street Journal Political Diary* July 8; http://online.wsj.com/article/SB10001424052702303365804576433912523446884.html

14 "Crossing Lines in California," David Broder, *Washington Post*, March 31, 2005.

Bibliography

Adams James R. (1981) "New York Moves to the Supply-side" A.B. Laffer Associates, April 8.

Altig, David, Auerbach, Alan J., Kotlifoff, Laurence J., Smetters, Kent A., and Walliser, Jan, "Simulating Fundamental Tax Reform in the United States," (2001) *American Economic Review,* Vol. 91 (3), pp. 574-595.

Auerbach, Alan (1995) "Tax Reform, Capital Allocation, Efficiency and Growth," Unpublished Draft, December 21.

Bankman, Joseph (2003) "Who Should Bear Tax Compliance Costs?" Berkeley Program in Law and Economics, Working Paper Series, UC Berkeley, http://www.escholarship.org/uc/item/2tt3c5dr.

Barta, Patrick (2009) "The Rise of the Underground" *Walls Street Journal,* March 14; http://online.wsj.com/article/SB123698646833925567.html.

Beach, William W., (1996) "The Case for Repealing the Estate Tax," *Heritage Backgrounder* No. 1091, August 21.

Block, Sandra (2007) "A taxing challenge: Even experts can't agree when preparing a sample tax return" *USA Today,* March 26; http://www.usatoday.com/money/perfi/taxes/2007-03-25-tax-preparers-hypothetical_N.html.

Blumenthal, M. & Slemrod, J, (1992) "The Compliance Cost of the U.S. Individual Tax System: A Second Look After Tax Reform" *National Tax Journal* 185.

Boskin M. (1973) "The Economics of the Labor Supply" in Cian Glen G. and Watts Harold W. eds Income Maintenance and Labor Supply. Chicago: Rand McNally.

Boskin M. (1978) "Taxation, Saving and the Rate of Interest" *Journal of Political Economy* Volume 86, April 1978 pp S3 – S28.

Boskin, Michael (1995) "A Framework for the Tax Reform Debate," Testimony before the Committee on Ways and Means, U.S. House of Representatives, June 6.

Brumbaugh, David L., Esenwein, Gregg A., and Gravelle, Jane G. (2005) "Overview of the Federal Tax System," CRS Report for Congress RL32808, March 10.

Buchholz, Todd G. and Hahn, Robert W. (2002) "Does a State's Legal Framework Affect Its Economy?" *U.S. Chamber of Commerce*, November 13.

California Business Roundtable (2002) "Twelfth Annual Business Climate Survey," *California Business Roundtable*, January.

California Chamber of Commerce (2003) "Survey: Migration Out of State Growing," *California Chamber of Commerce press release*, February 27.

California Chamber of Commerce, "A Growth & Jobs Agenda"; http://california.uschamber.com/agenda/.

California Public Utilities Commission (2000), "CPUC President Lynch and Commissioner Duque Statement," December 13.

Cataldo, Anthony J. and Arline A. Savage (2001) "US Individual Federal Income Taxation: Historical, Contemporary, and Prospective Policy Issues," Oxford: Elsevier Science, p. 146.

Case, Karl E., Quigley, John M., and Shiller, Robert J. (2004) "Comparing Wealth Effects: The Stock Market versus the Housing Market," May, Working Paper.

"CEOs Select Best, Worst States for Job Growth and Business: Texas, North Carolina, Florida Top List as Best States; California, New York, Michigan Are the Worst" *Chief Executive.net;* http://www.chiefexecutive.net/ME2/Audiences/dirmod.asp?sid=&nm=&type=Publishing&mod=Publications%3A%3AArticle&mid=8F3A7027421841978F18BE895F87F791&tier=4&id=D8BB1C4F12AE46EF9B7647E09E3253A6&AudID=F242408EE36A4B18AABCEB1289960A07.

Cobb, C.W. and Douglas, P.H., (1928) "A Theory of Production," *American Economic Review,* March, 139 – 65.

Congressional Budget Office (2001) "CBO's Method for Estimating Potential Output: An Update," The Congress of the United States: Congressional Budget Office, August.

Congressional Budget Office, (1996) "Labor Supply and Taxes," Congressional Budget Office Memorandum, January.

Coors, Andrew C. and Laffer, Arthur B. (2003) "Tax Trouble in Gotham City," Laffer Associates, May 6.

Coors, Andrew C., Laffer, Arthur B., and Miles, Marc A., (2002) "Dividends: Stop the Discrimination," Laffer Associates, December 16.

Douglas, P.H., (1948) "Are There Laws of Production," *American Economic Review,* March, 1 - 41.

Edwards, Chris (2006) "Income Tax Rife with Complexity and Inefficiency" Cato Institute, April No. 33;

Edwards, Chris, (2005) "Options for Tax Reform," *Cato Policy Analysis,* No. 536, February 24.

Elizabeth G. Hill, (2003) "Overview of the 2003-04 May Revision," Legislative Analyst's Office, May 19.

Engen, Eric, Gravelle, Jane, and Smetters, Kent (1997) "Dynamic Tax Models: Why They Do the Things They Do," *National Tax Journal,* Vol. 50, No. 3, pp. 657–82.

Erblich, Christopher E. (1994) "To Bury Transfer Taxes Without Further Adieu," *Seton Hall Law Review.* Vol. 24, pp. 1931-1968.

FairTax "Replacing the U.S. Federal Tax System with a Retail Sales Tax – Macroeconomic and Distributional Impacts," *Report to Americans For Fair Taxation,* December, 1996.

Fleisher, Michael P. (2010) "Why I'm Not Hiring" *Wall Street Journal,* August 9.

Forman, Jonathan (2001) "Simplification for Low Income Taxpayers" Joint Committee on Taxation: Study of the Overall State of the Federal Tax System.

Fox, Joel, *The Legend of Proposition 13: The Great California Tax Revolt,* Xlibris.

FreedomWorks, "Top Ten Reasons to Scrap the Code" FreedomWorks, http://www.freedomworks.org/scrapthecode/topten.php.

Gale, William G. and Holtzblatt, Janet (2000) *The Role of Administrative Factors in Tax Reform: Simplicity, Compliance and Enforcement.*

GAO (2005) "Tax Policy: Summary of Estimates of the Costs of the Federal Tax System" Government Accountability Office, August, GAO-05-878.

GAO (2007) "Tax Compliance: Multiple Approaches Are Needed to Reduce the Tax Gap" GAO, Statement of Michael Brostek Director, Tax Issues Strategic Issues Team, GAO-07-391T.

George, Henry (1998) *Progress and Poverty,* New York: Robert Schalkenbach Foundation.

Gillen, Michael A and Packer, Steven M (2009) "New IRS Strategic Initiative: Increased Audit Activity on Its Way?" *The Legal Intelligencer Duane Morris*, September 1.

Gravelle, Jane (1997) "The Joint Committee on Taxation 1997 Tax Modeling Project and 1997 Tax Symposium," Joint Committee on Taxation, November 20.

Guyton, John L., O'Hare John F., Stavrianos Michael P., Toder, Eric J.(2003) "Estimating the Compliance Cost of the U.S. Individual Income Tax" Presented at the 2003 National Tax Association Spring Symposium.

Gwartney, James, Lawson, Robert and Holcombe, Randall (1998) "The Size and Functions of Government and Economic Growth" Joint Economic Committee, U.S. Congress, April.

Heller, Walter (1978) "Testimony before the Joint Economic Committee of Congress, 1977" as cited in Bruce Bartlett (1978) *National Review*, October 27.

Hill, Elizabeth G. (2003) "Overview of the 2003-04 May Revision," Legislative Analyst's Office, May 19.

Holtz-Eakin, Douglas and Donald Marples (2001) "Estate Taxes, Labor Supply, and Economic Efficiency," American Council for Capital Formation Center for Policy Research, January.

Hood, John (2003) "Moore on America's Tax Revolt," *Carolina Journal*, June 16. http://www. carolinajournal.com/issues/display_story.html?id=822.

IRS (2008) "2008 Annual Report to Congress" *National Taxpayer Advocate*, Volume 1, December 31.

IRS (2009) "2009 Annual Report to Congress" *National Taxpayer Advocate*, Volume 1, December 31.

Jansen, Bart (2000) "Overhaul ordered by FERC," *The Associated Press*, December 16.

Jasper William F. (2003) "California's collapse: California's woes high taxes, costly energy, burdensome regulations, and more are all symptoms of government run amok" *The New American*, October 6.

Joines, Douglas H. (1980) "The Kennedy Tax Cut: An Application of the Ellipse" A.B. Laffer Associates. September 25.

Joint Committee on Taxation (1997) "The Joint Committee on Taxation 1997 Tax Modeling Project and 1997 Tax Symposium," November 20.

Jorgenson, Dale (1995) "The Economic Impact of Fundamental Tax Reform," Testimony before the Committee on Ways and Means, U.S. House of Representatives, June 6.

Jorgenson, Dale W., (2001) "Accounting for Growth in the Information Age," Working Paper.

Kadlec, Charles W. and Laffer Arthur B. (1978) "The Jarvis-Gann Tax Cut Proposal: An Application of the Laffer Curve" A.B. Laffer Associates. June.

Kadlec, Charles W. and Laffer, Arthur B. (1979) "A General Equilibrium View of the U.S. Economy" A.B. Laffer Associates. December 14.

Keating, David (2010) "A Taxing Trend: The Rise in Complexity, Forms, and Paperwork Burdens" National Taxpayers Union, 127, April 15.

Keating, Raymond J. (2010) "Small Business Survival Index 2010," *Small Business Survival Committee*, December.

Keynes John Maynard (1972: Reprint) *The Collected Writings of John Maynard Keynes,* London: Macmillan *Cambridge University Press.*

Kirkland, Katie, (2000) "On the Decline in Average Weekly Hours Worked," *Monthly Labor Review,* July.

Koenig, Evan F. and Huffman, Gregory W., (1998) "The Dynamic Impact of Fundamental Tax Reform Part 1: The Basic Model," *Federal Reserve Bank of Dallas Economic Review,* First Quarter.

Kotlikoff, Laurence J. (1993) "The Economic Impact of Replacing Federal Income Taxes With a Sales Tax," *Cato Institute Policy Analysis* No. 193, April 15.

Krause, Kate (2000) "Tax Complexity: Problem or Opportunity" *Public Finance Review,* Vol. 28, No. 5, 395-414.

Laffer, Arthur B. and Stephen Moore (2011) "Boeing and the Union Berlin Wall," *The Wall Street Journal,* May 13.

Laffer Arthur B. (1980) "A California Tax Update" A.B. Laffer Associates. March 28.

Laffer Arthur B. (1980) "The Ellipse: An Explication of the Laffer Curve in a Two Factor Model" A.B. Laffer Associates. July 28.

Laffer, Arthur (1984) "The Complete Flat Tax" A.B. Laffer Associates.

Laffer, Arthur B. (1990) "Is the California Tax Revolt Over? An Analysis of California's Proposition 111," A.B. Laffer Associates. May 17.

Laffer, Arthur B. (1978), Revitalizing California's Economy: A Discussion of the Impact of Proposition 13," United Organization of Taxpayers, March 22.

Laffer, Arthur B. and Laffer, Melissa (1998) "A Study of California's Housing Prices," Laffer Associates, November 19.

Laffer, Arthur B. and Thomson, Jeffrey (2003) "California in the Crosshairs," Laffer Associates, May 21.

Laffer, Arthur B. McNary, Mark and Lance Vitanza, (1994) "California D.P. (During Pete)," A.B. Laffer Associates. June 8.

Laffer, Arthur B. (1990) "A Proposal for California Complete Flat Tax," A.B. Laffer Associates.

Laffer, Arthur B. (1991) "California Dreaming," A.B. Laffer Associates, June 25.

Laffer, Arthur B. (1992) "The Complete Flat Tax 1992 Style," A.B. Laffer Associates.

Laffer, Arthur B. (1993) "The Great California Tax Experiment," A.B. Laffer and Associates, May 28.

Laffer, Arthur B. (1993) "The Great California Tax Experiment: From Karl Marx to Adam Smith and Back Again," A.B. Laffer Associates, May 28.

Laffer, Arthur B. (1995) "Jack Kemp Letter," Laffer Associates, October 17, 1995.

Laffer, Arthur B. (1995) "The California Flat Tax Proposal Tax Amendment," Laffer Associates, October 20.

Laffer, Arthur B. (2001) "How to Mark Dubya a Winner: The Flat Tax," *Wall Street Journal*, May 31.

Laffer, Arthur B. (2002) "Russia's 12-Step Recovery Starts With the Flat Tax," Laffer Associates, June 6.

Laffer, Arthur B. (2003) "Will Gray Davis Survive" Laffer Associates, August 6.

Laffer, Arthur B. (2003) "A Flat Rate Tax for California State and Local Governments: Presentation to the California Commission on Tax Policy" Laffer Associates, April 28.

Laffer, Arthur B. (2003) "Proposition 13: The Tax Terminator," Laffer Associates, June 27.

Laffer, Arthur B. (2003) "The Only Answer: A California Flat Tax" Laffer Associates, October 2.

Laffer, Arthur B. (2004) "Flataxism: Western Europe Under Fire," Laffer Associates, February 12.

Laffer, Arthur B. (2006) "California Who Are You?" Laffer Associates, February 17.

Laffer, Arthur B. and Hammond, Christopher S. (1990) "Either California's Housing Prices are Going to Fall or California's In for One Helluva Rise in Personal Income," December 28.

Laffer, Arthur B. and Jeffrey Thomson (2003) "Tax Amnesty: A Win/Win For All," Laffer Associates, May 12.

Laffer, Arthur B. and Moore, Stephen (2008) "California, Who Are You? Part II," Laffer Associates, January 18.

Laffer, Arthur B., Winegarden, Wayne H. and Donna Arduin (2010) "Competitive States 2010: Texas vs. California, Economic Growth Prospects for the 21st Century" Texas Public Policy Foundation, October 10.

Laffer, Arthur B., Winegarden, Wayne H., Arduin, Donna, and Ian McDonough (2009) "The Economic Impact of Federal Spending on State Economic Performance: A Texas Perspective" Texas Public Policy Foundation, April 1.

Laffer, Arthur B., Marcal, Pedro and Mark McNary (1993) "Rosa Californica," Laffer Associates, January 28.

Laffer, Arthur B., Moore, Stephen and Jonathan Williams (2011) "Rich States, Poor States: The ALEC-Laffer State Competitiveness Index" American Legislative Exchange Council.

Laffer, Arthur B., Winegarden, Wayne H. and John Childs (2011) "The Economic Burden Caused by Tax Code Complexity" The Laffer Center for Supply-side Economics, April 14th.

Landau, Daniel L. (1983) "Government Expenditure and Economic Growth: A Cross-Country Study" *Southern Economic Journal*, 49: January;

LAO (2001) "California's Tax System: A Primer," California Legislative Analyst's Office, January.

Mankiw, Gregory N. and Weinzierl, Matthew, (2005) "Dynamic Scoring: A Back-of-the-Envelope Guide," Working Paper, Revised: April 7.

McQuillan, Lawrence and Hovannes Abramyan, (2010) *U.S. Tort Liability Index: 2010 Report* Pacific Research Institute.

Mitchell, Daniel J. (2005) "The Impact of Government Spending on Economic Growth" Heritage Foundation, Backgrounder #1831, March 15;

Moody's Investor Services Global Credit Research (2001), "Moody's Lowers the Senior Unsecured Debt Rating of PG&E Corporation…" January 5.

Nellen, Annette (2001) "Simplification of the EITC through Structural Changes", *Joint Committee on Taxation: Study of the Overall State of the Federal Tax System.*

Plotkin, Joseph and Coors, Andrew C. (2005) "The AMT: Another Reason To Hate April 15th," Laffer Associates, February 7.

Reed, W. Robert (2003) "How right-to-work laws affect wages," *Journal of Labor Research*, Vol. 24, No. 4, pp. 713-730.

Report of the President's Advisory Panel on Federal Tax Reform (2005) November.

Robert J. Barro (1991) "Economic Growth in a Cross Section of Countries," *Quarterly Journal of Economics*, Vol. 106, No. 2 May;

Rossotti, Charles O. (2006) Commissioner of Internal Revenue, 1997-2002 Testimony before the US Senate Finance Committee, September 20.

Saxton, Jim (2006) "Costs and Consequences of the Federal Estate Tax," Joint Economic Committee, United States Congress, May.

Saxton, Jim and Mac Thornberry (1998) "The Economics of the Estate Tax," Joint Economic Committee, United States Congress, December.

Scully Gerald W. (2008) "Optimal Taxation, Economic Growth and Income Inequality in the United States" National Center for Policy Analysis, Policy Report No. 316, September.

Scully, Gerald W. (2006) "Taxes and Economic Growth" National Center for Policy Analysis, *NCPA Policy Report* No. 292, November.

Seiler, John (2001) "The Electricity Crisis and California's Economy," Laffer Associates, April 6

Setze, Karen (2004) "DOR Says 23,000 State Employees Filed No 2002 State Returns," *State Tax Notes, Tax Analysts*, July 12.

Slemrod, J. & Blumenthal M. (1996) "The Income Tax Compliance Cost of Big Business" *Public Finance Quarterly* 441.

Slemrod, J. & Sorum, N., (1984) "The Compliance Cost of the U.S. Individual Income Tax System" *National Tax Journal*, 461.

Staff of the Joint Committee on Taxation (2001) "Study of the Overall State of the Federal Tax System and Recommendations for Simplification, Pursuant to Section 8022(3) (B) of the Internal Revenue Code of 1896, Volume III: Academic Papers Submitted to the Joint Committee on Taxation" Joint Committee on Taxation, April.

Stathopoulos, Peter (2003)"DOR Targets Delinquent Taxpayers to Attack Budget Woes," *State Tax Notes, Tax Analysts*, October 6.

Sullivan, Martin, (2004) "Practical Aspects of Dynamic Revenue Estimation," *A Report of The Heritage Center for Data Analysis*, June 14.

Taylor, Humphrey, Krane, David and Amy Cottreau (2002) "U.S. Chamber of Commerce State Liability Systems Ranking Study," Harris Interactive, January 11.

The American Institute of Certified Public Accountants, "Guiding Principles for Tax Simplification"

Treasury Inspector General for Tax Administration (2002) "Management Advisory Report: Taxpayers Continue to Receive Incorrect Answers to Some Tax Law Questions" Treasury Inspector General for Tax Administration, April; 2002-40-086.

Tritch, Teresa (1997) "Why Your Tax Return Could Cost You A Bundle: We Asked 45 Tax Preparers to Fill Out One Hypothetical Family's Tax Return – And We Got 45 Different Answers. Here's What You Can Learn from the Pro's Many Mistakes" *CNN Money.com*, March 1; http://money.cnn.com/magazines/moneymag/moneymag_archive/1997/03/01/222962/index.html.

Uhler, Lewis K. (2001) "We have done everything possible to limit supply: We're paying for years of wrongheaded policy," *The Orange County Register*, January 7.

United States Government Accountability Office, (2005) "Tax Policy: Summary of Estimates of the Costs of the Federal Tax System", August.

Varshney, Sanjay B. and Dennis Tootelian (2009) "Cost of State Regulations on California Small Business Study," Varshney and Associates, September.

Wanniski, Jude (1980) "An Authentic Guide to Supply-side Economics" A.B. Laffer Associates. May 2.

Biography

Arthur B. Laffer, Ph.D

Arthur B. Laffer is the founder and chairman of Laffer Associates, an institutional economic research and consulting firm, as well as Laffer Investments, an institutional investment management firm utilizing diverse investment strategies. Laffer Associates' research focuses on the interconnecting macroeconomic, political, and demographic changes affecting global financial markets. Laffer Investments' investment management strategies utilize some of the economic principles and models pioneered by Dr. Laffer as well as other unique offerings managed by the firm's portfolio management group. The firms provide research and investment management services to a diverse group of clients, which includes institutions, pension funds, corporations, endowments, foundations, individuals and others.

Dr. Laffer's economic acumen and influence in triggering a worldwide tax-cutting movement in the 1980s have earned him the distinction in many publications as "The Father of Supply-Side Economics." One of his earliest successes in shaping public policy was his involvement in Proposition 13, the groundbreaking California initiative that drastically cut property taxes in the state in 1978.

Years of experience and success in advising on a governmental level have distinguished Dr. Laffer in the business community as well. He currently sits on the board of directors or board of advisors of a number of companies, including Alpha Theory, Armor Concepts, Atrevida Partners, BAP Power, BridgeHealth Medical, Consensus Point, Cubit, Dataium, Executive Trading Solutions, LifePics, and Pillar Data Systems.

Dr. Laffer was a member of President Reagan's Economic Policy Advisory Board for both of his two terms (1981-1989). He was a member of the Executive Committee of the Reagan/Bush Finance Committee in 1984 and was a founding member of the Reagan Executive Advisory Committee for the presidential race of 1980. He also advised Prime Minister Margaret Thatcher on fiscal policy in the U.K. during the 1980s.

He was formerly the Distinguished University Professor at Pepperdine University and a member of the Pepperdine Board of Directors. He also held the status as the Charles B. Thornton Professor of Business Economics at the University of Southern California from 1976 to 1984. He was an Associate Professor of Business Economics at the University of Chicago from 1970 to 1976 and a member of the Chicago faculty from 1967 through 1976.

During the years 1972 to 1977, Dr. Laffer was a consultant to Secretary of the Treasury William Simon, Secretary of Defense Don Rumsfeld, and Secretary of the Treasury George Shultz. He was the first to hold the title of Chief Economist at the Office of Management and Budget (OMB) under Mr. Shultz from October 1970 to July 1972.

Dr. Laffer has been widely acknowledged for his economic achievements. Recently he was noted in *Time Magazine's* March 29, 1999, cover story "The Century's Greatest Minds" for inventing the Laffer Curve, which it deemed one of "a few of the advances that powered this extraordinary century". He was listed in "A Dozen Who Shaped the '80s," in the *Los Angeles Times* on Jan. 1, 1990, and in "A Gallery of the Greatest People Who Influenced Our Daily Business," in the *Wall Street Journal* on June 23, 1989. His creation of the Laffer Curve was deemed a "memorable event" in financial history by *Institutional Investor* in its July 1992 Silver Anniversary issue, "The Heroes, Villains, Triumphs, Failures and Other Memorable Events."

The awards that Dr. Laffer has received for his economic work include: two Graham and Dodd Awards from the Financial Analyst Federation for outstanding feature articles published in the *Financial Analysts Journal*; the Distinguished Service Award by the National Association of Investment Clubs; the Adam Smith Award for his insights and contributions to the *Wealth of Nations*; and the Daniel Webster Award for public speaking by the International Platform Association. Dr. Laffer also earned the Father of the Year award from the West Coast Father's Day Committee in 1983.

Dr. Laffer is the author of a number of books, including *The End of Prosperity: How Higher Taxes Will Doom the Economy—If We Let it Happen*, which was a nominee for the F.A. Hayek book award in 2009, and most recently *Return to Prosperity*.

Dr. Laffer received a B.A. in economics from Yale University in 1963. He received a MBA and a Ph.D. in economics from Stanford University in 1965 and 1972 respectively.

Wayne H. Winegarden, Ph.D.

Wayne Winegarden is responsible for analyzing and writing the firm's industry-based policy studies. Prior thereto, he worked as an economist for Altria Companies Inc. in Hong Kong and New York City. In these roles Dr. Winegarden analyzed the impact of the economic environment in East- and Southeast-Asia on the company's operations, and integrated these insights into the company's strategic planning process. Additionally, Dr. Winegarden examined the impact of tax and regulatory polices on the company's operations and supported its government affairs objectives. Dr. Winegarden also has experience analyzing federal and state budget, regulatory, and financial sectors for policy and trade associations in Washington D.C.

Having further served on the economics faculty at Marymount University, Dr. Winegarden is a columnist for Townhall.com, and has been interviewed and quoted by Bloomberg and CNN. He is frequently invited to deliver research findings at policy conferences and meetings. Dr. Winegarden received his BA, MA and PhD in Economics from George Mason University.

Acknowledgements

Without the assistance and dedication of so many, this book would not have been possible. A special thanks goes to the Pacific Research Institute for the vision to publish this book. PRI has risen to become the premier think tank on California issues. I want to extend my deepest thanks to Sally Pipes, President and CEO of the Pacific Research Institute, Rowena Itchon, my editor and vice president of marketing, Dana Beigel for graphic design, and PRI's Christine Hughes, Cindy Chin, Laura Dannerbeck, and Chrissie Dong for their hard work in making sure that *Eureka!* gets the attention of all Californians who care about turning the state around.

I also deeply appreciate the work and insights of Wayne Winegarden, my co-author and partner at Laffer Associates, the excellent research by Nicholas Drinkwater, and Ford Scudder, who shepherded this project along.

Finally, I am so very grateful to a very special group of supporters of PRI who made it possible for us to undertake a project of this magnitude and importance.

About Pacific Research Institute

The Pacific Research Institute (PRI) champions freedom, opportunity, and personal responsibility by advancing free-market policy solutions. It provides practical solutions for the policy issues that impact the daily lives of all Americans, and demonstrates why the free market is more effective than the government at providing the important results we all seek: good schools, quality health care, a clean environment, and a robust economy.

Founded in 1979 and based in San Francisco, PRI is a non-profit, non-partisan organization supported by private contributions. Its activities include publications, public events, media commentary, community leadership, legislative testimony, and academic outreach.